THE GREAT
ROAD CLIMBS
OF THE
SOUTHERN ALPS

For Simon Mottram, onlie begetter of these books

With death at my side
I strive to live with fresh insight,
seeing the better, taking hold of the worst.

© Rapha Racing Limited 2013
First published in Great Britain in 2010 by
Rapha Racing Limited, Imperial Works, Perren Street, London NW5 3ED
www.rapha.cc | +44 (0) 20 7485 5000

ISBN: 978-0-9558254-2-2

Cover: The drama of riding the high mountains. France into Italy… Col d'Agnel… Colle d'Agnello.

Design: Jonathan Bacon
Production: Joe Hall
Illustrations: Ben Aquilina
Printed in St. Albans, UK by The Manson Group Ltd.

Volume 1 – '*The Rapha Guide to the Great Road Climbs of the Pyrenees*' is also available
Volume 3 – '*The Rapha Guide to the Great Road Climbs of the Northern Alps*' is also available

THE RAPHA GUIDE TO

THE GREAT ROAD CLIMBS OF THE SOUTHERN ALPS

by Graeme Fife
photography by Pete Drinkell

Rapha

CONTENTS

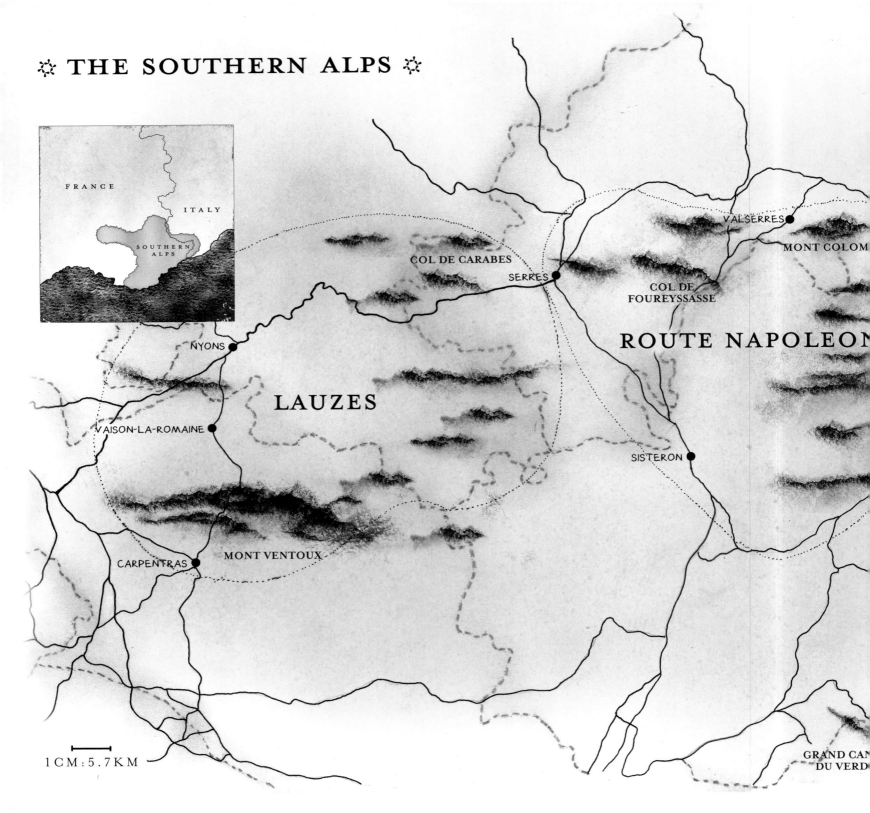

☼ THE SOUTHERN ALPS ☼

FRANCE

ITALY

SOUTHERN
ALPS

COL DE CARABES

SERRES

VALSERRES

MONT COLOM

COL DE
FOUREYSSASSE

NYONS

ROUTE NAPOLEON

LAUZES

VAISON-LA-ROMAINE

SISTERON

CARPENTRAS

MONT VENTOUX

GRAND CAN
DU VERD

1CM:5.7KM

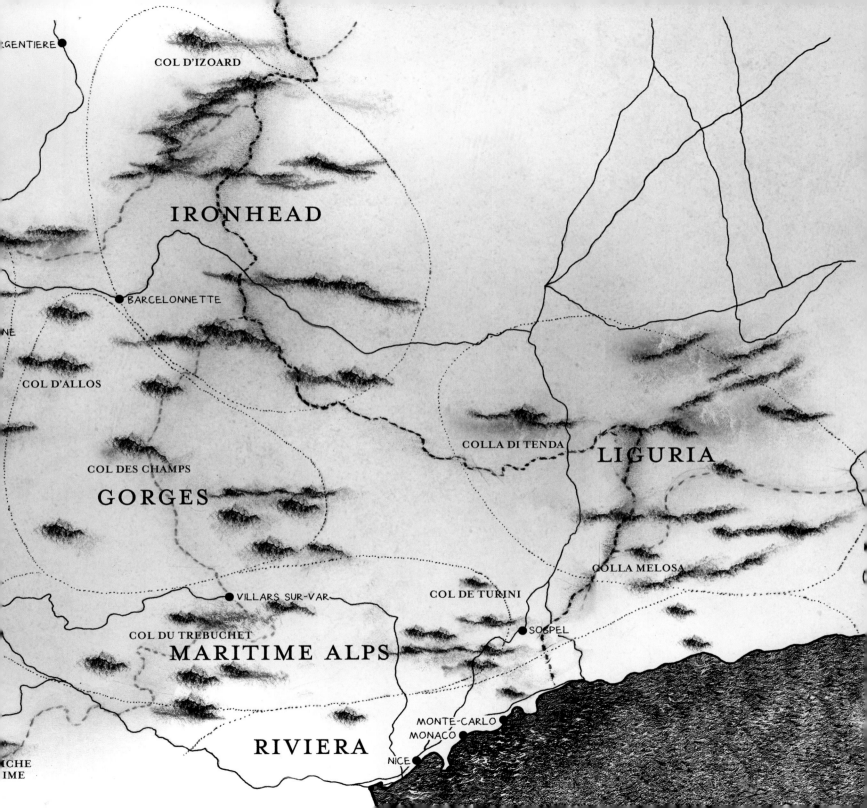

GENTIERE

COL D'IZOARD

IRONHEAD

BARCELONNETTE

NE

COL D'ALLOS

COLLA DI TENDA

LIGURIA

COL DES CHAMPS

GORGES

COLLA MELOSA

VILLARS SUR-VAR

COL DE TURINI

COL DU TREBUCHET

SOSPEL

MARITIME ALPS

MONTE-CARLO

MONACO

RIVIERA

NICE

CHE
IME

INTRODUCTION

Alp, strictly, refers neither to any peak or ridge of the mountain chain but an upland mountain pasture just below the snow-line which reappears each spring when the snow melts. These meadows are of great antiquity – recorded as early as the 8th century AD and subject, one assumes, to the same kind of measurement as the fertile alluvial mudfields of the Nile's banks after the annual flooding, the importance being to mark out the exact same dimensions of each allotment of ground as it became available, for planting or pasturage. (The origin of geometry: measuring areas of the earth.) Hay is cut in lower fields but in insufficient quantity to support herds and flocks all year round. The *Alpgemeinden* of the Swiss cantons (communes – *gemein* meaning 'common' and *Gemeinde*, 'community') are composed of those who have a right to take their cattle up to the alpine grazing every summer, the right being traditionally attached to certain plots of ground in the valley or houses in the village or to certain families. The size of the alp is determined by how many animals it can support: one cow or two heifers, three calves or sheep, four pigs or eight goats.

The Alps are not continuous like the Pyrenees, and consist of numerous ranges separated by comparatively deep valleys. The mountain mass describes a broad band, convex in form towards the north, the lie of the valleys mostly west to east and south-west to north-east. Many of the ridges are intersected transversely by deep clefts ranging from full-scale valleys to tight passages through crowding rock. Known in French and Provençal as *clues* (or *cluses* in the Jura mountains) from the Latin *claudere*, 'to close or stop up', they have not only been used from earliest times for the passage of man and animals but also act as air vents which moderate the otherwise sharp differences in climate on adverse slopes.

The full extent of the Alpine ranges includes Austria, Germany (Bavaria), Italy, Switzerland and France. For our purpose here, we must concentrate on subdivisions within what a basic topographical system designates as the Western Alps – the others are Central and Eastern.

The Western Alps comprise:

Maritime Alps: from the Col di Tenda to the Col de Larche
(sometimes called Col de l'Argentière)
Cottian Alps: from the Larche to the Mont Cenis Pass
and west to the Col du Galibier
Dauphiné Alps: from the Col du Galibier westwards and southwards
Graian Alps: from the Mont Cenis to the Little Saint-Bernard

*These last are further subdivided into three groups: Central – the watershed between
the Mont Cenis and the Little Saint-Bernard, Western or French, and Eastern or Italian.*

The Cottian Alps were named by the Romans after Marcus Julius Cottius, son of Donnus, king of fifteen Ligurian mountain tribes whom the emperor Augustus befriended during the pacification of the Alpine regions during the last years of the 1st century BC. Augustus granted Cottius sovereignty over twelve of these tribes with the title of *praefectus civitatium* (that is, state prefect… 'the man put in charge'). Cottius erected a triumphal arch, which survives, in Augustus' honour at Segusio – Susa, in the valley below Mont Cenis – and improved the road over Alpis Cottia, now Mont Saint-Genèvre, east of Briançon, and thought by some to be where Hannibal crossed with his elephants [see IRONHEAD]. The emperor Claudius conferred the title of king on the son of Cottius and on the former's death, the kingdom was made a Roman province, Alpes Cottiae, by Nero.

The Graian or Greek Alps, were so named by Pliny the Elder (born AD23/24, died, overcome by fumes from the cataclysmic eruption of Vesuvius, which he came to observe, in August 79) in his *Natural History*. He refers to a legend concerning some Greeks ('Graii' in Latin) who had followed Herakles (Hercules) across the mountains but, their limbs frostbitten, had remained behind and settled.

The Dauphiné Alps are situated in the ancient French province of that name, an area now comprising the modern *départements* of Isère, Drôme and Hautes-Alpes.

In the 12th century, the local ruler, Count Guy IV of Albon, sported a dolphin as a heraldic device to puff his reputation as a caring leader of his people. The dolphin, used as an ornament by the Greeks, was, in mediaeval art, a symbol of sociability and familial love, from the behaviour of the notably friendly marine mammal. Guy was nicknamed '*le Dauphin*' (French for 'dolphin'), the sobriquet stuck and his successors were known as Dauphin Viennois. (The family seat was in Vienne.) In 1349, Humbert II, Dauphin without a son and heir, flogged off the inheritance, the whole caboodle, to the French king Philip IV on condition that the heir to the throne of France should keep the title of Dauphin alive *and* that the territory now known as the Dauphiné should be excused payment of a substantial number of royal taxes and imposts. Such exemptions of aristocratic privilege were a major source of the furious popular unrest which sparked the Revolution.

COMPOSITION OF THE ALPS

The action of heat, water, ice and pressure transforms the fundamental matter of the earth's body into metamorphic rock. Igneous rock, by volcanic combustion; crystalline rock, composed of crystals or crystalline particles, such as mica (Latin for 'crumb'); schist, whose component minerals are arranged in a more or less parallel manner; gneiss, composed, like granite, of quartz and mica but distinguished from it by its foliated or laminated structure; limestone, composed of conglomerated fragments of shell and chalk; sandstone, from the compressed bed of an ocean which has receded. Sedimentary rock is that dumped by the movement of a glacier, rivers or the withdrawing of waters, while conglomerate rock is comprised of the debris of pre-existing rocks, rounded or waterworn, broken down and cemented together. (Cement comes from *caedimentum*, 'cutting' and, thus, broken or pounded stones, tiles etc. mixed with lime to make a hard-setting mortar.) Amorphous rocks are those which are uncrystallised, massive, and without stratification, cleavage or other division into similar parts.

The Alps present a geological medley of all these processes and types, a blotch picture, if you will, of the immemorial time-scale of the great lifting, shoving, grinding down, wearing away, compacting and compounding which resulted in the mountains as we see them today. And, during the clash and shift of their formation, a depression sank north-east/south-west between the crystalline central massifs and the foothills known as the Préalpes [see VENTOUX page 113] which, in the course of erosion, became a long furrow cut through marl (clay) known as the Alpine trench.

The Alps are lacerated by a number of great rivers which, beginning as mountain torrents, played a crucial role in the shaping of the ranges and the watering of the resultant valleys: the Rhône and its great tributaries, Isère, Romanche, Drac, Durance, Verdon, the Var, the Vésubie and the Tinée feeding the Alpes Maritimes. Those valleys acted as conduits for people on the move, too, and along them were built towns to obstruct the people whose movement was unwelcome: in the Durance, for instance, Castellane, Digne-les-Bains, Sisteron; in the Var, Entrevaux.

Mediterranean rivers are usually parched dry in the summer from lack of rain and evaporation in the extreme heat, but in spring and late autumn they swell with water from violent storms or the post-hibernal thaw and pound through the gorges and down the valleys, bursting their banks and often in times past wreaking havoc, until they were contained in flood by dams and artificial lakes. Easy to see, therefore, how, in the prehistoric era, their rampant power added to the rough hewing of the alpine landscape.

The Alps were formed as part of a massive crumpling of the earth's crust, a general upward flexure known as geanticlinal, from the Rif mountains in Morocco to the Himalayas. The tegument was rucked and folded in a complex series of ridges and pleats both anticlinal (the inverted V of a ridge) and synclinal (the cleft of a valley) on which ice, water and atmosphere worked further to mould mountain ranges and the intervening plains between them, such as the gap between the Alps and the Carpathian mountains of Central and Eastern Europe, the largest European range [see also ROUTE NAPOLEON page 166].

One section of the crystalline schist layer of the African tectonic plate – what is now Italy and the Balkans – shifted northwards, eventually shunting one section of the Alpine flexure sideways to form the foothills known as the Préalpes, and forcing itself up through the sedimentary rock layer, deposited below the sea, that covered that part of the continent [see LAUZES page 96].

Glaciers carved out *cirques* (huge, natural rock-formed amphitheatres) and U-shaped valleys consisting of a series of smaller valleys rising up like a flight of locks from the main trench below. This relief was later smoothed out by the erosion by water when the glaciers melted

Connecting gorges opened up the bolts – this seems to be a use of the Yorkshire word (in a Whitby glossary) meaning 'trench' or 'gutter', thus narrow passages or archways between houses, hiding holes – and ironed out the connections between the hanging (i.e. upper) valleys and the floor.

In the Préalpes, the *cluses* cut across the axis of the folds, some mountain torrents having carried down debris from the upper reaches and dumped it at the end of the main valley in what accumulates to become an alluvial cone – as at the foot of the Carabès [see LAUZES].

HISTORICAL AND POLITICAL

In the shaping and consolidation of France from a mosaic of warring kingdoms which emerged after the Romans left and the prolonged battering of strife – both internal and from outside – which ensued, the disputed alpine frontier region played a significant role. The fertile hexagon of France, inhabited and cultivated first by the Celts whose artisanal skills were unmatched in Europe, then brought to civic order by the Romans who built fine cities, aqueducts, bath-houses and a vast network of roads in stone, drew a procession of peoples across its vulnerable borders. The Alps, forbidding in aspect, nevertheless proved to be a surmountable barrier, surprisingly porous. The lush valleys of the region promised easy living, the big rivers coursing through supported a busy, to-and-fro commerce, while some well-trodden passes offered tempting routes for trespass, the precedent of military adventure from Hannibal on impelling emulation. Kingdoms, duchies, counties of one stripe or another lorded it in turn, power was taken, held, tussled for, the back and forth of armies across the alpine ramparts to wrest power from or preserve it against other armies marking the history of the region indelibly.

The Romans had established themselves in southern Gaul in the 2nd century BC. At the commencement of his Gallic Wars Julius Caesar, governor of Cisalpine Gaul – north-eastern Italy bounded by the Graian, Cottian and Maritime Alps – also took over Gallia Transalpina (originally Gallia Narbonensis) to which he refers, in his Commentaries, as 'our province', namely Provence. (The incumbent governor had died.) He opened hostilities in 58 BC beyond the boundaries of his governorship, a questionable arrogation of responsibility, to protect Transalpine Gaul from the exodus of the Helvetii tribe en masse – he reports a third of a million on the move from their homeland round Geneva. He led five legions on the fastest route to block them but does not say which crossing of the mountains he took – probably either the Larche or Montgenèvre. By 51 BC, all Gaul was pacified and Roman and, battered by the protracted wars, remained thereafter quiescent until the end of the Empire in the late 5th century AD.

The Franks (who gave their name to France), a Germanic people living north and east of the Lower Rhine, moved south, took Burgundy and invaded Provence. In 800, the Frankish king Charlemagne became Holy Roman Emperor, as secular ruler of what amounted to a recrudescence of the ancient Roman Empire, in notional tandem with its spiritual head, the Pope in Rome. Charlemagne was much preoccupied with incursions of Moorish armies, mostly fleet-footed light cavalry, into southern France from their territories in Spain, famously (though not historically) in the Pass of Roncesvalles in the Pyrenees. (See the earlier *Rapha* volume on those mountains.) In 732 an army of heavily armoured Franks with their throwing axes under their king Charles Martel ('The Hammer') had crushed an invading force from the Emirate of Cordoba at Tours, deep inside the Frankish kingdom. Tours was a decisive victory: it almost certainly prevented Europe from becoming Islamic. However, it was not until the 10th century that Provence, now subsumed into the kingdom of Burgundy, was freed from the threat of Moorish pirates along its coast.

The Burgundians, probably of Norse origin from the island of Bornholm ('Burgundarholm' in Old Norse), east of Denmark between Sweden and Poland, established themselves in Gaul before the advent of the Romans who knew them as 'Burgundiones'. Their power grew during the final years of the Roman Empire and, for a while allies of the Franks, their kingdom was eventually taken over by the more dominant kingdom in the 6th century AD. It kept its name and covered an area pretty well that of the landscape described in this book. When Charlemagne's empire broke up, Burgundy revived and absorbed Savoy. When the kingdom of Burgundy in its turn collapsed in the 11th century, it was divided between France and the Habsburgs who had inherited the Holy Roman Empire, Savoy being parcelled out among a number of lesser counties, including Provence.

In the 14th century, The Holy Roman Emperor Charles IV split the County of Savoy from the kingdom of Burgundy, and from then on the House of Savoy grew to become one of the major players in the fortunes of southern France, an ever stronger and dominant dynasty. Centred round Geneva, succeeding dukes of Savoy expanded the dukedom in all directions by a series of dynastic marriages and artful quid pro quo diplomatic alliances, adding territories on both sides, west and east of the Alps, including Piedmont and part of Liguria. Control of the three most accessible passes, Mont Cenis and the two Saint-Bernards, gave Savoy a prime advantage. Decline and fall ensued, the inevitable pattern: the blood of the dukes of Savoy got watered down by complacency and indolence, until in 1536 François I of France invaded and reduced Savoy to French rule. In 1557, the Savoyard heir, Emmanuel Philibert, whose blood was fierier – he'd learnt generalship and resolve fighting with the Spanish armies against France – beat the French at Saint Quentin and the treaty which he subsequently imposed on them restored to him his hereditary possessions. He moved his capital from Chambéry to Turin.

Several times occupied by French troops during the European wars of the 17th century, Savoy retaliated by invading the southern Alps in 1692 and reclaiming Nice.

The French king, Louis XIV, sent his master military architect, Commissaire générale de fortifications, Sébastien le Prestre, the future Marshall of France and *seigneur*, afterwards Marquis, de Vauban, to plan, update and oversee the fortification of key towns in the region: Briançon, Sisteron, Colmars and Mont-Dauphin (midway between Briançon and Gap) Subsequently Vauban also improved the defences at Toulon, the port of Antibes, Entrevaux and Besançon.

Vauban

Born in Burgundy into the minor nobility in 1633, Vauban began his military career aged 17, and in 1655 he received his first commission as '*ingenieur du roi*' (king's engineer). The king personally noted Vauban's courage and ingenuity in the conduct of the sieges of Douai, Tournai and Lille (1667) and his intellectual brilliance, diversity of interests, potent energy and above all his inventiveness in the matter of defensive masonry, consolidated a career of remarkable achievement. He advised the king more broadly on the defence of France's borders and his extensive work in the Alps alone is testimony to the confidence Louis XIV placed in him.

Like a number of French *savants*, as scientists were called, Vauban's intellectual curiosity encompassed a range of disciplines: agriculture, the rearing of farm animals, forest and canal management, the census, colonial government. Short, thickset and stocky with a truculent air, he had little grace, being described by one commentator as somewhat churlish and vulgar. Despite the king's high opinion, Vauban was not averse to speaking his mind with the forthright manner of a man who deals in practicality. His treatise criticising the king's levy of taxes – printed without the necessary royal imprimatur – was condemned, albeit Louis XIV blocked prosecution of his master military builder. He died in 1707.

The Genius of Vauban

This was demonstrated in both aspects of his siege-work: building forts strong enough to resist attack and exploiting the weakness of enemy strongholds.

Vauban could read terrain – contour, dip and rise, aspect, perspective and relative lie of ground – and take the best strategic advantage of what it offered in terms of protection from, and opening to, attack, and visibility or concealment. He devised – or adapted from a Saracen model – a system of parallel trenches for the carrying of enemy citadels and refined the 'star fort' developed in Italy during the 15th century to counter the destructive force delivered by 'black (i.e. gun) powder': his walls were built lower and made of brick, which does not shatter and fragment unlike stone. Brickwork was strengthened with compacted earthworks. Sloping revetments deflected the full impetus of cannon fire.

An effective fortress must keep the enemy out and its own garrison safe. Starting with the core curtain wall, the girdling *enceinte* (the same word means 'pregnant'), Vauban improved and elaborated it, using a complex geometry of angles and faces, walls, projecting bastions, salients and outworks to supply maximal possibilities for denying an attacker close access while not only protecting the defenders but simultaneously allowing them to direct fire against the assaulting army from the main gun positions and enfilading (flanking) fire from the angled projections – notably arrow-shaped, projecting *demi-lunes* (solid half-moons) jutting out from the *enceinte*.

Vauban was a tireless overseer of the building works – all carried out by manual labour, picks and shovels, wheelbarrows and carts, cranes and explosives, amid the dust and smoke from the lime kilns, a racket of noise, from 5am until 7 pm with breaks totalling three hours. 'Remember,' growled Vauban, 'Vitruvius [the Roman writer on architecture] said that the best mortar needs to be doused in sweat.' He also instituted recruitment and training of military engineers and founded an Engineers Corps.[1]

After the Revolution

Savoy was occupied by Republican troops of the revolutionary armies in 1792 and became the *département* of Mont-Blanc. Nice became the *département* of Alpes-Maritimes. Napoleon invaded Italy, marching his army and heavy guns across the Col du Grand-Saint-Bernard in May 1800. 'We are battling with ice, snow,

---

1 The familiar English term 'Sappers' points to their main preoccupation in cutting tunnels underneath defence works and placing mines to demolish them. (Late Latin *sappa*, whence French *sappe* – a spade, spadework.)

blizzards and avalanches,' he wrote in an official despatch to Paris. 'The Grand-Saint-Bernard, astonished to see such a volume of people crossing its pass with so little ceremony, puts a number of obstacles in our way. In three days, the entire army [of 55,000 men plus artillery and baggage train] will have gone through.' A brilliant victory at Marengo delivered all Piedmont to him. After his final defeat in 1815, Savoy reverted once more, to its duke, Victor Emmanuel I, who, thanks to an earlier treaty concession, was now also King of Sardinia. (He abdicated in 1821 in favour of his brother and, for the next 40 years, Savoy's interests were bound up with those of Italy.)

In 1858, Napoleon's nephew, the emperor Napoleon III, struck a deal with Camillo Paolo Filippo Giulio Benso, Conte di Cavour, the prime minister of Piedmont-Sardinia and one of the architects of the Risorgimento for the unification of Italy, to drive the Austrians out of Italy in return for the cession of Nice and Savoy to France. In the conflict, France took Lombardy but exchanged it for Savoy, although Victor Emmanuel II, duke of Savoy and Piedmont, and king of Sardinia, declared that the deal should be honoured 'without any constraint on the will of the people'. Thus, in 1860, a plebiscite voted overwhelmingly for the union of Savoy and Nice with France, and so were born the two *départements* of Savoie and Haute-Savoie. The slice of land west of the southernmost Ligurian Alps, below Tende and La Brigue, however, remained in Italian hands. As for the House of Savoy, it retained its Italian Lands and its dukes became successively kings of Italy, beginning with Victor Emmanuel II who ascended the throne in 1861.

Cross-border tensions heightened when Italy (unified on 20 September 1870) aligned itself with Germany and Austria after France's defeat in the Franco-Prussian war of 1870. In a new era of artillery, breech-loading, higher-calibre ordinance made of highly tempered steel delivered explosive shells from barrels rifled for greater accuracy, and General Séré-de-Rivière, secretary of the Committee for Defence, was charged with updating France's alpine defence system. (An interesting word, artillery: from mediaeval Latin *articula*, a diminutive of *artem,* 'craft', whence French *artiller*, an artisan, specifically a bowyer, who made weapons.)

Séré-de-Rivière oversaw the construction of 166 forts, 43 second-line strongholds and 250 batteries in a line from the North Sea to the Mediterranean. Adapted to the new power of ordnance, the forts are squat, prison-like edifices placed on cliffs and promontories, often furnished with steel-reinforced gun embrasures, with many, in more remote locations, provided with haylofts and stables for the mules essential for transport, all built to house a garrison in low-walled barrack blocks.

The building of Fort Suchet, near Sospel in the Alpes-Maritimes, between mid-April and mid-October 1883, gives some idea what went into the labour of blockading France's eastern frontier. Steel turrets weighing 21 tons apiece were laid on 10-ton open trucks drawn by a steam locomotive of 17 tons. Long stretches of track had to be enlarged, bridges strengthened with extra props, embankments underpinned to support the passage of the 48-ton convoy the 30 kilometres from Menton on the coast to the fort at 1283 metres above sea level. Travelling at a speed of 700 metres per hour, the locomotive's boiler consumed a cubic metre of water every 2 kilometres and a stockpile of coal every 3… a precious fuel eyed greedily by local peasants.

The Corps of Engineers augmented by Alpine troops also constructed new roads to facilitate the movement of troops and armaments at gradients which made the slopes accessible to heavy *matériel* – 37 kilometres over the Restefond, for example, and the road through the Casse Déserte below the Col d'Izoard. Think of yourself, therefore, as comparable to a field gun with limber, or a howitzer, as you slog up to the highest metalled pass in Europe.

After the First World War, Franco-Italian relations continued sour and André Maginot, Minister for War, introduced a law allotting finances to the building, between 1932 and 1940, of the line of fortifications which took his name. The lessons learned during the earlier conflict, notably the hammering the great fortress of Verdun had taken, ameliorated the form of the new emplacements – generally much smaller, sunken into the ground with a minimum of superstructure, curved in shape, fashioned in concrete up to 3.5 metres thick, with additional dense armour plating.

Italy declared war on France on 10 June 1940 and, a week later, invested the alpine frontier with an army vastly superior in numbers to those of the French. Alpinists were drafted to help in the combat. The Italian assault was repelled and a German advance stalled at the river Isère.

The French government, however, unwilling to submit to the kind of bloodletting the nation had suffered in the '14-18 war, signed an Armistice with Hitler in the Forest of Compiègne on 22 June 1940 – a symbolic venue, for it was here that the German surrender had taken place in 1918 – and the Italian western offensive got no further than Menton. (The Tende and La Brigue territory was conceded by Italy to France in 1947 so that she could extend her frontier to the line of the mountains.) The heroism of the French resistance fighters in the region through the summer of 1944 is recorded throughout this book.

Crossing the Alps

Many of the roads built by the Roman legions across the southern littoral of the Mediterranean followed existing tracks beaten long before the serious business of wider conquest began. The expression 'All roads lead to Rome' is generalised enough to have no solid antecedent. There is the mediaeval Latin *'Mille viae ducunt homines per saecula Romam'* (a thousand roads lead men to Rome through all time), and in his *Treatise on the Astrolabe* the English poet Geoffrey Chaucer writes: 'Right as diverse pathes leden the folk the righte wey to Rome', but wherever the source the sentiment is rooted in a powerful reality: the network of roads built by the Roman legions – one legion of around 5,000 men could build a mile a day, foundations, full paving, gutters and side stones – across the expanding Empire did indeed lead to and from Rome. They were the arteries of power. Along the metalled highways flowed the Roman war machine, in its wake the systems and infrastructure of law, tithing and governance, the commerce, the engineers, the architects, the peoples of the *Imperium Romanum* – the sphere of Roman rule. It is well said by the great historian Ronald Syme that 'the Romans thought in terms of road'. Thus, the Via

Aurelia ran 175 miles (the Latin for mile is *millia passuum*, 'a thousand paces') up the west coast of Italy from Rome to modern Pisa. It was extended round the coast to Ventimigilia by the Via Aemilia and some time in the dying years of the last millenium BC, the emperor Augustus, as an essential part of the pacification of a number of alpine peoples after the chronic lawless upheavals of the civil wars, ordered the further lengthening of the Aemilia by the road named after his patronymic (from his adoptive father Julius Caesar) the Via Julia Augusta. This was later extended by another section of road, the Via Julia, to link with the existing Via Domitia, tracing what had been a very ancient route from the Rhône to Spain. For the moment it stopped at Cemelenum – now Cimiez, a suburb of Nice to the north-east – which became capital of a new province named Alpes Maritimae. To mark the pacification, a hefty, imposing triumphal monument was erected on rising ground by the Via Julia, with views of the sea in both directions (near the Col d'Eze), by what is now La Turbie – from the trophy's Latin name, *Tropea Augusti*. Its inscription honoured Augustus 'because under his leadership and auspices all the alpine tribes from the upper (i.e. Baltic) to the lower (i.e. Mediterranean) sea had been brought under the rule of the Roman people'. In particular, Augustus subdued the Salassi tribe which had controlled the two Saint-Bernard passes and exacted tolls, which the Romans called brigandage. Most of them were sold into slavery and, from now on, the tolls on alpine passes were levied by Roman tax officers, who did not call it brigandage.

Even in the latter stages of the Roman era, the Alps sustained a network of inns and relays for travellers to which were added charitable hospices for the welcome of pilgrims heading for the Holy Land. In the late 10th century, Bernard de Menthon established two such on the cols which bear his name. Later sanctified and not to be confused with Saint Bernard of Clairvaux, founder of the Cistercian order of monks, he is the patron of alpinists and mountaineers as well as giving his name to a Swiss breed of very large brown and white working dog with a huge head and a smallish brandy barrel slung under its neck.

Most people travelled on foot or by mule or horse but other modes of transport appeared as people who could afford to pay for a journey arrived at the foot of the mountains and pointed up at the top. These included litters slung on poles between two horses, and wheelchairs – the *chaise roulante à deux roues* i.e. on two wheels or else mounted on runners like skis, with two levers for the driver standing at the back to direct the contraption, with the additional aid of digging his heels in to bring it to a halt. For steeper descents, the driver attached chains knotted five or six times to trail behind in the snow as a decelerating drag. Madame Royale's secretary who travelled in one of these *ramasses* in 1643, says that they made a descent of around four miles in about quarter of an hour with '*une rapidité incroyable*'. The German *berline*, a luxury four-wheeled coach of very solid construction, conveyed four passengers in Pullman-coach comfort. The diligence (from a primary meaning of the word 'haste, speed, despatch') was for the public who paid a much lower fare and, crammed in like luggage, endured what must have been considerable discomfort.

When the French revolutionary army arrived at the banks of the Var in 1792, the only method of crossing the wide stream was on the back of porters. General Anselm therefore ordered the immediate construction of a bridge across which his men could march. Napoleon's plan to link Nice and Genoa by a main road – what became the Route de la Corniche – had at its root a similar military ambition. He declared, somewhat exorbitantly, of the roads built across the mountains: 'The crossings of the Alps surpass in hardihood, grandeur and technical endeavour, all the works of the Romans.' He was, surely, *not* echoing what the mystic poet William Blake said in a different context: 'Great things are done when men and mountains meet.'

The railway arrived at the end of the 1840s. A line joined Aix-les-Bains and Saint-Jean-de-Maurienne in 1856, stage one in a grander project, the cutting of the first great railway tunnel in history, by boring apparatus powered by compressed air, the Fréjus – north of the Col de Montgenèvre, not that other Fréjus (Forum Augusti) on the coast. This opened in 1871, a stunning feat of technology, with seven tunnels, three covered galleries and eight kilometres of corrugated iron tubing to protect trains from snow and avalanche. The trains were fitted with a new system of braking, devised by John Barraclough Fell (1815-1902) an English railway engineer: two jockey wheels beneath the locomotive could be activated to grip a third, central rail, by means of levers and bevels and thus enable the engine to climb or descend slopes as steep as 1 in 12, (8+%). Other tunnels followed – including the Simplon and the Gotthard – pierced by means of hydraulic cutting machines.

The motor car soon arrived. The Touring-Club de France conceived a grand scheme to open up the mountains with its Route des Alpes in 1909 and financed road-building in the Hautes-Alpes. Until 1914, roads were cut by workers using no more sophisticated tools than picks, shovels pails and occasional small batches of explosive. The engineers applied wondrous ingenuity to negotiate chasms, valleys, irregularities of contour with bridges, viaducts, revetted embankments and so on.

The Route des Alpes from Thonon-les-Bains to Nice crossed the Col des Gets, on through Cluses, Megève and Maurienne to the Col du Galibier, thence to Briançon, Col d'Izoard, Col de Vars, Barcelonnette, Col de Cayolle and the coast. On 1 July 1913, the Paris-Lyon-Méditérranée (PLM) company inaugurated the first full crossing of the alps by autocar (open bus) from north to south in five, one-day stages. By 1933, PLM had conveyed 250,000 passengers across the Alps.

A lawyer from Grenoble, Henri Ferrand, waxed enthusiastic about driving over the mountains: 'Thanks to the car, one's pleasure is doubled with an exquisite sensation of following the most varied routes… there is a transport of true physical well-being in crossing beautiful landscapes which, at a speed of 12 to 18km/h unfurl before one's eyes like the backdrop of a diorama.' Marius Berliet, born in Lyon in 1866, advertised his sleek saloon crossing a packed earth mountain road, in 1825: 'Nothing stops it, not extremes of temperature, not the steepest gradients, not poor roads… it's a Berliet.' A slogan Henri Desgrange might well have applied to his Tour de France which first crossed the Alps in 1912.

Grame Fife 2009

How to get there

Access to the area covered in this book is relatively straightforward. Fly either to Nice or Grenoble. Marseille airport is far west of the city but, at a pinch. Flights are available to Cuneo on the Italian side, otherwise there is no very handy airport on the Italian side – Turin is just a little too far away. The European Bike Express (www.bike-express.co.uk) operates a coach service with trailer for bikes and delivers cyclists to a number of destinations, on both the French and Italian side. The TGV rail system is also a convenient alternative to car and bike rack, and gladly accommodate cyclists and their machines.

Emergency numbers in France

Pompiers (First Aid): 18
Police: 17
SAMU (Services d'Aide Médicale): 15
Weather (Sp. Météo): 3250 (mobiles only)

Emergency numbers in Italy

Carabinieri (Police): 112
Medical Emergencies: 118

1. IRONHEAD

The sector takes its name from the Tête de Fer above the Larche to the south-west and reinforces the presence of some of the grandest cols in this volume, iconic climbs of both Tour de France and Giro d'Italia, mighty challenges to any cyclist bent on the ultimate test in riding mountains.

The region embraces two large national parks on the French side: Queyras just south of the Izoard and the Mercantour whose northern tip sits just below the Larche. Both parks, created by the central government principally to stimulate tourism – the Queyras in 1977, Mercantour in 1979 – cover areas ringed by mountains which had long preserved a certain independence, enclaves apart. The territory of the Queyras (local patois for 'the huge crag') was originally occupied by the Quariates, one of the tribes mentioned in the accord between Augustus and Cottius in 8 BC. (See Introduction p.2) Thanks to their command of a number of strategic alpine passes, their successors, the Queyrassins, secured significant privileges, largely in the matter of tolls for the passage of goods, and eventually royal franchises, bestowed on them by the Dauphin, the heir to the French throne. (There are various references to Dauphin and the Dauphiné in the following text.) Such freedoms granted by the Crown may be seen as forerunners of the fundamental civic liberties demanded by the revolutionaries in 1789.

Fleeing Catholic persecution, a large number of French Calvinists, otherwise Huguenots, took refuge in the Queyras and the protestant faith became well-established in what, for a long time, remained a safe haven. Huguenot is a word of disputed origin but, in France, it bears the taint of subversive politics and, during the bitter Wars of Religion which ravaged France from 1562 to 1598, between Catholics and Huguenots, a protestant army seized the fortress of Queyras, a potent symbol of their resistance. The uneasy peace enshrined in the Edict of Nantes, 1598, ended the wars but not the swill of intolerance. The ravages of plague and the depredations of the Thirty Years' War left the Queyras desolate. Louis XIV's vicious pogrom, the infamous *dragonnades* (raids by dragoons), to persuade protestants to convert,

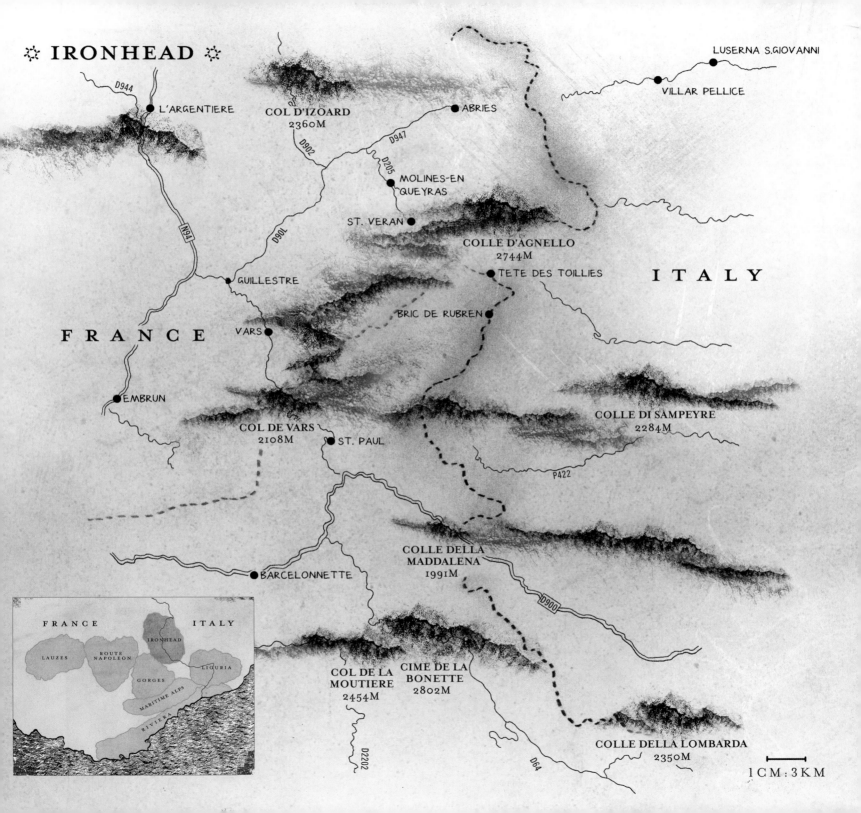

✿ **IRONHEAD** ✿

LUSERNA S.GIOVANNI

VILLAR PELLICE

D944

L'ARGENTIERE

COL D'IZOARD
2360M

ABRIES

D902

D947

D205

MOLINES-EN
QUEYRAS

ST. VERAN

COLLE D'AGNELLO
2744M

I T A L Y

D90L

TETE DES TOILLIES

BRIC DE RUBREN

GUILLESTRE

F R A N C E

VARS

N94

EMBRUN

COLLE DI SAMPEYRE
2284M

COL DE VARS
2108M

ST. PAUL

P422

COLLE DELLA
MADDALENA
1991M

BARCELONNETTE

D900

COL DE LA
MOUTIERE
2454M

CIME DE LA
BONETTE
2802M

COLLE DELLA LOMBARDA
2350M

D2202

D64

1CM:3KM

FRANCE   ITALY

LAUZES   IRONHEAD

ROUTE
NAPOLEON   LIGURIA

GORGES

MARITIME ALPS

RIVIERA

and his revocation of the Edict of Nantes, 1685, prompted widespread emigration and, with it, depopulation. Occupied by the Austro-Sardinians after Waterloo, by-passed by the industrial revolution – the first metalled road, between Guillestre and Château-Queyras, wasn't laid till 1857 – and badly smashed up by German artillery and bombing in the desperate fighting between the FFI and the beleaguered Nazis in 1944-5, the Queyras has, finally, been restored as an area of great natural beauty.

The Mercantour, which had been part of the Italian royal hunting estates until 1861, revived that trans alpine link in 1987 since when the work of maintaining it has joined in cooperation with the administration of the Italian Parco naturale delle Alpe Maritime with which it shares 33km of common border, south-east from Isola. The Mercantour boasts a rich abundance of flora and fauna: red and roe deer, blue hare, stoats and marmots roam the lower wooded slopes, chamois, ibex and the mouflon – a wild sheep with distinctive curved horns and reddish fleece imported from Corsica – inhabit the upper reaches. Black grouse and snow partridge cluck in the thickets, short-toed and golden eagles cruise the thermals and wolves are being reestablished from across the border in Italy.

CIME DE LA BONETTE 2802M

Northern approach from Jausiers 1213m

LENGTH: 23.8KM	
HEIGHT GAIN: 1589M	
MAXIMUM GRADIENT: 10%	

Jausiers, population 1001 at the last census, was the smallest of nine new start/finish towns to host the 2008 Tour de France and has, since 1995, been twinned with Arnaudville in Louisiana. Why? I hear you say. In 1805, Jacques Arnaud of Jausiers, then 24 years old, set off for the French American colony of Louisiana hoping to get rich. He married a Cajun woman, was joined by his brothers, founded the settlement later named after them, went on to Mexico, opened a clothes shop and got zotzed by a disgruntled local in 1821. As we know, when it comes to the fashion business, tempers can run exceedingly high. However, their pioneer's fate notwithstanding, other residents of Jausiers followed in his wake to seek their fortune in textiles and banking and came to be known as the altogether homely 'Barcelonnettes'. In the Place d'Arnaudville in Jausiers stands the ancient family home, Lou Filadour, the old silk mill where the Arnaud brothers were born. To its wall is affixed a plaque commemorating their 'instigation of the emigration to Mexico, source of the Ubaye valley's prosperity'.

The D64 rambles gently out of Jausiers for a thousand metres or so to the big toe of the mountain's foot, houses, chalets, sheep's cheese and honey for sale, gîtes, a walled cemetery in a field apart in Lans (1402m, 4km), the first of a number of named settlements over the first 13 kilometres, signs for off-road mountain

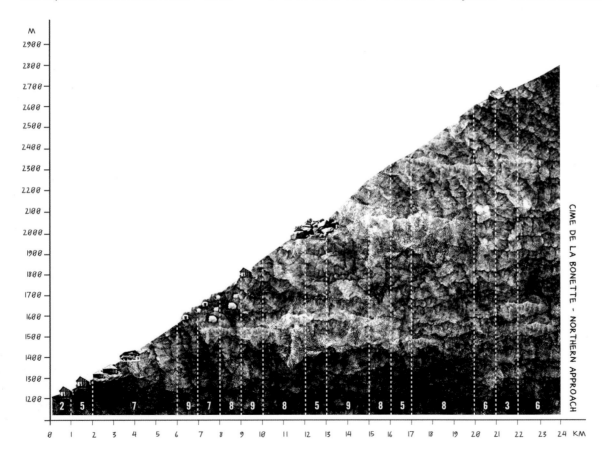

CIME DE LA BONETTE – NORTHERN APPROACH

CIME DE LA BONETTE *continued*

walks and, very likely, cyclists both laden with tourist panniers and slick as hair gel on racing machines. Gradually the valley closes in hustling the road up onto the slopes. It may look reluctant as, indeed, you yourself may feel, but here is the bite of the climb and a sign admonishes you: 'ROUTE DE HAUTE MONTAGNE… PRUDENCE RECCOMANDE'. Prudence, for sure. The gradient is a fairly steady 5–7% with a judder of 8–9 around La Chalannette at 6km, 1555m. The road is finding its hold in the inlet to the valley, the river below, a cascade supplying a full gush of water, a sign to a lake off to the right.

The gradient dips again but, from 8km it resumes at the steeper crank of 7–8% with a dollop of 9 here and there. These minor variations in gradient don't signify so much on the ground, however: there is a sort of accumulated pressure of climbing to which you adjust by the medium of patience and gradual inuring to toil.

Around 12km, 2000m, the road spills into the open plateau of the upper mountainside, steep grassy slopes to left and right, the banks of the river off to the right broadening, the moorland of the plateau made lumpy by outcrops of rock and boulder, poking up like giant petrified molehills.

This is a militarised zone used as a training area by the Centre d'instruction du combat en montagne de Barcelonnette and formerly home to the famous chasseurs alpins, the elite mountain infantry of the French army, also deployed as specialists in urban warfare. The terrain is similar to that encountered by allied troops in Afghanistan and you are likely to see scary-looking individuals with black-daub face paint in flak jackets toting bulky items of weaponry looming out of the broken ground of the hillside. There will probably be armoured personnel vehicles in attendance and aloof coves scanning the distance through binoculars.

Crags along the skyline, deep gullies in the

mountain walls, a torrent passing under the road and the inkling of a high pass way up ahead where even clouds have to heave themselves with an effort over the dizzying altitude of the massif itself. The rocks form a circular rampart, reminiscent of a dam wall and the great Cirque de Gavarnie in the Pyrenees.

The mood of aggressive intent is not something you would immediately associate with a rather less obtrusive resident of these bleak uplands, the marmot. When the 2008 Tour de France passed through this north-easterly corner of the large national Parc du Mercantour, strict orders went out to team cars and following vehicles not to use their klaxon, thus to preserve some ambient peace and quiet – invaders of the habitat enjoined not to disturb its native fauna. The marmot, which can be induced to stop for photo calls by the enticement of high-pitched short-burst whistling, seems to be a mild enough critter. Indeed, one sun-kissed afternoon on the Agnello, your photographer and I spent a happy quarter of an hour engaged in a delightful close exchange with one of the more laid-back brothers, his head cocked in curiosity, and I do swear he smiled – photographer clicking away, me sibilating most tunefully, like a Swannee whistle, to prolong the colloquy. The image is cosy but, sad to report, your marmot is known to engage in fights which, on occasion, can end fatally. Sex and power at the root, for sure. For the moment, let us leave the bellicosity to the human species in their *Caserne* (barracks) de Restefond, a bullet-head blockhouse with mean-eye loopholes at 19km, 2530m, looking very out of place in this natural, freestyle wildness.

The gradient, round the large sweeping bends and the long transits in between, keeps to its preferred 7–8% but, at some 4 kilometres from the top, eases a little. Pray that you feel the slackening. It is bleak up here, snow will cling on even in late June, banks of it

lining the side wall. Just below the summit a pill box at the side of the road, grim post for sharpshooters on guard for interlopers. The thought impinges: does Bjarne Rijs, much taken with the disciplines of hard-core military toughening, as we know, bring his CSC team members up here for nocturnal Nordic bonding sessions, long nights on a bare mountain?

The full height of the massif, at the Cime de la Bonette (2860m) sits atop the crest up a loop of road sprouting from the col. At the col (2715m), the road flattens very briefly between two sizeable buttresses of rock, through what is called, baldly, 'La Porte' (the gate), a sign indicates 'NICE' towards the yawning abyss which is the southern approach and the gale blows strong. From this stony whithering height (Anglo-Saxon whitha is a squall or blast of wind) the far, far off southwards holds promise of the blue waters of the Mediterranean, the sun-roasted beaches of the Côte d'Azur, journey's end for the Route des Grandes Alpes on which the Bonette, the insurmountable roof of the Tour de France, lies.

Now, from October 1961, in advance of the Tour's debut here, smarting at the fact that the Bonette's 2715m was below that of the Col d'Iseran (2770m) as well as two of the Giro's favoured climbs, the Stelvio (2757m) and the Agnello (2744m), the extended road teetered up to the Cime. From here the panorama is unassailable: towering peaks and, on a clear day, the sea and, to the west, Mont Aigoual, the high point of the Cévennes. A veritable rooftop. It begs a further kilometre of climbing and gradients of around 12 and 15%. In 1962, the Tour itinerary named the passage as Col de Restefond, an appellation preserved, whimsically, in the official guide for 2008, the Tour's fourth crossing, from the southerly direction. In fact, the Col de Restefond, a short distance below the true summit, sits on a military track between two fortified installations in a restricted zone.

Southern approach from Saint-Etienne-de-Tinée 1144m

LENGTH:	23KM
HEIGHT GAIN:	1658M
MAXIMUM GRADIENT:	10%

On the side of the school in Saint-Etienne, a sundial reads: *'Bel soulélié soulélio l'ubac è l'adret'* (A warm sun shines on north and south alike).

Into the gorge and some steep lifts heave you onto a ledge road, the river Tinée running below. At 8.2 kilometres, the river bed is wide, stones and rocks form the banks and the valley becomes a spacious wide-throated gorge – a long sight of the road ahead creeping round the mountain's flank. At 10km, 1650m, Le Pra ('the meadow'), a shanty town of houses with tin roofs and a church. The surface is good, as all roads must be when the Tour issues its diktats on the prevailing state of asphalt, and it winds along, a good open balcony towards the big knuckle of massif ahead. The general surroundings are attractive, the pastures are kempt, cattle-cropped and sheep-nibbled, another settlement of houses sits on the grassy slopes, trees stand erect. A stony fissure contains the downward flow of a torrent which is dammed at intervals to increase the pressure of the flow. At 13km, 1850m, where the gradient has stiffened to between 7.5% and 8%, Boussiéyas is a diminished outpost of sociability – a derelict hotel/bar – and a view of the snaking road just travelled below. At 14 kilometres look up, right, to the crags, including the Col des Fourches looming over the ridge at 2261m. Moorland opens out, now, together with a mighty perspective of mountains all round. There are distance and altitude signs all the way.

At 16km, 2090m, a spasm of 8.5% as you near the crags which hang over the road, the lower skirts of the Cirque du Salso Moreno at 2250m overhead.

At 17km, 2345m, the abandoned Camp des Fourches, indicated some way below by a black marble monument standing up the hill from the road. This signals: 'Camp des Fourches 15 Sept 1950' and 'Boussiéyas 21 July 1950' in the form of a shield surmounted by a crested helmet, the latter similar to that warn by the ancient Spartans, and elaborate tracery enclosing a '7' (7th battalion presumably). A short way along stands the ruined barracks of the camp, at the entrance to the line of hutments, a stone slab engraved with the Chasseurs Alpins' hunting horn motif (like that used by the Spanish Correos) enclosing '28 CAMP DES FOURCHES'. At the far end of the barracks a sign marks the 'Col de Pourriac frontière d'Italie'.

The stone buildings were constructed in 1890 to house a battalion – 800 men – together with stables for mules. In winter, the garrison was reduced to 40 men, all trained skiers, but what a miserable posting it must have been, cut off by snow and cold, provisions hauled up in baskets by rope and pulley, cabin fever rife. Murals painted by stir-crazy troopers – exotic women, sunny scenery, palm trees – attest to their hibernal hankerings. There also survives a graffito 'Fuck the army', though presumably of later date and, perhaps, by a passing civilian rather than a squaddy risking martial punishment.

The soldiers were known as *'diables bleus'* (blue devils), from their reputation for fearsome courage and, more prosaically, from the navy serge of their uniform (although it should be noted that from 1840 young recruits in the French army were called *'bleu'*, so too in the French Foreign Legion, for the blue blouse with which they were issued on coming to the Legion barracks in Marseille). The Chasseurs' motto: *Jamais être pris vivant…* Never taken alive.

Towards the summit on the northern side of the mountain, there are further signs of Chasseur interest hereabouts: a stone engraved with a horn and the number 15, further on, the same horn motif with *'14ême et 6ême Cie 1905'* (14th and 16th Company) painted on a rock in yellow on a green ground.

The Chasseurs are easily recognised by the wide beret they wear in parade dress, nicknamed 'tarte' (pie). The British Army adopted the beret in the 1920s mimicking similar headgear sported by the 70th Chasseurs Alpins (now disbanded).

The road continues along a shelf cut out of the rock and a short way up there is a memorial stone recording military manoeuvres in the summer of 1936. The 14th Army Corps were stationed on the south side and the 5th Army deployed north, over the Col de Pourriac, to mimic incursion by Italian troops. One General Jacquenot was in overall command. On the morning the manoeuvres were due to begin, a local man called Martin read the sky and warned his immediate superiors that an electric storm was brewing. The General ignored the warning and walked up to the Camp des Fourches with an officer of ordinance to observe the day's action. The electric storm broke and both men were fatally struck by lightning. Serves (you might say… I do) the General, at least, bloody well right.

At the col stands a shrine to Her again in another of her multifarious guises. Here she is *Notre Dame du Très Haut…* Our Lady of the Extremely High.

The road across the Bonette, the Route de Nice, was classed as an imperial road on 8 August 1860 by the Emperor Napoleon III. The Col and the Cime de Bonette were inaugurated in 1960–61.

Via Col de la Moutiere 2454m

This is a side route to the top via the D63 which branches off the D2205, 4.2km out of Saint-Etienne, towards Saint-Dalmas-le-Selvage. It's very narrow, although the tarmac gives way at the col itself (17.3km) to a track, rideable, to the Restefond.

The High Life

There is kudos attached to crossing a summit for the first time and Tour legend inscribes the names of the great pioneers with some reverence: Octave Lapize, dominant in the Pyrenees, 1910, first inclusion of those mountains, led over the Ares, Aspin, Peyresourde, Tourmalet, Portet d'Aspet, Port and winner in Paris... Emile Georget, (3rd overall 1907, 1911) the triple of Télégraphe, Galibier, Lautaret in 1911... Federico Bahamontes, the Restefond in 1962, and again in 1964. Raymond Poulidor said: 'I don't remember it being very hard but it was very long, it went on forever. And then, at that altitude, it was difficult to breathe. Also, it was very hot that day and we had to change wheels because the tar was melting and clogging between the rim and the brake blocks.'

Riding his first Tour in 1983, Robert Millar crossed the Restefond ahead of the field, an exploit that made him, as they say, one of the revelations of the Tour. It was an early marker of his extravagant talent: King of the Mountains and 4th overall the following year, 3rd in the Mountain competition in 1985 ahead of Greg Lemond, Millar's climbing may be said to have reached its apogee that day on the Restefond in his début Tour. Solo, in complete command, the perfect eloquence of letting the bike speak for him, he matched the brilliance of the great climbers who made the mountains their domain and stamped their exuberance and class on the history of the great race. He never had a nickname, he was, perhaps, too prickly to win that kind of affection, no Eagle, no Angel of the Mountains, no Pedaller of Charm but up there with the best? For sure.

In only the fourth time of crossing the great massif of the Bonette/ Restefond in the 2008 Tour, another neophyte, the young South African John Lee Augustyn, riding for Barloworld, was first over, ahead of the entire field, and seemed in with a good chance of taking the win at the foot of the climb in Jausiers. He attacked over the last kilometre of the climb – and the last 2 kilometres are severe, upwards of 12% at the end of a 25 kilometre slog. Hurtling off onto the twisty descent, he overcooked a bend, flew off the road onto the verge between the tarmac and the ravine, and somersaulted off his bike. A spectator rushed over to help him up, he was unhurt, not even scratched, remounted and set off in pursuit. But, his chance was gone and the – luckily, in the event, rather comic – fall detracted from that glorious moment when he rode across the roof of that Tour, the highest stretch of asphalted road in Europe, in the lead, on his own.

Colle della Maddalena (Col de Larche) 1991m

Western approach from Barcelonnette 1130m

LENGTH: 31.5KM

HEIGHT GAIN: 861M

MAXIMUM GRADIENT: 7%

Barcelonnette was founded in 1231 and, the naming of towns and provision of market charters and sundry civic privileges being in the gift of royal and ducal authority at that time, the original name, Barcelone, reflects the patronage of the prevailing man of influence, Raymond Bérenger IV, Count of Provence and Barcelona. The House of Savoy moved in next but ceded it to France in 1713, by the Peace of Utrecht – which carved up the Spanish Empire in Europe, as part of the exchange for the Dauphiné. The people of Barcelone, newly united to France, clamoured to join the Parlement de Provence as citizens of Barcelonnette, Barcelona's younger cousin. This valley of the Ubaye, (Provençal uba means 'north, exposed to the north') in which the town sits, was ever a major source of disquiet for whichever power happened to be in the ascendant. The suzerainty of the dukes of Savoy bound it to the interests of Piedmont in Italy and, when power switched, old loyalties and antagonism persisted. But the to-and-fro hostility dates back into those benighted times even before the Romans recorded their incursions hither in the Latin. The road over the Larche is, therefore, one of those major arteries of invasion which pumped hostile force backwards and forwards across the Alps time and time and time again. Eastwards from Barcelonnette at 15.4km, the Fort de Tournoux testifies to the need for constant vigilance, preparedness and visible armed force. Its fortifications, built over 20 years from 1843, are the latest of a number of other military installations placed along this end of the valley. A whole series of enclosed galleries, gun platforms, batteries and lookout turrets linked by tunnels stretch some 1300m from the barracks at the bottom to the highest emplacement at around 2000m.

The road up which mules hauled double-ended

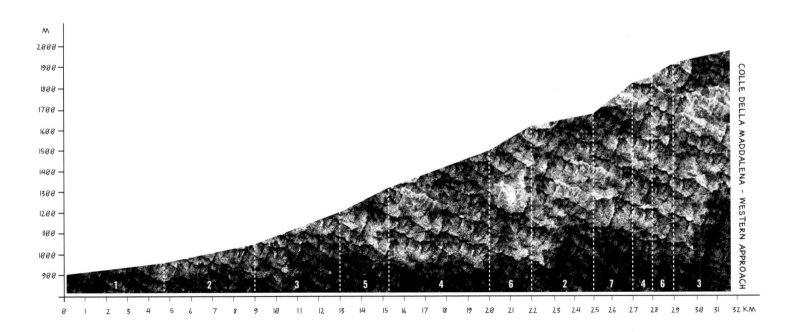

COLLE DELLA MADDALENA - WESTERN APPROACH

carts loaded with materials were so constructed that at each hairpin the muleteers could park the cart, unhitch the animals, bring them round to the rear of the cart and re-hitch them. This obviated the jolting of a tight turn and the danger of losing the load. Between 1920 and 1930, as part of the extension south of France's major frontier fortifications the Maginot Line (brainchild of the Defence Minister André Maginot, died 1932), two ancillary forts were built on either side of the Larche close by Tournoux, at Roche-la-Croix to the south and Saint-Ours to the north. Looking back to the bluff on which the Tournoux perches and from which it hangs like a concrete landslide, one can see how its fearsome armaments dominated the approach.

The Tournoux barracks are now derelict, gutted, windowless and dilapidated… an example to the war buffs whose narrow perspective and violent disposition ought, by now, to be following suit.

The D900 from Barcelonnette is easy, its continuation up the Larche being a main route into and out of Italy and thus invested with traffic, although periodically shut to heavy lorries in the summer months. However, pick your time of day and the nuisance will be diminished. Even so, we include it here for limited interest, largely as a handy way of crossing from the big climbs of High Provence to the big challenges of western Piedmont. The valley, along a climb which imposes no great stress, a steady swing of around 4 and 5%, is pleasant, green and cared for, and the road has a good surface. At the village of Larche (1675m, 24.7km) stands a former French customs post and to the side of the col itself – a bleak enough place, though there is a café – stands a memorial to Fausto Coppi set up by *Gli Amici di Coppi*, Cuneo 5 June 1982. A commemorative eulogy, handwritten on paper, is tied round the obelisk.

Eastern approach from Vinadio 904m

LENGTH: 31.8KM	
HEIGHT GAIN: 1087M	
MAXIMUM GRADIENT: 8%	

The valley on the Italian side is narrower, more closely attended by settlements and lures to linger, including the Therme di Vinadio – hydromassage, antistress, facials, lymphatic drainage etc – and the vinously-seductive village of Sambuco.

Best part of the climb is the final 5 or so kilometres which swish through 21 tornante (hairpins) and hoist you around 200m in a stretch of 3.3 kilometres between number 7 at 1740m and number 21 at 1920m. The bends are sharp, the hillside tonsured – a derelict building to the left may have been an old sheep farm or else a ruined border post for the detention of smugglers and their contraband – and the view back down really very fine: a splendid squiggle of road which finally straightens out into the funnel of the valley into the Province of Cuneo.

COL DE VARS 2108M

Northern approach from Guillestre 1000m

LENGTH: 19.7KM

HEIGHT GAIN: 1108M

MAXIMUM GRADIENT: 9%

Guillestre, an old fortress town whose mediaeval fortifications have largely disappeared, is an agreeable place to stop. Not a view shared, one assumes, by the captured English seamen and marines held prisoner here during the Napoleonic Wars. Many of the houses still show open granaries on the top floor with extending arms for the pulleys to winch up the sacks of grain. There are sundials on walls, too, a particular feature of this region, sundials with moral injunctions to make the most of time, ever passing time, localised variations, some in Latin or French, often in the Provençal patois, on the tempus fugit and horas non numero nisi serenas (I don't count the hours unless they are tranquil) theme, some bleak, some wry, all hortatory:

'lou tems passo lacte [actually *l'acte*] *resto'*
Time passes, get on and do

'lou tems passo, passo lou ben'
Time passes, pass it well

'C'est l'heure de bien vivre'
Now is the hour: live well
[whether morally or gastronomically]

'utere praesenti, memor ultimatae'
Make full use of the present hour,
mindful of your last

'Le temps enchaîne la lumière guide'
Prisoners of time, day's light our guide

'Solo horare do, in deo spem vides'
I count but hours, you look for hope to God.
(And words issuing from the mouth of an angel:)

'Toi qui me regardes, écoute, accorde le rythme de ton coeur aux battements de mes instants, comprends-tu maintenant comme il est temps d'aimer'
Thou who look upon me, listen: attune the rhythm of your heart to my movements and understand, now, that it is time to love

'O tempora currere talis torrens'
O, the ever onrushing torrent of time.

And others:
'Mets la joie dans ta vie Aime travaille et pri'
Instil your life with love, work hard and pray

'La vie passe comme une ombre'
Life passes like a shadow.

One sundial warns:
'Je passe et je reviens, Tu passes et ne reviens pas'
I pass and return, You pass and do not return.

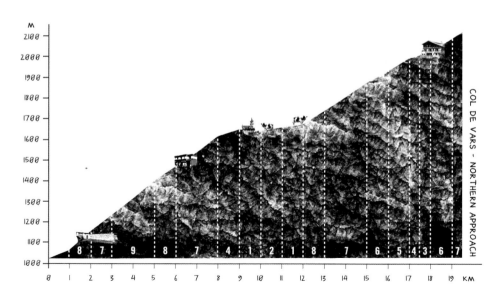

COL DE VARS - NORTHERN APPROACH

The D902 sweeps broad and steep in wide bends out of town, some 8 kilometres of upwards of 8 and 9%. It does, if you allow the unsettling thought to filter in, have the feel of a road built for skiers in coaches and cars. However there is, to distract you, a strong presence of mountain, wide views, a number of small communities en route to catch your interest. The surface is good, the knowledge that there is an intervening flat step of 3 kilometres to come, perhaps a small encouragement, and the stiffish gradient is, at least, regular. Contrarily, there are long straight stretches, too, which can be tiresome.

At 8.6km the slope flattens to a modest 4% or so, the road crossing three bridges in quick succession and then dropping into the first outcrop of the Vars consortium of hamlets, Saint-Marcellin-de-Vars (1635m, 10.4km), all of old foundation and now expanded to accommodate the seasonal tourist influx, although Saint-Marcellin exhibits no evident contamination. Sainte-Marie-de-Vars marks the last of this interim of easy riding with a snap of gradient, beginning 4 kilometres of up to 7.5% to the ski station of Vars itself. Idle ski lifts and their attendant commercial outlets, housing and appartmentalisation don't do much for the limited attractions of the village, long since encrusted with all the appurtenances of the winter invasion, at least a peaceable invasion.

Pleasantly situated beside a lake fed by a stream (1960m, 17.4km), the Refuge Napoleon opened on 28 August 1856, one of six (eight were planned but funds ran out). They were constructed on the order of the Emperor Napoleon III from moneys bequeathed by his uncle the Emperor Napoleon I (who died in 1821), in accordance with his posthumous wish to thank those three alpine *départements* of the Isère, the Drôme and the Hautes-Alpes which welcomed him after his return from Elba. Napoleon III acted, he said, 'for durable and friendly institutions in the heart of the region to perpetuate the holy memory with which Napoleon I honoured them.'

There are other refuges on the Cols d'Izoard, de Lacroix, du Noyer, Agnello and de Manse.

The Vars Refuge offers rooms and a restaurant as well as a range of facilities for those who wish to explore the area. The open moorland between it and the col is sweet relief at the top of the climb on a reduced slope of around 6%.

Southern approach from Fort de Tournoux 1308m

| LENGTH: 14.7KM |
| HEIGHT GAIN: 800M |
| MAXIMUM GRADIENT: 11% |

Note: There are col signs, altitude and distance, on both sides, all the way up.

A short way along the D902, branching from the D900 out of Barcelonnette, lies the Redoute de Berwick, the only one left of seven forts built by Vauban. The fort is named after James Fitz-James, first Duke of Berwick, an illegitimate son of the Catholic king James II of England. He was born in France and returned there after the succession in 1688 of the Protestant Dutch king, William III, to the English throne. A brilliant soldier and general, he became a Marshal of France. After his crushing victory in the War of the Spanish Succession at Almanza, northern Spain, in 1707, he was created Duc de Fitz-James by Louis XIV. Almanza is remarkable: an Englishman at the head of a Franco-Spanish army defeating a Frenchman – Henri de Massue, Marquis de Ruvigny, Earl of Galway, a Protestant exile and mercenary captain – at the head of an Anglo-Portuguese-Dutch army.

This is a flat valley approach through verdant meadows and pasture, small farmsteads, somnolent cattle grazing, big bosses of rock lowering over the tree-lined banks of the river Ubaye. The Vars and the Larche both tend to lose their winter snow quite early and for that reason alone, this valley of the Ubaye was, for centuries, a favoured route for invasion. Whichever flank melted first offered the prompt to a sally of arms and baggage trains for plunder.

At 3.5km a turn left leads back round to the Fort de Tournoux and at 4.4km, a tunnel with open embrasures looking out over the river and the sheer sides of the mountain, trickling streams of fresh water down their melancholy scored and furrowed stone face. And another tunnel, no windows but lit. The first 6 kilometres into Saint-Paul-sur-Ubaye (1450m) run at a leisurely pace, no stiffer than 4.5% with a bit of a kick up into town – hotel, auberge, chalets. The D25 to the right follows the upper course of the Ubaye and fades out into a footpath which treks to the source. Now the climbing proper begins on a regime of 6–7%.

The gendarmerie (the national rural police force, military in organisation, the word gendarme means 'armed man') has a barracks at 6.8km, 1480m, close by a sign indicating 'Col de Vars'. Off to the right, dominating the skyline, the great chain of the Chambeyron massif and, somewhere in amongst its jagged peaks, the Aiguille de Chambeyron at 3412m.

The road begins to levitate off the valley floor, bold ramparts of rock off to the left, a long view ahead and the road has a friendly, ambling feel to it, despite the statistics of gradient and despite this being one of the major climbs of these mountains and imbued with some ferocious incidents in cycle-race history. At 9.8km, 1660m, a small church below to the right in Les Prats ('the leas') and the gaunt

ridge of the Tête de Paneyron directly ahead. At a
hairpin here, in June, the lilac is in abundant bloom
and profuse of sweet scent. Across two small bridges
and onto the serious final assault of the col: brace
yourself for some nasty business… upwards of 11%
and no relief for just over 4 kilometres.

The ground is open, hummocky, grassy,
blisters of exposed earth and rock, and the line of
the col is in view, quite shallow with bare slopes
of scree draped like a muffler round the wattled
throat of the ridge. There is contentment and a
spur to effort in the tantalising sight of the pass,
the goal, the destination.

At the col, a souvenir-covered stall – buy your
whistling stuffed toy marmot – and L'Igloo, a bar/
restaurant/crêperie run by a charming and obliging
woman who will cook you an omelette to order
and tempt you with various scrumptious fruit tarts,
strawberry, apple, almond and pear… do not resist,
you owe yourself the treat.

A large commemorative stone by the road to the
west records a brief history of salient moments in
the shenanigans hereabouts.

1369 Vars sacked by a band of routiers (originally
      'freebooters', later independent cycle racers…
      draw your own conclusion.)
1383 The col is designated as part of the frontier
      between France and the state of Savoy.
1515 In July, an army led by King François I
      of France invades Italy over the col.
1518 Ubaye becomes French once more.
1559 The col marks the new frontier.
1692 A battle on the col (26 July) between the
      Milices du Dauphin (heir to the French
      throne) and the army of the Duc de Savoie.
      French victory. Savoy returns to France on
      21 September.

1713 Peace of Utrecht. Ubaye becomes definitively
      French sovereign soil.
1744 On 1 April a combined Franco-Spanish force
      under Louis François I, Prince of Conti, and
      Philip, heir to the Spanish throne, advances
      into Savoy over the Vars and on to Nice.
      On 21 April their combined expedition crushes
      the Piedmontese-Sardinian army at Villafranca
      (Villefranche-sur-Mer) on the Mediterranean
      coast east of Nice.

Another stone records the construction of the
road by various elements of the French army –
alpine troops, elite mountain infantry, engineers
– and its opening in 1891.

Hinault Fights Back

The Col de Vars was first included in the Tour de France in 1922, in tandem with the Col d'Izoard, also initiated that year. In 1933, the Frenchman Georges Speicher rode down the Vars heading for eventual victory in Paris with the aid of a new secret technological advance: a rear brake whose stirrups were fixed inside the rear stays instead of on the outside. This avoided snatching and delivered a smoother application of the blocks. In 1938, Speicher's Tour career came to an ignominious end, prefiguring that of his compatriot Jacky Durand in 2002: he was caught hanging onto a car door on a climb in the Pyrenees and disqualified.

In 1986, Bernard Hinault's Tour nearly ended on the Vars. Hinault was in fearful pain from a pulled muscle in his knee. (He had, in the past, been badly afflicted with tendonitis – in 1980, he'd had to abandon.) It was, he said, the only time he ever cried on a bike. Although he had promised to work for his lieutenant Greg Lemond's victory, on the face of it he had been doing quite the opposite, attacking incessantly and shaking the American's trust. Indeed, Robert Millar, the specialist climber, said that they had never ridden the mountains so fast. (Hinault won the Mountains prize.) Urs Zimmerman and Lemond, now in the hunt for yellow, ahead, Hinault, in obvious distress, overheard a moto-cameraman say to his driver: 'Stay with him – he's going to pack.' Hinault was stung. He fought back, so far beyond any crowding thought of pain or discomfort that he limited his day's losses to four minutes on Lemond. He started the next day still in considerable pain, but if pride is no certain cure it is a powerful anaesthetic and, at the end of that celebrated 18th stage, Hinault drove himself and Lemond in a decisive lead, the pair of them alone, up to the finish at l'Alpe d'Huez.

Surely not referring to Speicher's super-duper component, Hinault once said: 'No technology can increase the willpower of a rider, nor can it lessen the doubts which sometimes overwhelm him.'

Colle d'Agnello 2744m[1]

Western approach from Ville-Vieille 1400m

LENGTH: 21KM	
HEIGHT GAIN: 1344M	
MAXIMUM GRADIENT: 10%	

The D902 east from Guillestre passes through the narrow ravine of the Combe du Queyras, cut by the river Guil to Château-Queyras, another stark example of Vauban's work, dominating the Guil valley to the west of Ville-Vieille. Backing up this defence-work constructed by man, divine support is sought from a rocky peak, l'Ange Gardien, just to the south. Ville-Vieille, the town that existed long before this intervention of military engineers, at the start of the Agnello is tranquil and the Hôtel Gilazur offers fairly basic accommodation and a very friendly welcome. The Bar du Village, next door, serves excellent tuck (although the Gilazur does have a restaurant) and I urge you to try raclette if you have not sampled it yet. From a dish of boiled new potatoes pluck one onto your plate and onto it scoop cheese – the local cheeses are perfect for cooking – from a big slice which has melted under an overhead hot iron. Scrape off the goo, leave the harder layer underneath to melt in its turn. Eat with cornichons (gherkins) and, perhaps, thin slivers of blood-red, locally-cured ham marbled with white fat. Delicious. Round off your supper with a slug of the liquor digestif génépi (a Savoyard word for the alpine yarrow or wormwood flower). Another word for absinthe – do I need to elaborate there? – and the basis of both a liqueur and a salve for wounds.

The Agnello pass has seen a lot of action, one way and another, details listed on a large rock stele up the valley.[2]

218BC Hannibal, his army and his elephants heading for Italy.

51BC Caesar's legions (from the reverse direction) a-conquering of Gaul.

1515 Chevalier Bayard, oft considered that last of the true knights in shining armour, le bon chevalier, who busied himself much with his king's interests in these disputed territories.

1578 Duc de Lesdiguières, Constable of France, more of the same [see Bayard] but he did secure the final submission to the crown of the then independent Dauphiné.

1579 Maréchal de Bellegarde, from a famous Savoy family. More interesting than his belligerence is the fact that the king Henri IV poached his mistress, Gabrielle Estrée, a woman of high intelligence and feisty temperament. The king showered her with money, honours, titles, even offering her the throne just to keep her. She remained unswayed. She wrote:

> *Strange thing to watch a great king*
> *In thrall to women,*
> *Honour forgotten,*
> *Seeing an angel in a whore.*

1712 Duc de Berwick [see COL DE VARS]
1743 Philip of Spain [ditto above]

A local heroine, Marguerite Eyméoud, is also celebrated here though the date of her exploit is given as 1692: other sources give 1792. I was at pains to find out who she was; the patronne of the Gilazur did not know, gave as her excuse that she is from the other end of Provence, but recommended a visit to the Maison de Presse in Aiguilles up the road as the owner was, it seems, a rare scholar. He hadn't a clue. I asked the garage man at Ville-Vieille, 'Do you know of a Marguerite Eyméoud?'

'Yes,' he replied, 'she's my cousin, she lives in Molines.'

Either I had stumbled on a miracle of longevity to rival the venerable Methuselah or she was a descendant. Sadly, the cousin knew no more and my search continued. It transpires that the widow Eyméoud, Marguerite, of Molines-en-Queyras, hailed originally from Costeroux, a mountain hamlet above Fontgillarde, up the valley. Seven of its houses were swept away by an avalanche in 1708, another eleven were destroyed by avalanche in 1788 leaving ten, only, until the village was finally abandoned shortly after 1824. The ever-present threat of destruction by snow and rock clearly put steel into Marguerite's will because, sick of the incessant depredations of brigands, she galvanized the inhabitants from round about to take a stand. Very Magnificent Seven. In a defile of the Aigue Agnelle, the river flowing down this valley, the villagers ambushed a wagon train of robbers, reclaimed the booty and saw the intruders off. Sadly, the bold Marguerite died in the affray.

---

1 The Agnello, in Italian, is known as the Agnel in French. The words are synonymous, namely 'lamb'. For reasons not entirely capricious – the Agnello has often featured in the Giro d'Italia – but to give the Italian side of this book the added weight of presence which it richly deserves, we have plumped for Agnello.

2 There is some dispute about the pass they crossed. Montgenèvre, Mont-Cenis, Saint-Bernard some way to the north are all proffered but the evidence seems to point most directly to the unpaved Col de Savine-Coche (generally known as the Petit Mont-Cenis, just south of its Grand cousin). The historian Livy, following the earlier writer Polybius, insists that Hannibal arrived in Italy in the territory occupied by the Taurini tribe, the environs of modern Turin. Polybius writes that Hannibal pointed to the great, fertile sweep of the plains in the Po valley and the well-ordered and prosperous communities of the Gauls who inhabited them and told his men – exhausted by the long trek – that life there would be good.

In November 1944, her shade was re-invoked by six volunteers who 'fell for liberty and the defence of Queyras'.

At Ville-Vieille, leave the D902 which continues as the D947 and follow the D5, 4 kilometres of variable steepness, 6–8%, and on into Molines-en-Queyras (1765m, 5.5km) after a short flat stretch. (At about 4km, to your right you will see one of the celebrated Demoiselles Coiffées, rock formations peculiar to the region and described more fully in MONT COLOMBIS).

Out of Molines, take the left-hand fork, D205, onto a long balcony of a road at a brisk 8% or so

to another more even stretch into Pierre-Grosse (1885m, 7.5km), a tiny mountain village with a very narrow street of bumpy texture, houses, many of them ramshackle, pressing in from both sides like eager fans. Imagine the Tour coming up through here as it did in 2008. Extra. A sundial on the outside wall of a gîte admonishes: *'Tant que tu vis, vis'...* Live life to the full.

There is a big presence of ski chalets in Pierre Grosse and Fontgillarde. Just outside Fontgillarde, across the hillside to the right, on the flat bank of the river, someone has spelled out 'STIEB' (German: 'rise up') in stones next to a large C inside a double

circle, also in stones. A plea, surely, to Christ?

There are lots of graffiti on the road, post-Tour, including '2018' – France is vying for that year's Winter Olympics.

As did the riders the first time the Agnello appeared on the Tour itinerary (but many times in the Giro d'Italia), you will see the big range which dominates the horizon, far, far ahead.

Beyond Pierre-Grosse, the land opens out into flower-spangled meadows, the river cutting its way over a scumble of boulders and large pebbles over to the right, the road snaking through like a causeway. Fontgillarde (1990m, 9.5km), low enough below Marguerite Eyméoud's vanished home hamlet not to be in imminent danger of avalanche, yet still alert to the threat of off-mountain jetsam, has transverse rain gutters set into its high street. A short lift out and into grassy meadow slopes, a flattish moorland, a scatter of chalets, the river below to the right and a bastion of rock pinning some history to the landscape, the Rocher d'Annibal.

Set back from the road to the left, near a bridge over the river, a small wooden cabin houses Chez Mem's, a buvette – French snackery.

The last 8 kilometres begin the true climb away from the riverine pastures and up into the bleak fastness of this border pass, slow to tighten but after 2 kilometres of warm-up, a steady smack, smack, smack of upwards of 9%. The mountain sides are more exposed too, loose scree for vegetation, the road hitting some sharp bends, the ridge often snow-streaked still in June and exhaling a chilly mist.

Here the climb feels wild, testing, the verdure of the lovely valley gone, the grass more scrubby and the marmot sentinels on the instant qui vive (look-out) for intruders. Perhaps their atavistic suspicion jumped the gene pool into that of the local humans.

The surface is good, the bends serious, the

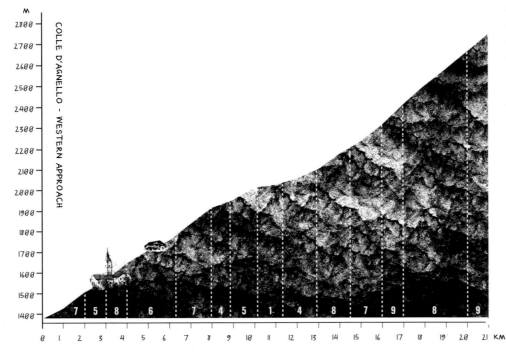

M

COLLE D'AGNELLO – WESTERN APPROACH

2800
2700
2600
2500
2400
2300
2200
2100
2000
1900
1800
1700
1600
1500
1400

7 5 8 6 7 4 5 1 4 8 7 9 8 9

0 1 2 3 4 5 6 7 8 9 10 11 12 13 14 15 16 17 18 19 20 21 KM

gradient hard and the tip of the road over the col most welcome. The Refuge Napoléon is now nought but a pile of ruins, although there is a large chalet-refuge off to the right below the pass and a visitor centre to the left.

A stone, placed here in 1823, marks the Franco-Italian frontier and the altitude. The view south into Italy is staggering, dramatic.

Eastern approach from Casteldolfino 1280m

LENGTH:	22.4KM
HEIGHT GAIN:	1464M
MAXIMUM GRADIENT:	14%

The road follows the course of the river Varaita di Chianale which flows some 75 kilometres through the Province of Cuneo, north-west Italy into the river Po. It rises at some 2,500m on the slopes of Monte Viso, in the Cottian Alps near the French border, not far from the source of the northward-flowing Ubaye.

This Val Varaita is the historical home of Italian winter ice climbing. The Ciucchinel Fall was the first icefall ever climbed in Italy, in 1977. On the way to the fall, west of Casteldolfino, lies the village of Bellino and a trove of antique sundials, all beautifully restored:

'Lou soulei nais per tuchi'
'The sun shines on all' (?) echoing the Biblical 'He maketh his sun rise on the evil and the good, and sendeth rain on the just and on the unjust.' *Matthew* 5:45.

'Vers le couchant je m'incline et vers la mort tu chemines'
I dip toward the west, you walk towards death

'Sine sole silet (sans soleil ne dit rien du tout)'
No sun… nothing to say

'Vulnerant omnes ultima necat ' (i.e. hours)
Every hour wounds us, the final hour kills us

'Le moindre nuage me trahit et le moindre souffle te détruit'
The thinnest cloud betrays me and the thinnest breath destroys you.

The climbing proper begins some two kilometres out of Casteldolfino, a 3 kilometre blast of 9% at worst to the Barrage in Castello (1590m) a little village off the road by the lake formed by the dam. A respite of some 2 kilometres into Pontechianale and a fine restaurant La Peiro Groso ('The Big Rock'), offering a subtler menu than any *Hard Rock*. Choose a bottle of Maero bottled in Castellar, a light fruity garnet in colour, from the Saluzzesi hills. In 1511, Marguerite de Foix (east of Carcassonne in the Pyrenees) and Marqhesato di Saluzzo (some 40 kilometres directly east of Pontechianale) gave Pope Julius II several bottles of the local vintage, a shameless bribe in return for an unimpeachable pedigree – 'Vintners to the Pope'. The fact that a princess of Foix was also Marquise of lands so far distant is an indication of how these territories were so distinct for so long, their autonomy deeply established, affiliations to the Papal See one thing, subjugation by monarchs quite another.

The ravioli hereabouts comes in a narrow tube shape, pointed at either end.

The church in Pontechianale, across a narrow stone bridge spanning the tumbling stream, bears an inscription in a frieze: 'La maison de Dieu est unne maison de priere est doreson ou les cretiens ni doivent antrer quavec crete est respect' (The house of God is a house of prayer and orison [also 'prayer' or, maybe, 'sermon'] wherein Christians should not enter save with awe [crete for crainte] and respect). The original is a charming example of phonic spelling. French orthography is problematic, largely because the

language contains so many homophones.[3]

A kilometre of 7.5% out of Pontechianale slackens into more manageable slopes, no worse than 4.5% into Chianale where the trouble starts. The view ahead is, however, stupendous. It's a huge mountain, the towering triangular bulk of it thrust up between two sloping valley sides which meet at the shallow V of the Varaita di Chianale. It is like a brusque memento mori, that massive presence of the very best that Nature can do with raw stone, and you on a bike on a winding road, the preamble to the hard ascent and that gaunt indicator of what has to be done looming in the centre of the main picture.

A sign tells you that the col is closed from 15 October until June. From Chianale (1800m, 12km), roadside signs impart extravagantly detailed statistical invoices: '1k 1809m 10.6% over 1.319k 9.45k to col…'

And here at Chianale stands the first of a number of powder-blue metal timing stations dotted about cols in the area on the Italian side, foot and top, all supplied with a card/microchip – in it goes, and off you go – 'Partenza'. The idea, instigated in 2005, is to time yourself and, thus, enter a league of best times. Go to the website www.rampignado.com and find, listed there, the best times recorded so far.

On 5 July 2008, ascending the Agnello from Chianale, one Leone Bruno recorded 33min 31sec and, less than 2½ hours later, he did the climb again and bettered that with 32min 49sec. Nutter.

Away from the self-inflicted pain clock-in machine, a left-hand hairpin takes the road over a torrent onto the climb proper. The tarmac is new and a sign indicates *'tornante'* (hairpin) at 1.8km, 100m. There is a breathtaking, wild view back right down

---

3 At Wareham, in Dorset, a similar frieze in a church will tell you how a sea captain 'died of a favour' – the local pronunciation of 'fever'.

the long valley and ahead to the steep sides of the mountain. This lump of rock has majestic attitude.

Another sign called 'Pra Nou' (new field) gives 1948m, 11.27% (over the next) 5km, 8.13km to the col.

Larch trees abound. Larch is *mélèze* in French, a Dauphinois word derived from vernacular Latin melacio from a pre-Roman *melix*, 'ice' – a homely notion, to name a tree from the way its lolling branches resemble the action of dripping. A 15th century melze is probably cognate with classical Greek μέλδειν – *meldein*, 'to soften by boiling, melt', though there is no obvious etymological link with the Old English meltan. The larch's resin is *térébinthe de Vénise*, i.e. Venetian turpentine, and its bark is used in tanning. The Italian is larice from Latin *larix decidua* – the larch is the only conifer which loses its leaves and its wood is hard and durable. The Roman poet Lucan records how the Psyllians, a people in North Africa famed as snake-charmers, added larch branches to fumigatory fires to keep enemy and evil spirits at bay.

At 3km a collection of ruined cabins and one new stone cabin sit to the right of the road, surely a byre used in the transhumance. Here the river swings right up the cleft of the lower slopes of Le Pain de Sucre ('Sugar-loaf'), the high peak dominating the range, the road turns left. A sign (Grange del Rio) shows 9.22% 904m 7.631km to go. Apart from the larches the roadside is pretty bare.

Sign: 'Tornante Carlo Emmanuele III 11.37% 850m 6.27km'. (The prince in question was duke of Savoy and king of Sardinia from 1730 to his death in 1773.)

A ruined building stares with blind windows from above up on soft, grassy slopes.

After the sign 'Roccio Skiapà 2183m 11.21% .458km 5.877km' the road traverses the deep and wide gouge of a stream bed which has spilled its course – long mounded spines of jagged stone interspersed with grass. A new stone building advertises 'BURRO FORMAGGIO' (butter and cheese).

At 6.8km, the steep rock-erupting grass of the slope plunges away from the road at mad angles, an overhead cable emits a whanging radio signal, a fizzling electric current bouncing between contacts. Now the road leaves the open gulf of the re-entrant to tackle the final assault, zigzagging round the close-hugged flanks, the last-gasp mano a mano. A sign 'Costa Rossette 2433m 10.61% .777km 3.3 to col'.

The multi-layered shale of the mountainside moves in on you, the very image of bare-toothed hostility, until the grass and soil cover and mitigate it. A sign – 'Valsecchi Alessandro 2610m 1.499km to col'. (He is possibly that bishop of Bergamo who died in 1879.)

The road narrows dramatically, hutched up against the mountain wall, most precarious. There are intermittent barriers and, scrawled in white and yellow chalk, (and this is the direction in which the 2008 Tour crossed): 'Ciaou Mama B.S.D.' coupled with an arrow pointing over the edge. This faintly sinister message goes, so far, unexplained. The 'Vai Damiano', by contrast, is clear, an injunction – 'Go' – to the Italian rider Damiano Cunego. Sign: 'Tornante L'A 2635m 10.79%. 904m 1.40km (from the col)'. Pulmonaires, of purple flower and blue at the base, sprout in the scant soil.

These last lifts to the col are shockingly narrow, the hairpins are murderously tight, a real helter-skelter of a chute off the col. On the road, 'NON AU LOUP' in green. Off to the right, just below the summit, is a Refugio Degli Alpini dedicated to one Mario Bottero and above it an oversize statue of the Virgin with a lamb at her feet (Agnus Dei... agnello... lamb, favourite prey of the wolf...) and an inscription voicing a prayer for universal peace and friendship between alpins (walkers) and chasseurs (hunters).

At the col, the blue machine to check your time, if contre-la-montre (time trial) is your style.

Saved by an Avalanche

In 1995, the Swiss Tony Rominger, having won the Vuelta a España a record three times in succession, came to the Giro d'Italia. At the conclusion of stage 18 he led by a healthy 5 minutes from Yevgeny Berzin and Pyotr Ugramov. Stage 19 was a classic Giro mountain killer: 202 kilometres from Mondovi to Briançon, via Borgo san Dalmazzo, over the Sampeyre and the Maddallena, up to Chianale and over the Agnello (as always for the Cima Coppi prime, or prize), then the Izoard.

The break went with nine riders, none obviously significant on GC (General Classification i.e. standings in the race). At 2.30, an hour before the race was due over the Agnello, an avalanche broke down the mountain side and injured a group of ten spectators, one of whom worked for the Giro. The organisers annulled the stage at Chianale (129km), to obviate danger to the caravan and above all the riders. Pascal Richard, who'd won a mountain stage at the 1994 Giro into Sestriere, took the win and Rominger cruised in, unthreatened. He took the pink jersey on without hiccup into Milan. This marked only the second occasion when a Giro stage was abandoned. They scoff at snow and unmade roads. (The other time was on the Passo Rolle in 1962.)

The 1994 Giro also went over the Agnello, scene of a rare ding-dong between Marco Pantani and Berzin. Pantani attacked again and again but the Russian wouldn't let go. He had his mind on victory and he made sure of it that day. Again it was Agnello, then Izoard, but on to a finish at Deux Alpes.

Col d'Izoard 2360m

Northern approach from Briançon 1210m

LENGTH: 19.6KM

HEIGHT GAIN: 1150M

MAXIMUM GRADIENT: 9%

The D902 leaves town at a steady 5% for around 4 kilometres. At 3.7km a by-road to the left leads up to the Fort du Goudran, part of the extensive fortifications of this key defensive position at the intersection of four valleys – Guisane, Durance, Cerveyrette and Clarée – and a mere 21 kilometres from the Italian border, north-west over the Montgenèvre pass. The old town, Ville Haute, circumvallated with a ring of forts, was laid out by Vauban and its steep, narrow streets are a great lure for tourists. The church of Notre Dame, in the shadow of Vauban's bastions, is girded with cypresses and dedicated to God rather than gunpowder though carefully sited to double as a defensive salient if need

be. Briançon, *petite ville et grand renom* (small town of great renown) held out for three months against a besieging Austrian army with a garrison of 300 in 1815. There are still barracks in the lower town and a military ski school for the *chasseurs alpines* (alpine infantry, literally 'alpine hunters') founded in 1904.

It is a long heave out of town along a narrow valley, some parts a bit of a highway, but the gradient has a fixed tempo and at around 4.3km, 1400m, it flattens and falls away for a while. Early in the climb such loss of height can be taken in stride. At 6km, in the company of wooded slopes, the climbing resumes, but for only a kilometre of 6–7% before a marked easing on the way up to Cervières (1615m, 9.6km) on a by-road to the left. The village was badly damaged during the final bitter fighting of the Second World War in this region, but the 15th century church survived.

The road continues through broad meadowlands, a great cordon of trees far in the distance like a

dense smoke screen shielding the flanks of the rock beyond. Two kilometres of the same 6–7% brings you to Le Laus (1750m, 12km), and a large, beetle-browed four-storey chalet, the Arpelin auberge and restaurant, a good place to stay – feather beds – and certainly to eat. Its speciality is open-hearth cooking, gigots hooked by their heels to a metal bar and roasted for some 5 hours over a fire of Scotch Fir (*pinus sylvestris*) and larch logs, assiduously basted by M le patron… 'tis a lovely sight and we had no time to stay to enjoy the result, pooh. You may sample the incongruously named 'La Tourmente' beer brewed from the pure *malte d'orge* (barley malt) of the region which is very far from a torment.

When Pete, the photographer, and I stopped for lunch that time, it was apparent that the waitress was not French. Indeed, her accent had a distinctly English note. I said to Pete: 'She'll be from Leytonstone.' She was, in fact, from Walthamstow, next door.

The final 7 kilometres head into the woods and negotiate a series of hairpins. The scent of pine and mountain beguile and perhaps distract from the sharp twist and turn of these hairpins at what now sets to a constant hammering at your legs, lungs, and possibly your back, too, of 8–10%. At around 1 kilometre from the top, the trees finish and the Refuge Napoléon pops out to the left like a Siren to seduce you to stop for warm cake and coffee and all manner of scrummy things with which to regale your suffering stomach and spirits but, should you wish to ride this col all in one, the final steep ramps on the helter-skelter that is the last kilometre beckon like a good deed in a naughty world and, hey, you can always scoot back down for tuck. Moreover, those last racks of the climb look horribly severe but are not, in truth, horribly severe. For, you have come this far, so what folly of indifference can suppress the adrenalin, the willpower, the sheer cussedness to go all the way in one?

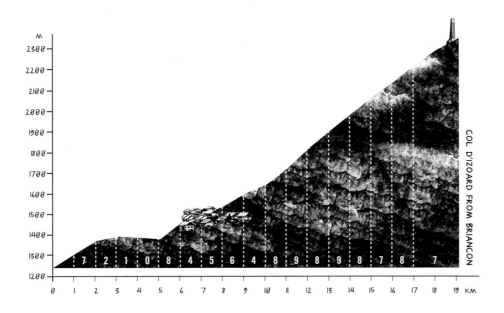

COL D'IZOARD FROM BRIANCON

COL D'IZOARD *continued*

Southern approach from junction of D902 with D947 1355m

LENGTH:	14.5KM
HEIGHT GAIN:	1005M
MAXIMUM GRADIENT:	10+%

The rock is up there, in full view, from the start. Apart from a sharp slope of around 7.5% into Le Pasquier (1530m, 4km), the approach is none too hard. The altitude signs are at odds with my altimeter reading but that is a commonplace of atmospheric variability and nothing, O reader, O mon frère, mon semblable (fellow creature), to get in a swither about. The string of wee communities, once mindful of their own business – as ever, survival – have been inundated with less pernicious influx than the destructive power of avalanche but quite as momentous: skiing. La Chalp (1670m 5.9km), has been overrun with squat chalets and, ski lifts poking out of the encrustation, rendered an ugly, sprawling mess. As if the road itself expresses its own distaste, the slope hits 7 and then around 10% and, all at once warming to its anger, does not relent from here to the top.

After another outcrop of chaletdom at Brunissard (1755m, 7km), you may say that the climb proper is on. The road, until now a meandering ramble through the foothills, meadows interspersed with built-up areas, hits the first big right-hand bend out of Brunissard onto a succession of shorter hairpins and a snaky approach to the real meat of the ascent. It noses forward into the tightening grip of the Izoard, round steep hairpins and fairly short interlinks onto a longer terrace from around 10.5km, 2030m. Stony ridges appear on the open side and the bends do the switchback to crank up the height – twiddle-gear 9% and more – with a dramatic lash of the tarmac whip. A long straight leads up to a viewing platform (left) and a hard right-hand bend and there… the Casse Déserte.

Here, at 12.2km, 2210m, you see the famous lunar landscape, the teetering slopes of the mountain to the right deep in scree and the huge rock stacks towering out of the rubble. It looks smooth, like grey aggregate, pulverized shingle, a slide of lava turned to stone. Everyone who rides this colossus of a climb will retain an indelible memory of it. And, if the ghosts of the Tour gather routinely anywhere on the route, you feel it must be in the lonely canyon of the Casse Déserte, amid the atavar menhirs, under the blazing furnace of the Dog Star. Those rock stacks might be the statue embodiment of the implacable *juges de paix*, the arbiters of human frailty who preside over the Tour, who punish the *jour sans* (off day) without pity, who oversee with a cold eye the terrible *défaillance* (loss of strength, physical and mental) and the superhuman acts of bravery, endurance and tenacity alike.

The road sweeps off for half a kilometre on a snort of relief past the ghostly presence of the primeval stone pillars and onto the final hard slog of the climb, 1.8 kilometres of 10%.

Atop the col, in a large, unpaved parking area, stands an obelisk memorial to one Général Baron Berge and units of Alpine infantry whose endeavours – with the cooperation of the *départements* involved – helped realise the Touring Club of France's dream of a Route des Alpes. By linking the Cols d'Izoard, Vars and Cayolle they opened the way north-south to the Paris–Lyon–Mediterranean railway company.

A souvenir shop serves moral uplift on postcards of sundial mottoes in praise of the sun:

'De tes rais raiou lou mel'
From your rays comes honey

'Lou sourey se levo per tutches'
Your smile alights on all

'Nihil sine sole'
Nothing without the sun

'Lumière est vie, vis dans la lumière'
Light is life, live in the light.

Thévenet Holds His Nerve

On the southern approach, just below that Shangri-La of the col where the roads dips away north, stands a memorial to two men who wrote their names into the history of the Izoard by crossing it alone: Fausto Coppi and Louison Bobet. Coppi rode over the Izoard in yellow, 1949, the year of his first Tour win. The year before, his great rival Bartali did the same on the way to his second win and in 1953, when the road over the col was still no more than a rustic track, thick with dust, littered with flints, Coppi stood next to the French directeur Marcel Bidot at the side of the road, where the plaque is now, with a camera slung over his shoulder.

As Bobet rode by, in yellow, he gave the campionissimo, his hero, a friendly nod and Coppi remarked to Bidot: 'Beautiful.' Years later, Bobet told Bernard Thévenet that the mark of a real Tour champion was to lead the race from the front through the awesome wilderness, in yellow. And, in 1975, Thévenet did just that. Merckx, who'd lost yellow to the Frenchman the day before, attacked him again and again but Thévenet didn't falter and finally pulled away. Nearing the top, he passed a young woman holding up a banner which read: 'Merckx, the Bastille has fallen.' It was 14 July. (Merckx, the five-times winner and dominant champion of professional cycling, who'd lost yellow to the Frenchman the day before, attacked him again and again but Thévenet didn't lose his nerve.)

Merckx in yellow claimed the Izoard in 1972, his fellow Belgian Van Impe took the Tour – and the Izoard, in yellow – in 1976.

The mountain entered the Tour in 1922. Its first conqueror was another Belgian, Philippe Thys, first triple winner, and in 1923, riding to overall victory, Henri Pélissier baptised the great col, as it were, with a mystic significance. Thévenet himself used the Izoard as an example of how a rider must parcel out his effort: to expend every iota of his strength up to the col, saving only a bare a fraction with which to jump-start recovery on the way down. Speaking of that day, when he reinforced his superiority over Merckx – albeit the lead was, as he put it to the author, 'no more than a speck of soot with someone like Merckx' – he said the experience of the crowds cheering him deliriously up and over the Izoard filled one of the great moments of his life.[4]

4 That day's stage, from Barcelonnette, which he won, alone, ended in Serre Chevalier, a ski complex to the west of Briançon. We see fit not to include it here, despite its moment of history. It's not worth the detour, nor does it feature in the official Tour de France list of summit finishes.

COLLE DELLA LOMBARDA 2350M

Northern approach from Vinadio 904m

LENGTH: 22KM

HEIGHT GAIN: 1446M

MAXIMUM GRADIENT: 10%

Vinadio, at the foot of the Stura di Demonte (stura is a bottleneck) where the stream widens into a full river, is the site of Il Forte Albertino, one of the largest fortifications in Piemonte, unique in that its walls enclose a substantial area of farmed land. The work was instigated by Carlo Emmanuele III [see above] and completed in 1847 in the reign of a successor, Carlo Alberto di Savoia, hence its name.

Some 400 of Garibaldi's followers, captured at the battle of Aspromonte, 18 September 1862, were held prisoner here for nearly a month. Gaunt and partially ruined, now, its precinct is the venue in summer for shows and concerts.

Go west for one kilometre out of town on the SS21 – which eventually crosses the Colle della Maddalena – and turn left over a bridge towards Pratolungo, a farming village, half a kilometre. There follow 800 metres of new tarmac daubed with a series of trident graffiti with the legend: 'Giro France le Tour' to one of which a local kid, Louis, has chalked his name. Then comes a string of quite

well drawn bike motifs and one large bike motif, at 1.2km, with 'DIDI'.

This is steep, 8–10+%, hairpins spaced at around 100m or 200m variably, shady acers (maples) and pines in attendance. At around 2km, there is an affectionate memorial to a 'dearly beloved' local padre Gourdanetto, Luigi, who died, aged 48 in 1947 'da fatal disgrazia'. Not, as you might think, stabbing cheerlessly at an ill-informed translation of the word, in community revenge for some scandalous extracurricular activity with a choirboy behind the sacristy, but in a fatal accident, presumably a fall. A short way on, by the road, a shrine to Santa Anna

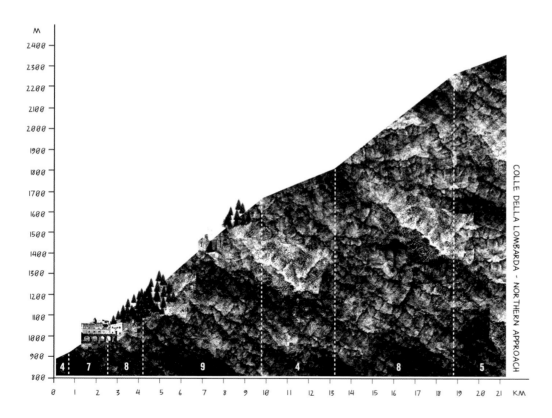

COLLE DELLA LOMBARDA - NORTHERN APPROACH

up whose side grows a rambling rose. (More of her, the Virgin Mary's mother, later.) Nearby, an ugly portakabin/hut for the men who worked on the resurfacing of the road ahead of the 2008 Tour's visit (its first) and graffiti on the road heralding their road-improving efforts: 'MERCI GRAZIE TOUR LE STRADE' and, further on, 'CICCIO' (with ITA i.e. Italia, written downwards from the first I) 'GRAZIE CRIKKIOLO' (the name of a radio station and an Italian form of Facebook).

The next 8 kilometres hit hard, never less than around 8% and long stretches of around 9–10%. At 3km the old tarmac comes back but it's in quite good condition then some more of the new. The road is fairly wide and develops a serpentine swing through tree cover. Across to the right, a steep slope strewn with a scree of big loose rocks, pines and poplars growing where they can out of the sliding ground cover. At 5km, a new stone cabin with wooden roof, window frames, doors. At 5.7km a fingerpost marks a Scorciatoria (shortcut) walk up to Santuario Santa Anna off to the right. (There are several such along the way.) Although little is known about the Madonna's mama, her numen is heavy hereabouts. Indeed, she has collared tutelary charge of most of the place: a shrine, the river and its vallone – a deep valley as distinct from your shallow val or valle – the sanctuary, the lake. Her name – Hannah in Hebrew – even resonates in a peak (Gran Capanna 1843m) up on the ridge, although a capanna is a mountain hut… the full set of blessed geographical trophies. She is the patron saint of women in labour and miners.

Of some saints, for whose very existence there is no historic proof, the Irish say that some are 'prayer-born'. The Golden Legend, a very popular medieval book of saints' lives, written between 1260 and 1275 by Jacobus de Voragine and a hot seller from its first edition, records fantastic events many of which Alban Butler, author of the standard work on lives of the Catholic saints, published between 1756 and 1759, pooh-poohs – for instance, about Saint Katherine, her of the heroic martyrdom on a wheel. There is no proof that she ever existed and one hagiographer says that her celebrated story 'is one of the most preposterous of its kind'. Why, in 1932, Pope Pius XI, formerly a keen alpinist, named Saint Bernard of Montjoux the patron of alpinists and other mountaineers. He also lambasted the fictions incorporated into the various hagiographies of Bernard. Indeed, one must treat many saintly legends of martyrdom with the sort of scepticism you would accord a banker – any banker, bankster – telling you that your money is absolutely safe with him.

At 6.2km, 1275m, the road widens and straightens before the hairpins kick in again, following the familiar pattern of hairpins like twists of the height ratchet and more even straights between. At 8.2km a ruined, perhaps demolished, stone building to the left has the look of a customs post or a military barrack/blockhouse. The concrete is of relatively modern date. To the right, a curious low-arched structure with shallow curved bays in reinforced concrete. For vehicles?

At 8.7km, 1500m, the Rifugio del Barracone comprises two ugly tin-roofed buildings in a wide clearing to the left and opposite, a melancholy memorial plaque in marble attached to a stone plinth with a black and white photograph: 'Bersezio Giovanni d'anni 22 di ritorno dal Santuario il 7.7.1968 con la bicicletta trovo tragicamente la morte su queste Pierre troncado la sua giovane vita'. The 22-year-old lad, cycling back down from the Sanctuary, swerved, crashed and hit this very rock, his young life truncated. (We did take the detour up to the sanctuary which stands at 2010m – don't bother. It's a gloomy edifice and the adjacent shop purveys only pietistic tat.)

A sluice to the left collects crystal-clear, jade-green water. Further on, adorning a side wall, a red, white and green graffito: 'Brus Ale Ballan Mattao'. Ballan we may posit, and this was before he took the 2008 road-race rainbow jersey in Varese. As for the others, remember, there are clubmen unknown to us strangers riding these ranges.

At 10km, 630m, on a boulder, sits a black marble plaque under a built pointy hat of loose stones: 'Pellegrino che a piedi passi segna il tuo cammino con sassi' exhorting the pilgrim on foot to mark his or her passing with stones and, correspondent to command, there is a goodly gathering of tiny rock piles like Neolithic gnomes scattered about. Since there are piles of stones everywhere about the place it isn't obvious which have been devotedly placed and which from random omnipresence.

Here, too, a shrine and, picked out in the ironwork of its grille: 'Voto di Guerra 1915–18'. (Voto, a vow, points to votive offering.) The inscription on a stone: 'Pellegrino da qui il tuo primo ed ultimo saluto alla celeste nomina' (Pilgrim, from here [make] your first and your final salutation of heaven). Two other plaques refer to '15–18', when the Italians and the Austrians fought here, and February 1941.

The road begins to curl round the upper valley at a gentler 4–6%, as if in contemplation of the last climb up to the col – why, it even tips downhill a ways, to gather breath and strength.

A ruined sheep and cattle byre attached to a building at 12.3km speaks of the summer pasturage up here and hairpins jink up into trees on a narrow and very steep strip of road (8.5–9.5%) to 13.2km, 1770m, where the mood softens marginally.

The turn to the Colle comes at 14km, 1855m – straight on winds up to the Sanctuary – and, as you climb, you see the pinched neck (stura) of the valley laid out below, the river muscling over boulders. Larches stand straight and still, their arms out-stretched gracefully a-droop below their waist, like classical ballet dancers poised in that position described in Enrico Cecchetti's system as arms demi-second, right foot coup-de-pied. He worked, as a teacher and mime artist, with the Imperial Russian ballet in Saint Petersburg and with Diaghilev's Ballet Russe, so there.

At 15km, 1950m, if you've a mind so to do, pause at a large right-hand hairpin where, from the balcony you may cast your view back over the long valley approach to the upper reaches. Below the balcony grows a lone rowan, a mountain ash, a tree which, from earliest times, enjoyed a reputation for inherent magical powers and efficacy against all manner of nasty charms cast by witches. For example, butter churns were commonly made of rowan wood for, if the butter were slow in coming (i.e. to clot), there was certain to be a witch's spell on it. The rowan saw off the evil influence. And an old rhyme says: 'If your whip-stock's made of rowan / Your nag may ride through any town.'

The road noses into airy altitude, and at 17.1km, 2100m, becomes a ledge and then a causeway across a moorland plateau littered with rocks and scumbles of stone. On that day we passed, in September, a small group of English cyclists, heading for Nice – mostly downhill all the way from the top of the Lombarda – straggled up the mountainside into a gelid white haze of thick freezing mist, ice and snow. They were shamefully ill-equipped: no tights, overshoes, some without even gloves. Be warned. Even in early autumn and late spring – you've seen pictures of the Giro – the weather up on these tops can be cruel. Go prepared, leg and arm warmers, gilets, hats, ear muffs, thermal knickers, the works. The stuff is all lightweight these days and you risk much by being under-insulated. And

the Colle della Lombarda, at 2350m, is very bleak and as prey to winds as an aerodynamics testing tunnel.

A website – www.memoriadellealpi.net – will give more information about the engagement, here, in August 1944 between the German 90th division of the Brigata 'Valle Stura' and the French resistance fighters of the FFI (Forces Françaises de l'Intérieur).

Pinned to a fence, there are several sheets of typed paper and pictures – tributes to Marco Pantani.

The undistinguished 5 kilometre scoot to Isola may best be served by cold statistics of kilometre marks: 2135m 7% (ski lifts), 2235m 8%, 2160m 7.5% (and a big right-hand hairpin), 2085m 6.5% (where we passed a guy on a machine fitted with time-trial bars, descending into the sleet…), more ski lifts as Isola 2000 appears, the usual scab of chalets, 2040m 5.5%, and onto the big two-lane ski highway. Here begins a great descent – visible bends, smooth and broad, a number of tunnels but they are short and number 6 has a side pass – but, truly, no draw as a climb. Isola 2000 was once used as a Tour finish in 1993 when Tony Rominger took the stage, and in 2008 as a transition to the Bonette.

In the village of Isola itself (16.6 kilometres down the valley, 873m), there is a Pepinière d'Isola Centre Expérimental sur le Châtaigner for studies on chestnut trees and nuts and all sorts of coniferous proliferation. Between Isola and Saint-Etienne-de-Tinée the D2205 follows the Tinée River and is accompanied, intermittently, by a brand-new cycle track.

Prato Nevoso 2744m

2008 Tour route

LENGTH: 9KM	
HEIGHT GAIN: 670M	
MAXIMUM GRADIENT: 8%	

The hot chocolate in the Bar Cometa on the blasted concrete wasteland that in winter becomes the Snow Field of the name is sensational: dense of texture, intense of flavour, almost as good as Salamanca's best, which is a nonpareil, and they serve an excellent Americano coffee, too, Italy winning hands down over France on the hot drinks front so far. However, this climb, up the 2008 Tour route, a hard enough ride to an ugly sprawling horrible vast ski station opened in 1966, has no intrinsic merit and, its place in the annals of cycle racing apart, need not detain us. It is, moreover, way off the track of our loci. From Miroglio (770m) it is 9 kilometres to the top (1440m). In the café there is a little wooden pub plaque for the POLLOCK Cycle Co., established 1883, proprietor Alexander Pollock.

There are some passingly interesting graffiti on the road: two circles enclosing an obvious phallus – a real bonk machine… lots of 'VV le Tour', the VV interlocked (i.e. 'Viva')… on a side wall, 'si scrive Tour si dice Ferruchio' (write Tour, say Ferruchio but surely not Ferruchio Lamborghini?)… and a terse memorial, 'Anton sempre con noi' (Anton ever with us).

The visit of the 2008 Tour was its first, Cadel Evans lost his yellow jersey to Frank Schleck, Denis Menchov lost his wheel on a wet daub of white graffiti and went down 5 kilometres from the finish and the stage was won by Evans' Australian compatriot, Simon Gerrans. L'Equipe's cartoonist showed Mother Tour standing over a boiling laundry copper with the caption 'Plunge Evans'. She dunks a faded yellow jersey into a cauldron brimful of the peloton drooling with envy and the jersey comes out bright yellow, like new, on the back of Frank Schleck.[5]

5 There is an excellent bike shop in Beinette, on the road between Prato Nevoso and Cuneo.

Colle di Sampeyre 2284m

From Sampeyre 971m

LENGTH:	16.3KM
HEIGHT GAIN:	1313M
MAXIMUM GRADIENT:	13%

This road was partially resurfaced for the 2003 Giro d'Italia, its first crossing, although the Gran Fondo Fausto Coppi has used it since 1997. (The Cima Coppi takes place in the Valle Stura i.e. between Cuneo and the Maddalena.)

The Sampeyre and the Colle dei Morti which follows it probe deep into very wild, remote country. The passes are narrow, the views stupendous – the great peak of Monte Viso towering to the north – the roads dwindle into that tough-nut, near rustic track beloved of the Italian racing fraternity who like to see their champions battling with the crummy surfaces which the campioni of old had to take in their stride. They test the will of the tifosi (fans), too: it takes real enthusiasm to make the trek up into these outlying, outlandish regions. The climbing is indubitably hard – 'spezzagambe' (break-leg) they say – the gradients rarely slackening below 8% and, for most of the way, nearer 9 and 10%.

Turn off the SP8 which crosses the Agnello onto the road heading south away from Sampeyre. A sign warns of flash floods and the movement of heavy vehicles:

'Fr Elva 930m ht 1354m 16.4k 8.3% max 15%' (i.e. for at least 100m).

The road winds lazily at first, the way ahead quite open and visible. At 1.8km, a cascade pours down over a stone shelf and the road swishes into two successive hairpins. The surface is terrible, beech, alder, birch, ash and larch supply ample shade. At 2.7km, a radio mast and small electric power hut/kiosk to the left and then a torrent to the right. At 3.1km, c. 1170m, the road breaks out into the

open. A house to the right and then a small shrine and below the road, ski button lifts and a view of Sampeyre. The road, very narrow here, now ducks back into trees. At 3.6km on a left-hand hairpin stands a white wooden box on a pole with a grille across its opening and a statuette of the simpering Madonna behind it.

Low-arched trees shelter a marginally better surface and, if you are lucky, jays flit from bough to bough. At 5.4km, through a succession of quite severe hairpins and under more ski lifts spanning the road and here (1428m) is the recently opened bar/ristorante Santa Anna – she supervises the catering, too, as well as keeping her eye on the metalling… there is 200m worth of new tarmac. Her influence wanes, however as the surface soon resumes its rougher state. Hairpins persist as, in the business of gaining height at full throttle, they must. At 7.7km, 1711m, in the guardianship of Madonna di Flour, a tiny settlement of stone buildings. A brief passage of open fields then back into trees though less thickly planted here. On one larch a sign trumpets 'AZIENDA FAUNISTICA VENATORIA' – a regulated hunting area – and a notice makes reference to articles in a legal code governing the conduct of 12-bore shotguns, air pistols and, no doubt, catapults and high-velocity bows. The pinus uncinata, a rare species of mountain pine, (French pin à crochets) is much in evidence. The road tightens to no more than one car width to 10.6km, the Rifugio Meira Garneri (1850m). It offers a bar, solarium, ristorante, camere (rooms). A ski lift mars the tranquillity of the spot. Around 11.1km, 1910m, the surface of the road is appalling, here and there like the edibility of the curate's egg, as if a crazed auto-moto-phobe has attacked it with a pneumatic drill and a kango jack-hammer. There is a small belvedere to the right at 13km, c.2000m, on a left-

hand hairpin, bel+vedere being Italian for French belle+vue, 'fine view'. Half a kilometre on, the road once more breaks out into the open on a stretch of fresh tarmac and on into sparser trees, rock pimples, shrubs, wild and high, vegetation blasted by the wind and cold, across a wide plateau (16.4km) and thence to the Colle (2284m). Here stands a green palm tree (or else a figurative larch) sculpted in metal with herself on top and an apostrophe: 'Nella bellezza della Natura affida a Maria la tua lode a DIO UNO E TRINIO'… To the beauty of Nature entrusted to Maria in your praise to GOD ONE AND TRIUNE. Puzzlingly, beneath this line of words, under the 'UNO' is a vertical string 'TEVENNER' with an 'I' next to the 'T' and the first 'E' framed thus 'ZES'. Any suggestions?

The road off the top is a tight squeeze and a number of graffiti on the road hail the late Marco 'Il Pirata' (the Pirate) Pantani with 'ringrazia e ricordia' (in grateful memory), next to a crude crossbones and 'PANTANI PIRATA LE'. (The odd spelling of some of these graffiti may be imputed either to marginal illiteracy or local dialect.)

As on the other side, it is moorland here, sparse trees, a rectangular stone building of no obvious current purpose. The road surface is better, the verge exposed. There are more trees in evidence at 2.4km and the mostly straightish road gives way to a few bends. At 3.2km a radio mast and, once more, moorland (2023m, 3.9km). Around 4.8km, 1971m, a road joins from the left, offering an alternative route into the gorge-like deep cut (north–south) of the Vallone di Elva whose stream feeds the west–east flow of the river Màira. Turn left for Stroppo.

An information board tells of an old legend which recounts how, early one morning, in the flower-spangled meadows which lie at the foot of the mountain, there appeared a young fairy with golden hair. From her comes the name Elva (presumably a play on the word 'elf' though that word is strictly Germanic in origin.) The local men, bewitched by this gorgeous apparition, dispersed to all corners of the globe in search of a woman whose curled tresses were of such golden beauty. So very romantic the Italians, or else they seized, here, on a copper-bottomed excuse for serial flirtation with blondes.

The road to Stroppo is pitted and scored, pitiable of surface and very narrow, and the hairpins which begin to snap at you are very sharp. Along with a veritable pattern of pins at around 400m and intervening bends, the gradient, upwards of 10%, is unrelenting. At around 8.4km, the road pitches you quite suddenly into a right-hand bend and the effect is abrupt: you might be going off the side of the mountain, a huge panorama yawning in front of you. Wow!

At 9.1km, c.1640m, San Martino consists of a lone house with a small *enceinte* (enclosure) grass and a vegetable plot by the roadside and, below it, the tiny village with its church perched on the bluff ('Nearer my god to thee…' as the hymn goes). From 10km, the trees reassert themselves and to the right, through their leafy cordon, appear occasional long views into the distant valley. There is, briefly, a flatter stretch, a balcony, from around 12.2km. At a junction (1350m), with a dead-end road leading to a Santuario Santa Maria di Morinesi past the hamlet of that name, an information board speaks of the local economy in ages past, when the inhabitants of these high pastures depended on two commodities: hemp from which to make coarse linen and sheep's wool for rough cloth.

At 15.4km, 1233m, a large tower and a church with blind windows loom up. The Chiesa di San Peyre dates from the 12th-13th centuries. The interior walls of the locked church (a notice informs us) are adorned with frescoes from the 14th-15th centuries which depict episodes from the life of Christ and a Transito (death scene) della Vergine by an anonymous artist identified simply as il Maestro di Stroppo, the village which guards the foot of this road, also known hereabouts as Strop. The unnamed Master flourished at the beginning of the 15th century and the frescoes, in pale pastel shades, show a marked influence of Byzantine icon painting. A stroppo is a sling, a nautical strop, a ring or band of rope or hide, its ends spliced together and used as a purchase for tackle, Latin strappus presumably made locally from the canapa hemp mentioned in the inscription quoted above.

At 16.1km, the road pitches down into a deep gorge flanked by trees, then onto a switchback series of hairpins which shoot you out into the small square in front of the church in Stroppo (1087m). Here there is a museum, L'Escola de mountanho – a reconstructed model of a mountain village school of the early 1900s, desks, wall-hangings, artefacts (a collection of dip-pen nibs, for example), signed documents, reports, photographs, books… it's used as a teaching centre for local schoolchildren and for research. Above the door of the Municipio (town hall, though Strop is no bigger than a village), a plaque names the heroes of Stroppo who died in the 1915–18 war, 16 of them called Abello and the whole number hailing from various tiny hamlets in the area, Stroppo being the chief community of the parish.

The chimney pots are square in form, with slab-built sides, and atop the rim sits a row of supports, like the uprights of a loggia supporting a flat lid.

The road scoots down a further 2.5 kilometres to Bassura on the long Màira valley road.

Alternative route up to the Sampeyre 2284m

LENGTH: 15.6KM

HEIGHT GAIN: 1329M

MAXIMUM GRADIENT: 17%

Go westwards from Bassura a bare 3 kilometres to a junction (927m), and there turn right into the throat of the Elva ravine. Rocks crowd in, overhanging with menace, occasional boulders spin off the beetling crags onto the road and bound across the barrier, the river rushes over the rocks below to the left. A dark and gloomy tunnel wherein such as goblins and kelpies may lurk claims 150m worth of your nerves and there is a bend midway along its stygian length to add to your anxiety, but cyclists do frequent this way, they have been seen and they whoop with the exhilaration of the descent, if not the hard labour of the ascent. Out in the open again, there follows a series of archways and, plain to be seen, way ahead, a snow tunnel and two archways hacked out of the living rock as the road creeps or crashes – depending whether your mood is bullish or timid – round the flank of the rock. This is an alternative way up to Gòria (1768m) and 10.8km distant, and on from there to join the road down from the Colle Sampeyre [see above]. The intermittent 15% of its gradient on the map is, I must warn you, no exaggeration.

Colle d'Esischie 2370m & Colle dei Morti 2480m

Northern approach from Ponte Marmora 944m

LENGTH TO THE ESISCHIE: 20KM

HEIGHT GAIN: 1536M

MAXIMUM GRADIENT: 12%

LENGTH TO THE MORTI: 21.4KM

Start from the Ponte Marmora on the valley road. Is there marble hereabouts? The river is the Marmora and this is its vallone but I do not know

of any quarries. Because of this road's association with racing, there is, at its start, a timing chip machine to both the Colle Esischie (20km) and the Colle dei Morti. There is also a hydro-electric station. The tarmac is new, this first stretch is gentle and there are kilometre signs, all named. At 1.3k stands the Ciaperase sign, quite close to which the babbling waters of the Marmora rough and tumble over the rocks of their bed to the left. Grangia Cumba indicates 4–5% and 17.6km to the

col. A snow tunnel, side-lit by open embrasures, at 2.9km and from here on the gradient cranks up. The sign named 'Bacino' tells us 8.5%, 16.6km. A dam, a waterworks and, 4 kilometres from the start, at 1223m, a junction with a road to Canosio up the Vallone di Preit off to the right. Here, too, is the Rifugio Vernetti. A left-hand hairpin ushers in a succession of them. This road, creeping up the north side of a sizeable massif is shaded, therefore cool and, after rain, inclined to hold the

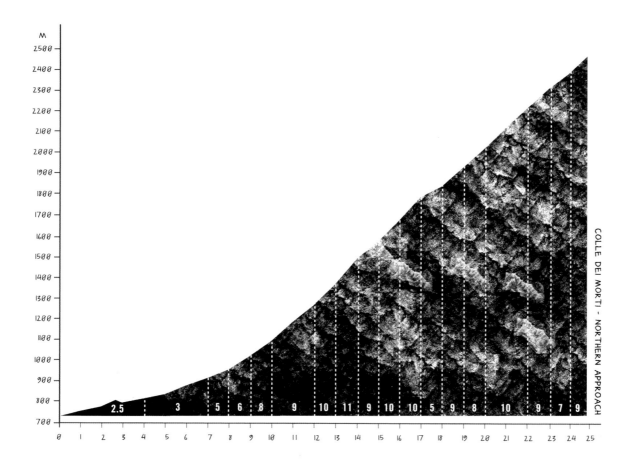

COLLE DEI MORTI – NORTHERN APPROACH

damp. Vernetti at 15.6km announces 7%, Marmora Bulu at 14.7km, 6%. The road emerges into open country with thickly wooded slopes to either side and crosses a succession of bridges over torrents. There is, I find, comfort in the murmuring and chatter of brooks. There follows a notional lull in the desire of the road to hurt you: the signs speak of 1.5% (at 13.8km) and 3% (12.8km) but these figures are manifestly inaccurate – the supposed 3% is much harder in fact. But, as in all circumstances, the thing is the thing – 'Ding an sich' is Immanuel Kant's way of stating the pragmatic case – and the minutiae of detail cannot either obscure or console the hard fact no matter how woozy you get during its action upon you. And Kant was no hard-boiled, sere-souled materialist. 'Two things fill my mind with ever-increasing wonder and awe' he wrote in his Critique of Pure Reason, 'the more often and more intensely the reflection dwells on them: the starry heavens above me and the moral law within me.' For, no matter that the thing is the thing, there are psychological landscapes for the exploration of which each and every of those things is a key.

The surface comes and goes, fair and broken. Urzio, 5% and 11.8 km to the col, then on into trees again and more torrents coursing off the upper rock as the road climbs up to it. Indeed, the torrents are as numerous as capillaries, the uppermost rocks perforated with their springings. Tolosano (1502m) consists of a few houses and a tiny church. The offered Tolosano sign gives 7.5%, 10.8km. And some way up at Cialanciette, (11.25%, 9.9km) comes a very bad surface and bad news, too. Perhaps the former has been repaired but nearby a large section of road had fallen off down the slope into the stream to the right and a slice cut out of the mountainside as a detour. At Rio Oliveto (4.54%, 8.8km), do not be fooled by the blandishment of the jocular sign-

writer: this soi-disant 4.54% contains a long stretch of at least 10–12%. Do not they say that there are lies, damned lies and statistics?

At Rocciasone (1781m, 9.6%,7.9km), the road pulls in its girth to one car width and, as lower down, there is plenty of shelter from trees, welcome on a hot day but inclining to damp and chill when there is no sun. Carus (6.5%, 6.9km) and a rare hairpin – the road is by and large fairly straight up to around 1700m. More broken surface and a certain scattering of detritus off the land together with the deleterious effects of rain and snow tormenting the tarmac. I am tempted to say: 'Ride this road as soon as you can – it's in the process of crumbling away and disappearing off the edge into the vallone,' but that would be to act the pessimist, entirely against my instinct. There is evidence of repair teams at their necessary task. Piecia brings 9.5% at 5.9km, La Bianca at 15.4 kilometres into the climb is a shepherd's stone hut and an AZIENDA FAUNISTICA while Lago Resile (1986m) marks a small pond off to the right, 7.22%, 5km. Here come grassy glades and stands of larch, a rocky meadow to the left below the road and a long cleft cut into the mountain, as it might be Roland had been this way with Durendal and delivered a swift hack at the rock. A ruined chunk of wall bears the legend: Divieto Accesso Proprieta Privata (No Entry, Private Property). Too late, my dears, too late. Siteita (7.5%, 4km). At 17.6 kilometres in, what looks like a refuge with 'Alpe Valanghe' (avalanches) painted on a beam from which is suspended a line of cowbells. The Alpe Valanghe sign itself offers no more than 3% with 3 kilometres to go. A short way on, a substantial double-arched bridge spans a stream to carry the road onto a moorland dotted with alpine dwarf vegetation and boulders protruding from furze and scrub grass. A sheer drop to the right. Buchet (8.55%,

2km), Terre Rosse (5%, 1km) and a run of bare earth and stone in patches brings you to the col and a sundial, whose message, no less sententious than offered by most, reads: 'Il tempo passa la Gloria resta' (time passes, glory lives on) but there is a secondary association for this is a souvenir of a bike race, LA FAUSTO COPPI 20th edition 2007. (This is one of a number of Gran and Medio Fondo local cyclo-sportive events which regularly cross these two cols. Fondo, a word with a number of shaded meanings, here stands for 'trial' as in 'time trial'.)

The Colle Esischie (2370m) is a windswept height of rugged beauty, and the Giro's passage here gives it status, a sort of blessing. A short way on to a T-junction. The left-hand road goes on – past a refuge pleasingly called 'The Marmot's Burrow' (La Tana della Marmotta) – to the Valle Grana and a steep 15 kilometre (approximately) descent to the valley head at Pradléves (822m) on the road to Cuneo, 30 kilometres from there. Turn right for a further kilometre to the Colle del Valonetto (2447m) and a further very narrow and precipitous 0.15 kilometres to the Colle dei Morti (2480m) overlooking the Vallone dei Morti. Amid the clutter of trophies and mementoes of Pantani, there is a picture of riders on the col during a Pantani memorial ride. Another col is named, the Colle Fauniera (2481m) with a memorial to Il Pirata, a statue of him with a Carlsberg tape as bandana tied round his temples, also a stone stele in memoriam Coppi and the blue timer-chip box. This is a rude and bleak spot, underlining, somehow, the sad demise of the man sculpted in grey, immoveable stone, his graven features forever fixed in a look of haunted inner suffering.

There is an annual race to the top of the Colle dei Morti.

COLLE VALCAVERA 2416M

South-facing route

LENGTH: 22.8KM	
HEIGHT GAIN: 1626M	
MAXIMUM GRADIENT: 11%	

The Tour de France has visited this province of Cuneo twice: in 1952 on the Sestriere–Monaco stage. Coppi was in yellow, Jean Robic (the 1947 winner) led over the Tenda, that pass on the big main road north of Menton which marks the Franco-Italian border, while in 1961, Turin–Antibes, Anquetil was in yellow and Imerio Massignan led over the Tenda. The two stages of the 2008 race brought the number of stages finishing or starting on Italian soil to 12 on what was the Tour's 22nd visit to the peninsula.

Cows browse even at this great altitude… extreme grazing, forsooth. The surface of the descent down the Vallone dei Morti is very rough to begin with, but 3.7km below the col there is new tarmac, albeit the asphalt is broken slightly here and there from the ravages of summer heat and winter cold, with stretches which seem to have missed out on the refurbishment altogether. The descent is twisty, wickedly steep and the drops off to the side are vertiginous. There is no shelter, either, on this exposed south-facing flank of the mountain. The Latin for south-facing is apricus from which we get 'apricot'. The Colle Valcavera (2416m, 2km) from the top goes unremarked. In the choice of cols for this book, the criteria were that the climbs should, if possible, be beautiful, historic and bloody hard. The Sampeyre and the Morti together net all three criteria in bag-loads.

From about 10km the tarmac is old and good in parts. From 14.2km, observe, across the valley whose head you are negotiating, the cattle on the sheer slope opposite: they must have special knee suspension to cope with the rake. From 16km the tree cover begins, at 17km another hydro-electric plant, attesting to the great volume of water pulsing out of this mass of rock, and the small community of San Giacomo. The tarmac of the last 9 kilometres to the bottom, that is 26 kilometres in all, to Demonte (780m) on the SS21 heading west for the Colle della Maddalena, looks pretty new, too.

Simoni Winds it Up

The Sampeyre has only recently featured in the Giro. The 2000 race crossed the Sampeyre, the Agnello, and the Izoard. Pantani – winner overall and of the mountains prize (his only green jersey) in 1998 – drew all the attention. He'd come to the Giro prepared to ride, (he said), for Stefano Garzelli, who was vying with Francesco Casagrande for the leader's maglia rosa (pink jersey). Italian racing is a complex affair, loyalties are rarely undivided, sworn promises written in water. Against his assurances and entirely careless of his leader's interests, Pantani attacked repeatedly on the Izoard. The Italian media painted the image of a generous Pirate riding himself into the ground for his captain, the gregario (domestique – team member) supreme at the call of Garzelli. Garzelli did not deign to contradict them. Thus the myth of Pantani the selfless was made and in the hysteria which greeted him at the finish no one paid notice to the winner, Paolo Lanfranchi.

In 2003, approaching the Esischie, (and the prize for the Cima Coppi) from the south, 13 riders led about 6 minutes ahead of Gilberto Simoni's pink jersey group. Over the top, five riders had broken clear by some 50 seconds but their overall lead on the chasing group had been trimmed to 4min 30sec, which gives some indication of just how steep and taxing the climb is. Moreover, since the Esischie is almost invariably taken in tandem with the Sampeyre, this double hit of gradient and distance is a real killer: the ascents are brutal, the descents highly technical and stressful, the respite between the two summits short indeed.

That day, although the escape group of 13 riders had, briefly, coalesced once more, the strain was telling and it was now fragmented even as Georg Toschnig broke away from Simoni's group. Simoni was winding up the pressure, however, and on the lower slopes of the Sampeyre he broke clear with Dario Frigo and Franco Pelizotti, this last hanging on grimly to a pace which was, evidently, pretty well at his limit already.

In the way of outstanding riders, Simoni had judged his effort to the scruple and his timing was on the button. Accelerating near imperceptibly, Frigo and now Toschnig on his wheel, he led towards the top of the Sampeyre and into wet snow across the road.

In former days, as Sean Yates told me, the daily pace of the Giro was geared to the appearance of the television helicopters late in the stage: 'On screen, boys, better show willing,' but times have changed. The pace this day is hot from the start – 46 kilometres in the first hour.

Simoni crosses the Sampeyre in the lead, Stefano Garzelli 45 seconds adrift and, with him, Marco Pantani. Into slush, the temperature very chill, descending a real pain and extremely perilous. Toschnig attacks, Simoni is more cautious. The sun breaks through, the road still awash and, into a turn Pantani slips and crashes heavily, taking Garzelli with him. There are ghouls, non-bike riders, who relish crashes. Little they know. Pantani, by now demoralised by what he saw as a savaging by the anti-doping agencies – he checked into a hospital less than a month later, suffering from clinical depression – sits in a miserable state of shock and pain for some time. Garzelli, lying second on General Classification, remounts almost immediately after a consoling tap on Pantani's shoulder.

Those who were there that day recall how many of the riders were in a shocking state coming over these two mountains, tired, wet, cold, strung out, nerves jarred by the terrors of the descent. One rider grabbed at the windproof top held out by a soigneur (trainer) but did not dare take both hands off the bars in order to put it on and rode down with the plastic jacket trailing like a banner.

Pantani eventually rode on, but he was, by now, a long way down. Garzelli, relayed by that great *gregario* (supporting rider) Eddy Mazzoleni (third in the 2007 Giro), managed to make up some of the time he had lost but still came in over five minutes' adrift and held onto his second place overall. Not so Pantani. Clearly in pain he struggled and finished the day nearly 16 minutes down.

The Giro organisers are generally loath to call quits on anything so wimpish an excuse as snow on the road, even on these narrow crossings of huge mountains.

ELEMOSINA

2. LAUZES

Defined by Mont Ventoux to the west and the Signal de Lure to the east, the LAUZES sector is named for the litter of small, thin, shale-like, chalk-white, limestone tesserae which cover the summit of both mountains and, from a distance, make them appear to be capped with snow. The word is Provençal lauza or lausa from a Gaulish word lausa meaning 'tile'. Our 'lozenge' has the same root. In Provence and the Cévennes, it applies not only to the natural scree but also to roof tiles.

Both Ventoux and the Lure belong to the region known as the Préalpes, the alpine foothills composed almost entirely of limestone. Located, broadly, along the Rhône Valley, the region originally lay under a vast, though relatively shallow, tropical sea. A submerged coral reef evolved, teeming with animal life. The debris of crustacean shells together with detritus falling into the sea from the land above the waters accumulated on the seabed, solidified and formed an imposing massif of hard, white rock, the calcareous stone which adorned the mountain relief of the Vaucluse when the waters receded.

At that point, Provence was shaken by significant tectonic shifts, the drift of the continental plates caused a folding of the Pyrenean and Provençal mountain chains along a west-east axis visible in the lie of both ranges. Later, when the bloc of the Alps was thrust up from the crust, the older chains were crunched, shouldered, hoisted in the mighty upheaval, like weaker props hoisted out of a scrum, and both Ventoux and the Lure attained their full prominence, bizarre outcrops in the flatter watershed of the Rhône. 'Crunch' is, though, really too explosive a word for a process of geological realignment spread over thousands and thousands of years.

The highest point in Provence at 1912 metres, Mont Ventoux is a sort of hub where several climates meet: the base of the southern slope is Mediterranean, the summit, blasted by winds, is harsh and alpine, and between the two, on the broad flanks of the exposed mass of the mountain, are represented most of the climate types of Europe, from the Mediterranean to Lapland.

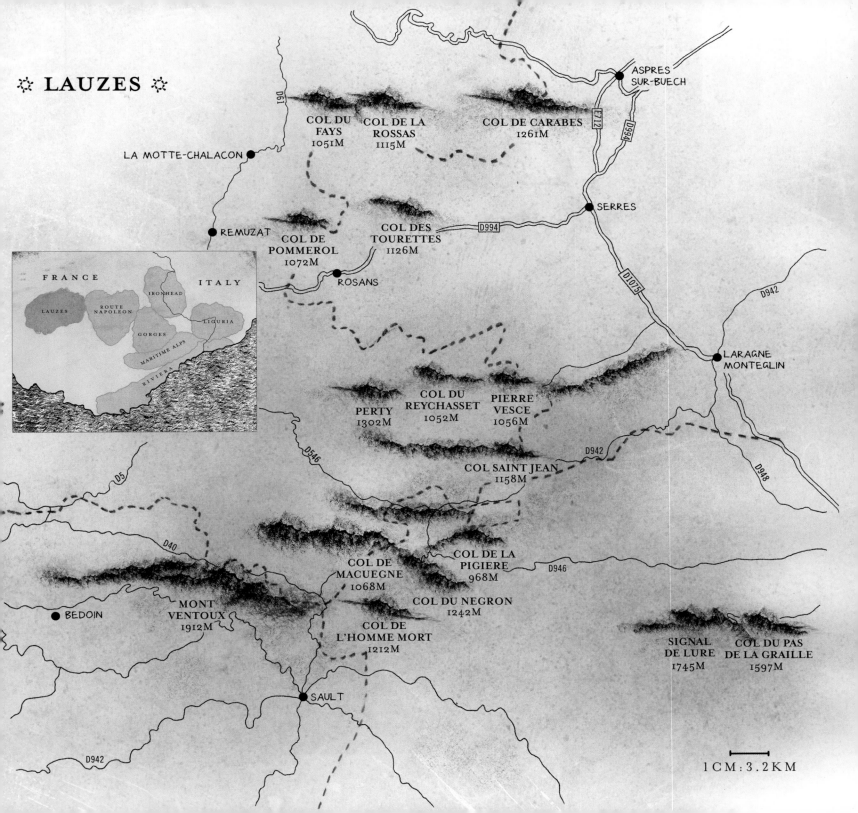

✷ LAUZES ✷

ASPRES
SUR-BUECH

COL DU
FAYS
1051M

COL DE LA
ROSSAS
1115M

COL DE CARABES
1261M

LA MOTTE-CHALACON

SERRES

REMUZAT

COL DE
POMMEROL
1072M

COL DES
TOURETTES
1126M

FRANCE   ITALY

IRONHEAD

LAUZES   ROUTE
NAPOLEON

LIGURIA

GORGES

MARITIME ALPS

RIVIERA

ROSANS

LARAGNE
MONTEGLIN

PERTY
1302M

COL DU
REYCHASSET
1052M

PIERRE
VESCE
1056M

COL SAINT JEAN
1158M

COL DE LA
PIGIERE
968M

COL DE
MACUEGNE
1068M

COL DU NEGRON
1242M

BEDOIN

MONT
VENTOUX
1912M

COL DE
L'HOMME MORT
1212M

SIGNAL
DE LURE
1745M

COL DU PAS
DE LA GRAILLE
1597M

SAULT

1 CM : 3.2 KM

Mont Ventoux 1912m

Known as The Giant of Provence, The Bald Mountain, and nicknamed *'Domaine des Anges'* (Domain of the Angels), it was known to the Gauls as Vintur after an obscure local god reckoned to live up there, presumably because he liked the ferocious gales of the Col des Tempêtes blasting through his frost-gelled hair. Ventoureso is the Provençal word for the north-east wind. There is also a claim for Ven-Top, 'snowy peak' in ancient Gallic. Mediaeval Latin records it as Mons Ventosus and Mons Ventorius. Ventosus (windy) transmutes into the French word. Ventoux is not, therefore, strictly an alp but its iconic status in the annals of bike racing attaches it indissolubly to this study of those mountains.

Today the lower slopes of Ventoux are thickly wooded, but at the end of the 18th century they had been denuded by centuries of depredation, the constant passage of men and animals and over-grazing. Flocks were driven up on all sides for the summer transhumance, trampling or cropping any burgeoning tree shoots. Since the droppings the animals left were insufficient nutriment for the soil, humus, mulch and ground box was gathered from the higher woodlands to rot down into compost. Timber was felled (without replanting) for the making of charcoal or to fuel lime-kilns. Add to this destruction the ravages of pigs, great devourers of acorns, the demand for wood by the naval shipyards and arsenal in Toulon for the French royal navy during the 17th century and by nascent industrial enterprises in the 18th century – glass-making factories, lavender distilleries, manufacturers of faïence pottery and tiles – as well as the trade that had existed for aeons, firewood for heating and cooking, timber for house-building. The French Revolution delivered the *coup de grâce*, because many tracts of forests which had been the privileged property of aristocrats were vengefully ruined by angry claimants to a new liberty, if not destroyed utterly. By 1838, the situation on Ventoux was catastrophic. On the southern slopes there was no woodland between 550 and 1150 metres of altitude, the zone dubbed 'locale of thyme and lavender' by two contemporary naturalists. To compound this disaster, the river Toulourenc, which flows along the northern base of Ventoux, flooded the whole area, devastated the agriculture of the valley and buried the fields under an alluvial mess. The floods of 1840, '41 and '42 were no less violent. In short, a concerted campaign of replanting, afforestation, rehabilitation and restructuring began in 1875 and continues still, with the result that Ventoux is now the most thickly wooded region in the Vaucluse *département* and supports a rich variety of fauna and flora. Its south face is covered with the largest gathering of cedars in Europe and the variety of its now-abundant woodland includes a number of pines – maritime, black or Austrian, Scotch, red – larch, spruce and fir, several species of oak, beech, maple, the service tree, mountain ash. Truffles from Ventoux go to the market in Carpentras but the culling of its mushrooms is forbidden without licence. Short-toed eagles cruise the winds, calm and at full spread of their wings, so too buzzards, ospreys, black kites, peregrine falcons and royal eagles. The long-eared owl – a comical-looking bird like a character in the Muppet Show – feeds on small furry mammals, the crossbill can crack open a pine cone to expose the juicy nut and the wheatear chomps on butterflies. The rare Orsini's viper lurks on the slopes of Mont Serein, a named peak on the north side, some 5km below the summit of Ventoux, its sole habitat in Provence. Your Orsini's viper can attain a length of 20 inches, according to some sources, but 38 inches according to others. It has coloration similar to that of a common adder, is docile some say, though others impute to it an irritable disposition, liable to strike if approached and deliver a bite that can cause fatal blood-poisoning. Or not. Don't chance it. The small-toed eagle relishes it for sustenance.

Southern approach from Bédoin 300m

LENGTH: 21.5KM

HEIGHT GAIN: 1612M

MAXIMUM GRADIENT: 10.5%

This, the way the races come, is the most interesting and the hardest.

Bédoin, founded in 1250, was burnt to the ground during the French Revolution and 180 of its inhabitants slaughtered on the orders of a young cavalry officer from Marseille, Louis Gabriel Suchet, later one of Napoleon's most brilliant and ruthless generals, and a local priest, in reprisal for the crime of *incivisme* (uncivic behaviour). Someone had sawn through the Tree of Liberty planted in the town square one night. (Plane trees were planted in towns and villages as meeting places and symbols of the new liberty and many still flourish.)

A bike shop *La Route du Ventoux* in Bédoin.

Take the D974 north-east out of town. On the distant horizon above tree-clad slopes sits that shocking peak of Lauzes like an unlanced boil. Cherry orchards, a Caveau de Vin in Sainte Colombe, a nursery garden, olive grove and Les Bruns, a tiny hamlet, shows off extensive vineyards laid out below to the right. Black poplars line the road between trim meadows and then on a shallow climb over the Col de la Madeleine (432m) through oaks and firs.

Near a restaurant Le Mas des Vignes a vulgar daub defaces the road, 'Pédales fuck you go home' which is homo- rather than cyclo-phobic, *pédale* meaning 'pederast'. As for 'Kono Flamshit' next to it, your

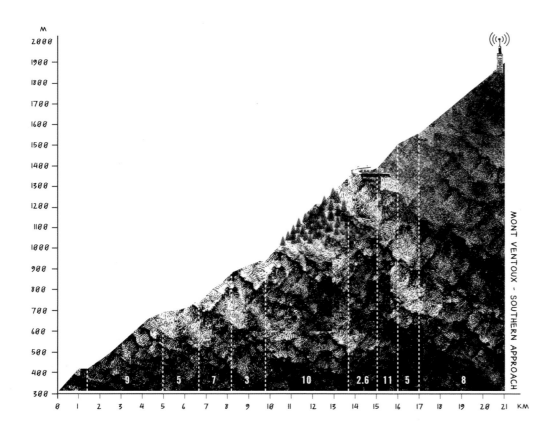

MONT VENTOUX - SOUTHERN APPROACH

guess is as good as mine.

(A *mas* is a farmhouse of the form typical in Provence, from the Latin *manere*, 'to stay', the same root which gives *maison* and mansion.)

The continuing re-afforestation, begun in 1861, gets lots of hearty notice on this road. Two varieties of oak, the ilex (French *yeuse* Provençal *euse*) and the kerm or scarlet oak, both evergreen species of oak, are good to see. The kerm is home to the kermes insect, *coccus ilicis*, whose dried carapace, a deep mulberry red, is used for the red dye cochineal. (Greek κόκκος – *kokkos*, Latin *coccum* is the scarlet berry of the kerm oak.)

The opening salvoes of gradient are harmless, 6 kilometres of nothing more sinister than 5.5%. Then, brace yourself: Thereon to the Chalet Reynard, it's upwards of 10.5% all the way, but, you get the hang of it, you absorb yourself in the task, you settle to it… what option do you have? Does this sign '15km 9.1% 630m' help? The surroundings are very attractive, the multifarious mix of trees is encouraging, a lovely sylvan route, nevertheless overlaid with grim history – the photo of Simpson riding this stretch is grim indeed. He looks horribly gaunt. There is no sight of Ventoux, but it's up there waiting, the sleepless giant balling up winds in its titanic fists, ready to hurl them into the emptiness.

Rocky fragments obtrude from the roadside and on one, a stone tablet fixed there by *Le Moto-Club d'Avignon* remembers '*Son regretté* (greatly missed) *champion Georges Berthier recordman de Ventoux le 20 sept 1936 le temps 15' 25*'. (Postcards in the souvenir shop at the col offer a number of grainy black and white images of those early racing cars hurtling round the bends on the upper slopes.)

At 10.4km, 989m, an abandoned mustard yellow building to the left bears the slogan '*Prouvenço Libro*' (Provence Free) and the road begins to step clear of older trees into a landscape of stunted scrubbier trees for a short distance. 12.6km, 1152m, reveals a board set up in a *hêtraie* (beech grove or plantation) on either side the road, alerting us to the presence of the *pic noir* – the black woodpecker – which shows an orange-red cap and a whitish bill. More boards follow singing the charms of other trees and heralding the *cerf* hart, the trickiest and most elusive runner of hunted game.

13.5km, a big left-hand hairpin and a small settlement of wooden chalets with another call for *Prouvenço Libro* addressed to the *Enfants de Bédoin* and we are at Chalet Reynard. The Pierre de Champeville commemorated by a plaque, was an artist-painter-poet-engraver, passionate about the mountains, born in Saint-Etienne, 1885 and died in Carpentras, 1950. He promoted a ski station on the slopes of Ventoux and described the mountain as '*une île éblouissante dans un océan d'azur*' …a dazzling island in an azure ocean.

Killed by Ambition

For all its iconic status, the Tour de France has crossed, or finished on, the Ventoux a mere 14 times since 1951. Lucien Lazaridès was first over but the day went to Louison Bobet. Ventoux hosted its first time-trial in 1958 when Charly Gaul, the Luxembourg rider who thrived in the cold and wet and usually did not prosper in heat, flew to the top in scorching temperatures, caught, dropped and put five minutes into Bobet, left Jacques Anquetil four minutes adrift and crushed that other superior climber, his arch rival Federico Bahamontes, by 31 seconds. His time for the 21.5 kilometres from Bédoin: 1hr 2min 9sec. Raymond Poulidor won on top of Ventoux, stage 14 of the '65 Tour, occasioning the remark recorded on page 121 below. The next time-trial to use the bald giant as its piste, 1987, set out from Carpentras (36.5 kilometres). Jean-François Bernard beat a clutch of ace anti-gravity coves – Lucho Herrera, Pedro Delgado, Fabio Parra – to win in 1hr 9min 44sec.

In 1970, Eddy Merckx took the stage on the Col des Tempêtes but the strain was so great that he needed oxygen. As Phil Liggett recalls, Merckx, straddling the bike, clinging to the bars of the podium structure to support himself, microphones thrust into his face, was scarcely able to speak, so jarred and in such distress that the whole thing shook with his trembling. On the way past the spot where Tom Simpson had died three years before, Merckx removed his cap and held it to his heart in salute of his former leader in the Peugeot team as Jacques Goddet laid flowers on the memorial stone. The melancholy story of Simpson's death is too well known to be recounted here but Merckx, who was one of the few continental riders to attend his funeral, spoke with passion about his erstwhile boss: 'It's unjust that his name should forever be so indelibly linked with drugs. The controls in those days weren't systematic and I don't pretend that Simpson didn't use a prohibited substance. He was far from being alone. He was a great rider who boosted me from his own experience… Not all older pros would do that with younger riders, especially with a rider they could see posed a threat to them… On the slopes of Ventoux, his ambition killed him.'

Simpson himself had been generously helped by another older pro, the great pioneer, Brian Robinson. Indeed, he paid handsome tribute to Robinson: that had it not been for his encouragement – 'they're just riders, like you' – he would not have lasted in the continental peloton.

Robinson crossed the Ventoux in his first Tour, 1955, and was party to another drama on the mountain. The 1950 winner, Ferdi Kübler, had never ridden the Ventoux and, 10 kilometres from the col, he launched a savage attack, as was his custom in the mountains.

The veteran Raphaël Géminiani, riding with Kübler in the break, warned him: 'Careful, Ferdi, Ventoux is no ordinary col. You can't tell it what to do.'

'Nor is Ferdi an ordinary rider,' the Swiss replied.

Higher up the climb he cracked, and Bobet, who had been making steady inroads into the leaders' advantage, went past. When Robinson came alongside Kübler – and Robinson was a fine climber but, with no pretensions to the mountains' prize, always conserved energy on the ascents so to recover time on the descent – Kübler was in a terrible state. '*Pushez Ferdi,*' he moaned, '*pushez Ferdi.*' Robinson's reply was terse and, that evening, when Kübler did crawl into Avignon, he collapsed. 'The Tour is finished for me. Ferdi's too old, too sick. Ferdi committed suicide on Ventoux.'

One of Bobet's team mates, Jean Malléjac, didn't even get to the top of the mountain. Six kilometres from the col, he fell to the ground in a delirium, the bike on top of him, his free leg pedalling on like an automaton. Unconscious for 15 minutes, he was revived with oxygen and an injection of the decongestant solucamphre.

Eastern approach from Sault 765m

LENGTH: 26KM	
HEIGHT GAIN: 1147M	
MAXIMUM GRADIENT: 10%	

Sault is a pleasant little town, the Hôtel-restaurant Le Signoret is a good place to stay and eat, while cyclists gather in the narrow thoroughfare either about to ride or having just ridden the Bald Mountain.

Take the D164 – a sign reads 'Le Mont Ventoux 26km' – and, if you look hard enough, you can see the radio mast of the observatory peeking above the far line of the ridges like a sentry over a parapet. The first 19.7 kilometres are easy enough, through broad hectares of farmland, descending gently a short way to 720m past lavender fields. As the climbing begins, stunted trees jostle the winding road and the foreground occludes any view of the ridges now, so there is that slight unreality juxtaposing the absence of menace *here* with what's in wait up *there*.

Old-style *bornes* (kilometre stones) show 4km 815m, 5km 850m, and into trees. On a wooden sign painted amber yellow, a stern rebuke for amateur fungus-hunters: '*Ramassage champignons interdit*' (Mushroom picking forbidden).

6km 908m, 7km 965m and, once again, the tarmac sets off downhill like spilled paint, throwing away precious metres, all to be retrieved. At 7.6km stands a tiny stone-built chapel on a small mound to the right – its dressed edging-stones holding in the cruder interlock of the walls' marl-like infill. 8km 1021m, and climbing resumes at a big left-hand hairpin, then eases a bit and on into the *Forêt Dominiale du Ventouret*. The road continues to wind as if it neither knows nor cares where it is heading, charged with doubt and rapt in introspection.

There are lots of *pique-nique* areas hereabouts for the idle non-cyclist and a 4 kilometre pause of *bornes*

for the introspective cyclist to brood on: try to stay focused, introspective cyclist, statistics do not triumph make.

12km 1250m brings the numbers back and here is the head of the valley, a deep cleft driven into the mountainside, a fissure, a cloven slit, a wedge-shaped rift. The road skirts all the way round and then climbs out with growing purpose, for here it is on the main block of rock and you are offered a big view down the length of the valley and beyond. 13km 1279m, and just before 14km 1302m, another huge panorama.

At 14.8km by a right-hand bend sits a low platform built of courses of stones, stepped into a slight bayed apron at the front like a mini stage or bandstand – in fact, a cistern.

On through scrubby woods, at 16.7km a sign for Chalet Reynard snack bar and restaurant and at 17km, 1403m, the geology changes abruptly – *lauzes* scattered like scurf from the bald head of the god, and the road, like his scalp, is bare and unprotected. 18km, 1412m, at a pinch of the road into the flank slopes of chalky shale over to the left and a wide long view opens out.

Here at Chalet Reynard just past 19km, 1420m, begin the bare slopes, the wind-scraped upper heights of Ventoux, the final stretches of road to the col. Those kilometres look fearsome steep and nasty. There is no getting away from it and better to tell it plain: they are horrible, a graceless causeway cut into the rock as it might be the ramp of an Inca sacrificial pyramid.

The road up from Bedoin joins from the left and, like Dante's '*Lasciate ogni speranza voi ch'intrate*' (Abandon hope all ye who enter here) a sign growls 'Le Mont Ventoux D974' at you.

A narrow cycle path runs up the left-hand side of the road – a dotted white line and pale green cycle symbol.

And there it is, the col, the radio mast, the observatory and the bleached, sun- and wind-flayed desert of *lauzes* and the big, hungry bends of the chute pelting you with a hail of gradient percentage. The arithmetic is guardedly mild – most of the way 6–8% and a leg-screw of 9% to the top – not as severe as the other side, but never underestimate the effect of appearance. There are no more signs for distance or altitude either, as if such banalities are irrelevant now that you are in the breakthrough to paradise or perdition.

Sight of the col atop the bare stone slopes comes and goes, a rash of dark green trees across the slope below and the road ahead, curving round the spurs of the mountain like a scar across knuckles.

The memorial to Tom Simpson, (24.1km), adorned with a cluttered heap of brightly-coloured bidons, has a new set of steps up to it, built with donations, particularly from the family of Bob Thom, mechanic for the British Tour team in 1955.

'*A la Mémoire de Tom Simpson, Médaille Olympique, Champion du Monde, Ambassadeur sportif Britannique.*'

A short way on there is another memorial: '*En mémoire du Gaulois P.Kraemer décédé en Ventoux 2.4.1983 Union Audax Français.*'

The radio mast towers up, like an early rocket on its boosters.

Just below the final metres, a turn-off and car park entice to a restaurant, Le Vendran, perched on the edge of the cliff, from where the road up is very steep, very bleak and as scary as a wintry squall on the old grey widow-maker, the sea.

It is quite a moment to arrive on the flat ground outside the observatory, to see the open sky beyond the big bend leading onto the descent by a sign 'Col des Tempêtes 1841m'.

There is a souvenir shop and an amply supplied stall vending variegated *saucissons*.

Petrarch

Two epitaphs on the observatory wall: one, 1875–1883, commemorates an early student of Ventoux, Professeur F Leenhardt. The second, placed by the Club Alpin Français invokes the walk up to the col made by the Florentine poet, Petrarch:

ma cime inviolée	*My virgin peak,*
et mes flancs dénudés et abrupts	*my flanks sheer and naked,*
ont été pour la première fois	*were for the first time*
décrits et poétiquement chantés	*caught and sung in poetry,*
après son ascension du 9 mai 1336	*after his ascent on 9 May 1336,*
par François Pétrarque	*by Francisco Petrarch,*
l'amant de Laure et ermite de Vaucluse	*lover of Laura, hermit of Vaucluse,*
qui unit la restauration des lettres antiques	*who united a revival of classical literature*
la première affirmation de l'alpinisme littéraire	*with the first essay in literary alpinism.*[6]

1336-1936

In a letter to his confessor, Dionigo Borgo San Sepolcro, Petrarch wrote:

'Today I made the ascent of the highest mountain in this region, aptly called Ventosum. My driving aim was to see what view such a high vantage point could offer. I have been thinking of doing this for a number of years having lived in this region since I was a child… the mountain, which is visible for miles around, was constantly in view… and my resolve hardened yesterday when I reread Livy's History and came upon the passage where Philip of Macedon, he who waged war against the Romans, climbed Mount Haemus in Thessaly, from whose summit he could, it is said, see both the Adriatic and the Euxine seas… The mountain is a very steep and almost inaccessible mass of stony soil. But, as the poet has well said 'Remorseless toil conquers all (and necessity sharpens the will in difficult times)'.'

[The poet is Virgil in the Georgics I.145: *…labor omnia vincit improbus et duris urgens in rebus egestas.*]

Petrarch lived in Fontaine-de-Vaucluse, south-east of Ventoux, 1334-41, and the fountain has come back to life after long being dried up, fed, it is now supposed, by an underground stream from the Montagne de Lure, and not, as it might seem to be, the source of the river Sorgue. Perhaps the fact that so famous a poet lived

---

6 Some sources say 26 April and it's not certain which route he took, although it probably followed a line
pretty well due east from Malaucène, with some divagations in search of a more accessible escarpment.

near the spring has endued it with something of the celebrity of that Pierian spring whose pure and bracing waters brought inspiration. 'A little learning is a dangerous thing' says Pope, 'Drink deep, or taste not, the Pierian spring.' Vaucluse's pool is very deep. In the 1950s, Jacques Yves Cousteau explored it in a submersible but did not find the bottom. More recently, a probe reached a sandy bed at a depth of 308 metres. 'There is' wrote Petrarch of this village where he wrote the Sonnets to Laura 'no place on earth more dear to me than Vaucluse.' Not at Laura's side? He saw her first in church. She remains otherwise anonymous though, on the internal evidence of the passionate love poems and sonnets work he dedicated to her, it is probable that she was married and, refusing intimate relations with the poet, nonetheless accepted his homage. We all know about one-way mail. 'Was it here,' he wrote, 'here in this small garden that my love began to fatten in its solitude, and ripen into words?' hinting, perhaps, at the line from Virgil's Georgics III, 291.

sed me Parnassi deserta per ardua dulcis raptat amor

Love swept me up into the high solitudes of balmy Parnassus.
[Parnassus is the mountain just north of Delphi in Greece, home to Apollo and the Muses.]

In one poem to Laura he writes:

ché co la morte a lato	*with death at my side*
cerco del viver mio novo consiglio,	*I strive to live with fresh insight,*
et veggio 'l meglio, et al peggior m'appiglio	*seeing the better, taking hold of the worst.*

This hints at a line in Seneca: *'Inferna tetigit possit ut supera assequi.'*
[He plumbed the depths so as to attain the highest reach.]

Mont Ventoux *continued*

From Malaucène 340m

LENGTH: 21KM	
HEIGHT GAIN: 1572M	
MAXIMUM GRADIENT: 10%	

This is a fairly routine climb for most of the way and, until the last few kilometres, offers nothing of the dramatic tension on the south side. The road is quite wide until those final cranks of the hairpins, long straights which eat into your will, a nasty spell of around 10% for 4 kilometres at halfway but, for those two contrary reasons on the way up, it does offer the best descent of the mountain. The views as you fly down into Malaucène are stupendous; as I say in a piece I wrote about Ventoux, you witness 'pure geography through eagles' eyes'.

An information board in a clearing to the right at 8.5km speaks of the various medicinal plants which grow on the mountain: *asperula odorata* (Sweet Woodruff – a nourishing restorative which, according to Culpeper 'is said to be a provocative to venery', that is aphrodisiac), *inula montana* (Asteraceae) often used in France instead of *arnica montana* for bruising, *hypericum perforatum* (St John's Wort – under the celestial sign Leo and, therefore, top notch to begin with – I speak from zodiacal

affinity – and particularly as an excellent vulnerary, that is its healing powers are sovereign for bruises, contusions and wounds 'especially in nervous parts'), *arctostaphylos uva ursi* (Bearberry – an efficacious astringent), *solidago virgaurea* (Golden Rod – ruled by Venus, this one, and 'long famous against hurts and bruises' though of the physical variety. Broken hearts, apply Venus? Probably not).

A short way on there is a belvedere if you've a mind to stop and drink in the amazing panorama to the north, the lesser sleeping infant giant of the Montagne de Bluye, no more than a sand-dune to this grown-up giant and from this superior altitude.

The last 5 kilometres break well clear of trees and negotiate three sizeable bends onto the final narrow ramp up beside bare rock and the final turn onto the Col des Tempêtes. After a brace of 7% they hit another brace of up to 10.5%. The observatory, viewed from this side, hangs over the mountain side more, the flanking slopes below it steep indeed though the pitch of the road cut across drops to 7.5%.

It may, perhaps, seem unduly disdainful to say that there is little drama in this approach. For sure, the drama of actually turning the corner onto the summit of Ventoux itself is always dramatic, from whichever direction you come.[7]

Personal Experience

When I first rode Ventoux the mistral – one of the 'three curses of Provence' – was howling in raw fury straight at me. The other two curses are the Durance River – see ROUTE NAPOLEON – and the Parlement in Province, or indeed any official body and there were several. Mistrau in Provençal means 'north-west' but also 'bailiff'. More than once it blew me to a standstill and all but wrenched the bike out of my hands. It was a gale out of the invention of primal wind. Aeolus or that vindictive Vin Tur, a local deity, had unleashed the entire sackful of the hurricanes that howl through elemental Chaos over that terrible rock. I straddled the frame, fighting to breathe in the blast of that ferocious gale. My shoes slid on a rink of wind, the bike leaped and bucked like a loose toe of canvas in a storm. Yes, Time died in my shoes. On the '69 Tour, the mistral smote the peloton at 70kph throughout a stage in the Camargue. Jacques Goddet and Félix Lévitan, the race directors, took pity and allowed the riders to tuck in behind the support vehicles for the last 50 kilometres. As Raymond Poulidor described it: 'An authorised en masse doping.'[8]

---

7 A short distance to the north-west of Malaucène lie the Dentelles de Montmirail, a ridge of delicately fretted rock (*dentelle* means 'lace') and two towns, names to conjure with in the nobility of wine production, Beaumes-de-Venise and Gigondas.

8 Ventoux, infamously, can be a torrid, airless place, as it was on the day when Simpson died, but the mistral is a cold, often bitterly cold, dry wind. Be prepared, therefore for quite savage extremes of temperature up there.

Col de Macuegne 1068m & Col de l'Homme Mort 1212m

Transitionals

MACUEGNE – LENGTH: 3.2KM
HEIGHT GAIN: 273M
MAXIMUM GRADIENT: 12%

HOMME MORT – LENGTH: 5KM
HEIGHT GAIN: 427M
MAXIMUM GRADIENT: 10%

These two minor cols are included as transition from the Gorges de la Méouges road (D542) running westwards from the Durance valley into the Vaucluse and the entrance to Ventoux.

Séderon (795m) at the start of the climb to the Macuègne, is a small village packed in round a narrow main street lined with shops and cafés. Enter over a little bridge spanning the infant Méouge. A war memorial honours the dead of 1914–18, a gendarme named Gamonet shot by the Gestapo on 22 February 1944, and six victims of an air bombardment, 10 August 1944. It is a constant theme in these areas: the scourge of war in its last throes that fell on innocent civilians and the combatants of the FFI (*Forces Françaises de l'Intérieur* – the French resistance fighters) in the bitter struggle to drive the Germans out of Occupied France. In the centre of town a water fountain stands next to a double-sided washing trough topped by a gold Marianne in a Liberty cap. Marianne is the national emblem of the French Republic, symbolic of the Triumph of the Republic and representing Liberty and Reason. During the Vichy period, 120 of France's 427 Mariannes were melted down and the hated Milice (the Vichy government's paramilitary security force) removed statues willy-nilly from town halls, so powerful an image did they present, an inspiring embodiment (albeit abstract) of Liberty.

From Séderon, the road sweeps up from a green valley and round to the right – where the D546 joins – for the 6 kilometres to the foot of the ascent to the Homme Mort on a good surface, gliding round short bends. The view of the slanting climb to the Homme Mort sits up ahead, none too daunting. Houses trumpet the sale of *miel* (honey), *fleurs* and essence of lavender, favourite snort of the bees hereabouts. The occasional sentinel Lombardy poplar stands tall and straight at the side of the road

Laborel deep in the gully, to the right Les Begues, with good food and lodgings at Les Céans on the recommendation from three American cyclists we met on Saint-Jean, two from Wisconsin, one from Idaho. (After my long ride in Mali to Timbuktu, the town known as 'The Ends of the Earth' which the peerless Tom Robbins calls 'Every man's Nowhere', I met an American friend whom I hadn't seen for a while. He asked me where I had been. 'Timbuktu,' I said. 'Timbuktu?' he said, in mock surprise. 'Doesn't exist. Where is it? Wisconsin?' Apparently, the thing about Wisconsin is that it's west of Pittsburgh and east of Seattle.)

The broad D542 sweeps past the smaller D63 with nary a look, as if it has much better things to do than dally over so niminy-piminy a stretch of asphalt muscling in on its flow from the left.

A bare 5 kilometres up the side of the Montagne d'Albion to the COL DE L'HOMME MORT, no more than 4%, a view across to the other side of a narrowing inlet of the rock mass. There is, about this climb, this agreeable amble, the crossing of the col, something almost offhand. You may see a checkpoint for a party of horse trekkers [see, too, page 123]. There is, however, a nagging knowledge that a real killer of a climb lies somewhere on its far side and, at a viewing point no more than 2 kilometres below the col, you will see it, on the

scenery backdrop painted along the horizon, that mystic peak capped with what looks like snow, incalculably vast and aloof, a preposterously large mountain jabbing at a torn sky, its naked summit white as alabaster. Roads going up there, you may think, must belong to different scales of tick-tock and map measurement, with time-locks between them and the road you are on. Higher, far, than Jack's Beanstalk, you know.

Scoot down the new tarmac narrow road into flat lands whose fields are lined with long mounds of lavender like *chenille*, which is French for 'caterpillar'. There are barrow banks of *lauzes*, too, presumably gathered from the surface of the soil as the earth works them free of its gums, like raspberry pips, and spits them out. [Off to the left is a grange called La Gabelle, the name for an ancient tax, particularly that on salt, and there is more about that in ALPES MARITIMES.] And so, on into Sault!

Col de la Pigiere 968m & Col du Negron 1242m

Negron ascent

LENGTH:	2.5KM
HEIGHT GAIN:	287M
MAXIMUM GRADIENT:	10%

Running parallel to the Homme Mort, the D18 leaves the D546 at the Col de la Pigière, 3 kilometres before the right turn to Séderon. The climb up to the Negron is severe, short – around 2.5 kilometres – but worth the effort because the views from the top are wide: Ventoux to the west, the Montagne de Lure to the east, the southern Alps and the long ridge of the Lubéron. Thereon, a pleasant 12 kilometre glide down to Revest-du-Bion and right to Sault.

Perty 1302m

Eastern approach from Laborel 827m

LENGTH:	8.5KM
HEIGHT GAIN:	475M
MAXIMUM GRADIENT:	7%

Out from Laborel, the D65 snaking into the portal of the valley, a few houses here and there, this ride has a jaunty feel, the slope is not hard, it swings round the side of the cut, a *borne* stone indicates 2km 959m, and here is an open shelf of road with a bumpy surface. 3km 1001m, and lots of cheery movement, 4km 1057m, then 5km 1120m and a large right-hand hairpin... mark the ratchet of pins and the milder winding between – like the tight snap of a whip and the flicker of the lash as it unfolds from the crack. Pale mauve, alpine, round-headed thistles grow aplenty, the *oursin* (sea urchin) *de Provence*.

At the col, a spectacular, three-way view: across the confines of the Ouvèze valley, bounded by the Montagne de la Clavelière, north, and the Montagne de Cros, south, the Ventoux massif and the Durance valley.

A fast descent on a swish of bends, into trees with occasional gaps where the view opens up. In Ruissas, 8.6 kilometres below the pass, the Hôtel Badiane offers Sauna, Hammam ('Turkish bath'), Piscine, open in summer but haunted by cats all year round – silent, staring grimalkins, on holiday from their seasonal job as familiars, perhaps.

Seek out Le Bougalou, a friendly pizzeria, restaurant and grill, with a terrace on the D546 just west of Saint-Auban-sur-l'Ouvèze. I enquire and am told that *bougalou* is a Provençal word for an ancient flute but it is not in my dictionary, though *bouco* means 'mouth'. The *patronne* tells us about the local-bred horse the *baracan du Vercors,* a strong creature used in the Drôme. There is much horse-trekking hereabouts and your *baracan*, like the sturdy, barrel-chested, short-legged garron native to Skye, is an ideal mount for the up and down of these steep, stony slopes. The Oxford English Dictionary defines a garron as an inferior breed and others call it miserable, but my daughter Lucy and I have ridden garrons, in driving rain too, then quite young, and our mounts were willing and sturdy creatures, quite uncomplaining.

Western approach from junction with the D546 611m

LENGTH:	18KM
HEIGHT GAIN:	691M
MAXIMUM GRADIENT:	7%

There is no real difficulty before the approach to Ruissas, past Montguers (642m, 3km) La Combe (702m, 5.5km), Montauban-sur-l'Ouvèze (730m, 7km). Perhaps this makes the later gradient the more taxing. You are not keyed up. You have relaxed. Excellent. Relaxing is to be encouraged. There is no call for constant agitation and hectic accelerando. There is place for *piano, piano,* too.

From Ruissas (844m 9.4km) the road climbs out of two bowls of valley separated by a central boss along a balcony with vistas. The approach to altitude is stealthy, then a hairpin and hop! – up to a sudden higher stratum, like a fillip of early promotion and advancement. A steady slope of 5–6.5%. This makes for a settled rhythm. Indeed, this pocket of cols between the Gorges de la Méouge and the D994 is a remote off-track area with excellent climbing on tranquil roads and handy loops for circuit routes.

COL SAINT-JEAN 1158M

A gentle way into more serious grimping duties.

| LENGTH: 7.5KM |
| HEIGHT GAIN: 371M |
| MAXIMUM GRADIENT: 7% |

From the D542, 2.5 kilometres beyond Lachau on the Gorges de la Méouge, turn onto the D170 and a flattish valley entrance to Eygalayes (753m, 1.9km) a tiny hamlet with a rustic road-cum-main street to suit. The Mairie is boldly decked with a tricolour and fulsome tribute to the release of Ingrid Betancourt, a French citizen who ran for president of Colombia in 2002. Openly and severely critical of FARC, the left-wing Revolutionary Armed Forces of Columbia, she was taken hostage by FARC rebels while campaigning in the jungle and held for 6 years. A letter signed by Josette Fournie, the mayor, invites Betancourt to the village and a plaque symbolises the 'Hope and Will of the municipal council of Eygalayes… to wish for a new millennium when the women of our world and our society will not have to fight for recognition, with a smile and solemnity we offer a place in the sun to Ingrid Betancourt (2000).'

On the *Place du 22 February 1944* a war memorial which bears the legend: '*Le Droit prime la Force*' (rights before force) in homage to the men of the d'Izon la Bruisse Resistance shot on that day. In so small a community there is powerful melancholy in such epitaphic brevity. Local men, farmers, shepherds, tradesmen, herded out like sheep into a field to be shot. Young, old, caught up in the wider struggle for freedom, their courage displayed and crushed in their small corner of the homeland. We must be grateful we were never called on to do the same. And another 1.5 kilometres on at 830m, a more substantial memorial names those 44 men of the d'Izon Maquis.[9]

'*Et s'il était à refaire je referais ce chemin*'
And if I had to take this path again, I would take it.

The line comes from Louis Aragon (1897-1882), surrealist, poet and novelist, who, amongst other oeuvres, translated Lewis Carroll's *The Hunting of the Snark*. All these men came from the immediate area – Izon lies on a road off to the west 7.8 kilometres away – one has no first name and there are five Jews.

On the curving climb away from the valley, and a sweet view of Eygalayes, there are a number of named *source*s (small springs) such as Bruis 8° (*bruire* is 'to murmur' as of a brook) though what the degree sign stands for I do not know.

At the col, around 6.5 kilometres from the junction, the road bends to the left and falls away. Above the hump of the pass itself, a shrine squats on a brow of projecting rock.

There follows a good rock 'n' roll descent on fast bends and pinched bends in succession, but visibility is not bad on the 6.5 kilometre drop at between 5 and 6% into Laborel (827m) nestling in the gully and Les Begues down the road to the right.

The American trio I met earlier confirm that the climb up to the Saint-Jean from Laborel is hard – so much for the innocuous gradient but the arithmetic attests to it if the legs contradict. This rural community has nothing to offer, a few gîtes signposted out a way, a hotel which offers neither bed nor beverage. The whole place looks sullen and forgotten. In fact, it was originally built up on the hillside and, during the 19th century, suffered progressive depopulation as farming dwindled and people left to make a living in towns. In 1900, the village was rebuilt in the valley bottom but was further hit by the drain on its men by the Great War. Tourism and second homes have partly revived its fortunes, during the summer, at least.

---

9 *Maquis*, the thorny and impenetrable scrub-and-brushwood-covered heath of Corsica, their *macchia*, the local name for a vegetation adapted to the dry conditions which follow the degradation of the Mediterranean forest of holm oaks and cork oaks. 'The Corsican *maquis* is an impenetrable thicket of evergreen oaks, junipers and arbutus,' wrote Maupassant and, for that very reason, the *maquis* was celebrated as a refuge for outlaws. The word was adopted as the name for the *résistants* of Provence who made their hideaway the stony *garrigue* (scrubland) of the region.

Pierre Vesce 1056m

Southern approach from Laborel 827m

LENGTH: 2.7KM

HEIGHT GAIN: 229M

MAXIMUM GRADIENT: 12%

Short but extremely hard (on both sides) in stony, dry-gulch territory, similar to most of the terrain hereabouts. As I have already hinted, these tracks over the mountains are very much part of Maquis country.

A sharp hairpin takes the D65B off the D65 west of Laborel, a narrow, very steep clamber into the armpit of the mountain. At 1.4km, a scatter of houses on the mountainside to the left, grey, like pumice whereas the bluff above is the creamy yellow of Cornish (or Devonian) clotted cream.

At 2.6km, a mini plateau – phew! – and at 2.7km the col (1056m) on a bare car-width of road.

The north-side climb up from a tiny hamlet, Villebois-les-Pins (850m), is equally demanding, equally brief and, looming over it, the conical Montagne de Pierre Vesce cloaked in trees, its peak at 1364m. The descent into Villebois-les-Pins is sharp and exhilarating.

Col du Reychasset 1052m

Eastern approach from Villebois-les-Pins 850m

LENGTH: 3.7KM

HEIGHT GAIN: 202M

MAXIMUM GRADIENT: 7%

You might begin the approach at 19.6km, 593m, from Eyguians where the main D1075, branching off the Durance valley, runs beside the course of the Buëch. Eyguians is the eastern terminus of the Route des Princes d'Orange, a strategic link between Buis-les-Baronnies to the west, in the Principality of Orange, and Orpierre – both of which territories were owned by the house of Orange-Nassau. (The counts of Orange were created by Charlemagne and took the title of prince in the 13th century, the city of Orange their capital.)

The D30 from Eyguians follows the line of the Céans River through Orpierre (682m, 7.8km) where the Céans and Armalauze rivers converge and continues on the D116 to Villebois. It's an attractive dawdle on a quiet road, almost flat, but part of the joy of this corner of the region is to nose into the wilder places and stiffer tests along easy byways.

Through Villebois the D116 follows the course of the Armalauze and at 1km, 918m, the gorge the waters have cut reveals itself. To this point the road seemed to be heading straight into the interfold of trees and mountainside but, round the corner, the folds fall away and there is the shaping of the low gorge. It's no more than 2 kilometres worth of 6 to 7%. Trees close in, a secretive road, this, and suddenly the col is there and you've hardly noticed the effort.

On the other side, a brilliant flash of open view like the sudden popping of a paparazzo camera as you emerge from between the curtains. The westerly approach is, ultimately, harder. Begin in Verclause and, if it's that time of day, seek out Saint-André de Rosans, just to the north, site of one of the most important Cluniac monasteries in Haute-Provence, founded in the 10th century and destroyed during the Wars of Religion 1562–98. The church was spared and is now undergoing restoration. In the small square opposite the tourist office and close by the ancient priory, you will find a welcoming and unpretentious restaurant that serves good grub and houses an excellent bookshop in an inner room.

After a 14 kilometre doddle from Verclause, the gradient springs at you like a woken guard dog and the final 4 kilometres vary from 6 to 6.5 and a blast of 9% before calming down onto the col itself. 1.4km from the col, a brown sign indicates 'Le Glacier' and a V-shaped plug of hill hoves into sight ahead, a stopper driven into the valley to stem the flow of water. Crossroads just beyond Laux-Montaux down where the road is hewn out of the rock of an oppressive cliff.

Verclause, an old fortified village, used to be part of the Dauphin's fief – the Dauphin being heir apparent to the throne of France – and the ruins of its castle and chapel dominate a bluff above the village. (More prosaically, a supermarket and café dominate the confluence of the D116 and the road below Verclause's historic ruins.)

Col de Pommerol 1072m

aka Col de Fromagère

LENGTH: 7.5KM	
HEIGHT GAIN: 402M	
MAXIMUM GRADIENT: 7%	

The old village of Rosans (670m) just off the D994 (the main road from Gap) west of Serre has a number of 15th and 16th century houses, while the tower commanding the main square dates from the 13th. Two plane trees flank the church door – revolutionary trees of Liberty, for sure [see page 114], chosen for the ample shade their spreading umbrella of branches provides. The Greeks planted them to shelter their cattle and flocks from the sun and the Romans called the plane tree *caeleb*s (our 'celibate'), 'unmarried' because it did not support vines, as did the elm – which is why the Romans brought the *ulmus* to Britain for their vineyards.

Up and out of town on the D25 and on down a way into a stand of spindly pines on either side, like the farewell committee of the village gathering in silent goodbye. A sign shows 'Col de Pommerol et de Fromagère' (the latter the village just below the col on the far side – the col is sometimes attributed 'de Fromagère', Pommerol itself lying a short way on.) A sign indicates one day in the year when the col is open exclusively to cyclists, at no charge. In 2008 it was 21 July.

Grass, rock, dwarf pines – the soil is thin and not of the best round here. The Roman veterans who were given free holdings of land in these parts after

their discharge cannot have been pleased. There is no obvious col height ahead which imparts its own attraction, that of riding a new road which keeps its purpose close, leading you know not quite where, a surprise, a route untravelled. With the heroic cols you know, of course, but these lesser, more obscure climbs have their own pull. At 1.7km the ridge does sneak into view and the gradient stiffens to 4.5%. At 2.7km a sudden break through the sparse tree cover but only briefly; the trees reassert and now the climbing kicks in at 6–7% for a couple of kilometres and a feeling of lift into the upper reaches. 3.6km, a big bald ridge rears up on the skyline, the Montagne de Raton. Now *raton* is a small rat but *mon raton* means 'my little darling'. Which extremity to make for? Which mood to evince? Verminous disquiet or romantic soppiness? The road shivers and heads with something like determination, now, for the eastern end, the V between the Raton and the Montagne de l'Archier.

5.1km, on easier slopes, an avenue of leafy hornbeams overhanging the road like an arcade in a *bastide* (country town) – see one such in Buis-les-Baronnies – about 900 metres long. Then bare road and narrow, metal barriers intermittently on the open side. Wild thyme grows here – remember Oberon in *A Midsummer Night's Dream* speaking of that 'bank whereon the wild thyme grows… There sleeps Titania sometimes of the night' so sends he Puck to fetch the herb called love-in-idleness (heartsease) with whose juice he will streak her eyes

and 'make her full of hateful fantasies' (Act II, sc. ii). Don't mock or eschew the poetic trance: it may get you through some hard times.

Acers and box (*buxus*) grow in clefts of rock, and oaks with a sharp-edged saw-tooth leaf, like Turkey oak, wild rose – eglantine, another element of the canopy over Titania's mossy divan – and pines.

The final 2 kilometres fade from 6.5% to 4.5% and, by the col (1072m 7.5km), an information board and a sundial which reminds us that '*Une secrete voix à toute heure nous crie que la terre n'est pas notre heureuse patrie*' 1777. (A hidden voice calls out time and again telling us that the earth is not our blissful – 'timeless' would convey the pun – homeland.)

Descend – a freewheeling drop on what has become the D338, tree-lined and twisty into farmland, orchards, grazing, a small clutch of houses which is La Fromagère.[10]

Towards the bottom, see a bluff ahead to the right of a tight gorge entrance, jutting out, its beetling walls cut into bastions like a natural fort. Opposite, to the left, a conical tree-clad mound on which is built a tower, the seeing-eye guardian of the village of Pommerol, a tight-knit huddle of houses, in the hollow below. Its church has an open belfry, elevated above the surrounding roofs, with two foramina (openings) but only one bell. A sward of neatly clipped grass that might be a bowling green by a lower fringe of the village, ringed by Lombardy poplars and other mature trees, as if Pommerol were hoping to be singled out in some best-kept mountain village competition.

---

10 Ascending this side, at 1.9km, 980m, the col is in view, then it disappears until 1km from top, when it shimmers in again like Jeeves peep-bo, coucou. Tantalising.

You know the myth of Tantalus? Suspended from a tree whose branches are laden with fruit he cannot reach, above a lake whose waters recede when he tries to drink.

However, he did kill and cook his son Pelops to serve as a dainty dish to the immortal gods to see if they could tell man-flesh from animal.

COL DES TOURETTES 1126M

The road is very narrow into and down the gorge between those projecting buttresses of rock, like the Symplegades, the clashing rocks at the gates of the Hellespont through which Jason's *Argo* passed, protecting the upper valley. From below the cliffs to the right, look up to see deep caves and galleries, a free-standing conical pillar, like a giant petrified termite colony, a ruined natural citadel of this underground stronghold, hacked out of the living rock which has silted down and solidified in its own rubble.

The 16th century chateau of La Charce (618m, 7.5km), where the D338 meets the D61, is an ugly edifice from the outside and, one imagines, damp, chilly and dark inside. It stands on a small promontory by the confluence of the Oule and the Establet of the gorge. It was the country seat of Philippe de la Tour du Pin de La Charce who rechristened herself Philis de La Charce after the heroine of a novel. She herself is remembered as a heroine in the latest flaring of war between the Dauphiné and the Dukes of Savoy. In 1692 she is reputed to have lead, sword in hand, an army of peasants to liberate Gap, the Diois and Les Baronnies (that region to the north and east of Ventoux) from the invading Savoyards. Reputed, I say… you know what suckers the French are for girls in armour sending foreign foes packing. And don't the Catholics of this region know Philis as their own Jeanne d'Arc?

The chateau has a new roof, thanks to its acquisition by the Mairie de La Charce.

Western side from La Charce 618m

LENGTH: 15KM

HEIGHT GAIN: 508M

MAXIMUM GRADIENT: 8%

The 6.1 kilometres to Bruis (705m) and a further 3.9 to Montmorin (765m) follow the course of a tributary stream through orchards and open farmland. In Montmorin a clock tower and a 12th century church with a sundial: 'On peut oublier le passé mais on n'évite pas l'avenir' (You can forget the past but you cannot escape the future). Do you find these pithy moral axioms to your taste or do you rebuff them as sententious tosh?

A non-potable water tap.

In a leafy stretch 1.8 kilometres out of Montmorin, a house called La Scie is guarded by a large white dog which will run and bark at you and, possibly, try to sink its teeth into your calf. It is not widely known that Eddy Merckx's nickname 'The Cannibal' was first used of Poulidor during the 1965 Tour (when he came second overall to Felice Gimondi). A journalist said of Poulidor's ride over the Ventoux that he devoured it 'with the voracity of a cannibal wolfing down the leg of an archbishop'.

2km, 860m, and a natural sculpture in a buttress of rock, possibly a two-horned rhinoceros – White, Black or Sumatran – and behind it a Great White Shark lunging out of the water, its head and jaw discernible. 3km, 925m, up and over a hump onto flat and a pond as the col and a radio mast appear way up in the shallow neck to the right. 5km, 1030m, and there is the col across the empty space, filled below with a thick texturing of trees in plantation. The surface is good all the way and the descent fast on both sides.

South side from Col de la Saulce 877m

LENGTH: 3.3KM

HEIGHT GAIN: 249M

MAXIMUM GRADIENT: 8%

Turn right off the D994 onto the D26 at the barely perceptible Col de la Saulce. After 300 metres, a sign shows 905m 8% good surface, bends and hairpins, then 4km 980m 7%, 5km 1050m 7% low trees, 6km 1120m (and a stone water basin with tap, then a house) and the col at 3.3km, 1126m. (The intermediate distances clearly relate to some other start point on a bike route, though I didn't find where it is. Possibly from L'Epine.) Although the gradient figures do shout, the climb itself is mild-mannered and a very agreeable loosener.

Col du Fays 1051m & Col de la Rossas 1115m

These two serve as transitional cols towards the Carabès

FAYS – LENGTH:	4.5KM
HEIGHT GAIN:	220M
MAXIMUM GRADIENT:	7%

ROSSAS – LENGTH:	5KM
HEIGHT GAIN:	315M
MAXIMUM GRADIENT:	6%

The rock hereabouts has a striated surface, similar to a coat of tile glue scored with a bonding comb. There are lots of upthrust chunks of mountain, giant rock molehills, the debris of a giants' rock-pelting mêlée.

Take the D61 north from La Charce, and 4.5 kilometres along a quiet valley road turn right onto the D106.

1km, 820m, a winding road of no altitude attention-grabbing in a valley entrance. 2km, 872m, round a generous right-hand hairpin and we heave away from the valley end for some 200 metres, swing back at a left-hand hairpin and into trees – holly, beech, hornbeam as well as stacks of cut timber. 4.4km, out of trees and a dilapidated hut of stone roofed with terracotta tiles which stands by the unmarked col, the timorous height no more than a hummock.

5km, 1050m, just below the Rossas, the road forges ahead into open country and on a long wiggly straight into Saint-Dizier-en-Dibis, meadows either side, then a short hop past the Bois de la Pigne to the Col de la Rossas (1115m – there is a sign but no 'la' in it) though you'd hardly feel the rise to it or the dip from it unless you were really concentrating or utterly worn out. To the right, an outcrop of blue-grey rock which looks like a low slag-heap, the colour of pottery pudding, a few trees growing out

of it, sucking its mineral and salts dry.

The 6.5 kilometres down into Valdrôme are a stiffer proposition as an ascent but no worse than 6%. In Vaugelas (952m), a hamlet halfway down, an old farm whose yard contains an open shed full of antiquated machinery and a venerable automobile. There are a number of granges, too, and a gîte in whose garden is penned a lama. Just beyond is Valdrôme, a ski station from which roars out a broad road up to a massive car park under the Montagne de l'Aulp for coaches in winter and campervans for the walkers who trek the high paths in summer.

Your photographer and I arrived at dusk one evening in September. Valdrôme appeared to be shut, discouragingly so. We scouted here and there and, in a tiny enclave of silent houses grouped round a cobbled street and minuscule square, like moping patients in a doctor's waiting room, we saw a building with a sign 'AUBERGE'. This was not swinging creakily in the wind, like that of the Admiral Benbow tavern one dark and rainy night in the first chapter of *Treasure Island*, but it had a dull-eyed look to it, a blind-patch dull-eyed look all right. However, nothing ventured, *finis coronat opus* (how a project ends is its crown), in for a penny and so on, I walked down its narrow courtyard to the door and peered in through the pane in the glazed front door. A feeble light spilled from within. I saw, inside the body of the house, two women and a man sitting at a small table under a single unshaded bulb. It might have been a scene out of Georges de la Tour. I tried the door handle, it turned, I entered.

'Good evening,' I said.

'Are you, by any chance, open?'

My accent is Parisian. Some folk distant from Paris take umbrage. Nothing to be done about that, and even though I can do a Midi accent, it didn't seem appropriate.

There followed a pause, not a hanging pause, more of a puzzled pause, a brief span of contemplation and, I don't doubt, of sizing up. The woman sitting nearer to me said:

'What were you looking for?'

'Food and a room,' I said.

She looked across the table to the man facing her. If her eyebrows went up like two question marks, I didn't register it. I did, though, register the man's reaction – between disappointment and resignation. He may have sighed. He did nod.

The woman turned to me and said: 'Yes.'

Never let it be said, thought or even dreamed that we do not push the boundaries hard, your photographer and I, the boundaries of time and space, when we work on your behalf. 8 o'clock in the mountains, miles from anywhere, no glims showing, no sound of merriment or even human activity, nothing plainly open? Commonplace to us, my dears, routine.

It transpired that they had shut for the evening, a night off before the arrival of a big party the following day. The room was adequate, the food fine, the company – they stayed to talk – engaging. Here, then:

Anny Noel and Alain Jacquat at L'Oustaou (Provençal for 'hotel', 'house') in Valdrôme. There is a website and they have a garage for bikes, a washing machine and a spin dryer. They will make sandwiches for you and Alain, who cooks, uses local produce.

COL DE CARABES 1261M

Northern approach from Valdrôme c.800m

LENGTH:	9.5KM
HEIGHT GAIN:	461M
MAXIMUM GRADIENT:	9%

The D106 out of Valdrôme follows the lazy bends of a riverside along a picturesque, leafy vale into a wider plain on grassy banks below a grassy, sloped hillside, the lea of the banks below the road amply furnished with trees and mown or nibbled close by sheep – cows eat to a rough cut and the sheep do the close work, like the razor after the scissors. Hawthorn, ash, oak, poplar, pine. A pretty flat meander. Gradually the trees take over on the bank and at 4km the road dips a short way into a left-hand bend like a springboard onto the climb – its line curving round the jut of the spur and out of sight, clearly detectable. At 5.7km a wooden stable and byre and then a tiny community, La Bâtie-des-Fonds, in trees with a wooden-slat walkway off into the woods. For mushroom pickers? Chestnut gatherers? Trysting lovers? It's a mystery.

A sign speaks of the col, the road is very narrow, the tarmac new, the solitude complete. Ah, but there is a thrill in going way off the beaten track.

Chemin Forestière de Lalaye (6.6km) and gravelled tarmac – most of the loose stuff has gone, but a quite precarious ledge develops with the surface broken here and there as the road inches its way round the cliff and, with a sigh, back onto safer ground with verges either side. Very lonely, the company of woodland, what creatures lurk, what fungus at its roots, what tales it could tell... a meadow with a carpet of flowers, as if the nymph of field-blooms, Flora, pursued by lascivious Pan – it has to be him in this wild place, Le Grand Pan – had let fall her cloak in her haste to escape. No chance.

At 9.5km the col, a yawning view enclosed within trees but 30 metres on and we gaze down onto a small community in the basin of the hanging Aiguebelle valley. (Provençal *carabès* means 'carapace' – familiarly, 'the back' or 'the shell'.)

As the trees thin out, hayfields spread below and the panorama opens up as if its wrapping had been unpeeled.

In Le Chateau, at the base of a stump of rock carpeted with grass, 4.5 kilometres from the col, there is goat's cheese for sale, also eggs, at a farmstead where the collie is very shy, no guard dog he.

The climb from this direction – the 6 kilometres from La Piarre – is well-shaded most of the way, too. The 4.5 kilometres up the low valley from Sigottier (c. 700m) to Piarre are gentle. Just before Piarre the road slips through a rocky defile, very much the portal to the upper valley. This southern approach has a very dramatic aspect, forging towards those natural rock bailey towers and on into the jaws of the valley like Aeneas into the Underworld. So here is Virgil to give us metaphor for this business of riding up mountains:

facilis descensus Averno:
noctes atque dies patet atri ianua Ditis,
sed revocare gradum superasque evadere ad auras
hoc opus, hic labor est

The way down to the birdless regions of darkness is easy. The gates of black Dis stand open day and night. But to retrace your steps back up to the open air, that is toil, that is hard (Aeneid VI, 126).

(La Piarre is *quibus* in French, meaning 'money, the needful, the wherewithal'.)

This Carabès is a peach on both sides, dramatic, interesting, hard, varied, remote.

Towards the bottom and Sigottier, grassy banks

of river and through another rocky defile where the Aiguebelle and Arron join.

West of Serres, a monument records heavy fighting, 19–20 June 1944, between the resistance fighters of the Maquis of Morvan and 300 Wehrmacht and Gestapo. The French inflicted heavy losses and then fell back on Rosans. On Wednesday 21 June, the SS burnt Montclus (a village up the road) in reprisal. (It is now rebuilt). 23 men were killed in the fighting, four were caught and shot later, nine prisoners died during deportation.

COL DU PAS DE LA GRAILLE 1597M & SIGNAL DE LURE 1745M[11]

Northern approach from turn onto the D53 off the D946 508m

LENGTH:	26.5KM
HEIGHT GAIN:	1237M
MAXIMUM GRADIENT:	8%

Even from the main road, the Montagne de Lure fills the skyline, a mighty chunk of rock whose parched solitudes were of long fascination to a local writer, Jean Giono. He wrote much about the ancient god of the wild places, shaggy, horned and goat-footed Pan, and pantheism, the heathen worship of all the gods. Pan's name is properly derived from the Greek pas-pasa-pan, πας. (This word appears in such English compounds as panacea, 'cure-all', panorama, 'all-embracing view', pandemic, 'affecting all people'.) The Homeric Hymn in his praise says that the immortals on Olympus christened the infant Pan 'because he

delighted all their hearts'. According to Plutarch, Pan is the only god who has died in our time.

The hamlet of Les Richaud (520m, 2.7km) sits tight in the loom of the Lure's towering curved escarpment. The surface is good to begin with, lavender, sunflowers, fruit trees under nets filling the flat valley floor. At 2.5km, into pines and out again as the wall of the amphitheatre broods weightily above. At 3.5km, 570m, the climb starts in mixed woodland – beech, larch, holm oak, black Austrian pines and there follows a sudden jolt of around 6.5% for a kilometre.

Every time the road breaks free of the woods, as it does occasionally, the bare rock ramparts lour overhead. The trees below cluster like a gathered crowd gazing up at the dizzy altitude and the emptiness of the sky waiting for a transfiguration. The gradient settles at a mild 4–5.5% and there are stretches which are almost flat. The

combination of riding through such handsome woodland on a winding, tranquil road and the intermittent glimpses of that skyscraper block of stone precipice above lend the ride both a gentle serenity and stark drama.

9.4km, 880m, the Jas des Bailles (*jas* in Provençal means 'gîte, bed, litter' or 'sheepfold') a cabin in the woods and after it an abrupt change of tempo, a brisk reminder that this is a climb and you need to be concentrating. (*L'Equipe*'s cartoonist greeted the first mountain stage of the 2008 Tour de France with a picture of a peak as a stone giant on whose chest could be seen a line of cyclists. The caption: 'At last, my yearly massage'.)

A ring of mountains to the north includes a Montagne du Pied de Mulet ('mule's hoof') and a Crête de l'Ane ('donkey's crest'), indicators of a mode of commercial transport not so long ago the only way of carrying heavy loads from valley to valley across these high ridges.

There is hunting in these woods and you may see hound dogs, with or without their owners. They are friendly creatures, inquisitive and ready to make your acquaintance. I guess it can get lonely, even for a hound whose job it is to flush out game in the direction of the waiting shotgun.

This road proves the unreliability of statistics. The arithmetic suggests no worse than 7.5% but at 17.4km, for instance, a right-hand hairpin unleashes a severe shock of steepness which a spacious view in snapshot through the trees over the land below may assuage. Another hairpin some 2 kilometres on hints that you are 'in for a mauling' as one of the men in a British square at Waterloo is said to have remarked as Napoleon's

11 French graille is a crow, and Provençal luro means
   either 'lure, decoy', or 'good-for-nothing large dog'.

Imperial Guard marched up towards them, late on that momentous day. All told, however, long as it is, this climb is a delight, a metalled forest track happily lost in a dappled green otherwhere.

'5km' (i.e. for the GPM – Grand Prix de Montagne, the mountains prize in any race) in white on the road (1450m here) signals the col and evidence that the pass is used for races. The slope flattens out onto shale-like ground by a rock wall and at 21.5km sweeps round on a full-circle bend to the col (1597m). A wide view to either side and a car pull-in on loose stones. A cairn sits above the col and signs indicate two GR tracks (long-distance 'Grande Randonnée' paths), one to Forcalquier – a town to the south-west – another to the Pas de Jean-Richard, not marked on the map.

The road here has a bike-unfriendly, granular, granite-chip surface and moves onto a more exposed ridge, the vegetation scrubby and low, a lesser Ventoux, the Lauzes concealed beneath grass as the summit of the mountain with the masts of the Signal (a military and naval term for semaphore or heliogram) above a stark, bleak, rude skyline. Its slope to a hummocked plateau below the road is covered with a limestone scree, as it were the petrified scurf on the Lure's bald pate, and an alopecia (ἀλώπηξ – *alopex* is Greek for 'fox') of mangy tufts of shrub and grass.

Raptors wheel overhead.

On the day we were there, three two-up, armchair Harleys roared by, headlights blazing.

The southern slopes of the mountain do indeed recall the bony Giant over to the west. Five hundred metres below the Signal, there is another pull-off for cars and a great wide panorama over the rim to the north and west, on a low ridge above it, three small cairns.

Southern approach from Saint-Etienne-les-Orgues 685 m

LENGTH: 18KM	
HEIGHT GAIN: 1060M	
MAXIMUM GRADIENT: 9%	

This is a ski highway, a fast and easy descent but, as a climb, not a patch on the rustic way just described. Two French women cyclists taking a breather below the Signal confirmed this opinion.

A Word on Astronomy

A stele 4.5km from the top:

*'A la mémoire du savant astronome
Belge Godefroy Wendelin 1580-1667
qui rendit à ce ciel un homage des plus
anciens en édifiant en 1603 à Lure le
premier essai d'observatoire français'*

*To the memory of the learned Belgian astronomer
Godefroy Wendelin 1580-1667 who, in 1603,
bestowed upon these skies a homage to the
astronomers of the ancient world by setting up the
first observatory in France on the Lure.*

This Flemish astronomer (also spelt Vendelin) in 1630 measured the distance between the earth and the sun using the method invented by Aristarchos of Samos (early 3rd century BC). He first postulated the movement of the earth round the fixed stars and sun and, in his copious spare time one assumes, he also invented the hollow spherical sundial, added $1/1623$ of a day to Callipos' estimate of $365\,1/4$ days as the length of the year. (Quite a mathematical laboratory, Samos: home of Pythagoras.) The value Wendelin calculated was 60% of the true value (243 times the distance to the moon – the true value is about 384 times, Aristarchus calculated about 20 times). The Vendelinus crater on the moon is named after him.

In 1643 he saw that Kepler's third law applies to the satellites of Jupiter.

Kepler's three laws of planetary motion:

1. Planets revolve around the sun in elliptical orbits. The Sun sits at one focus of the ellipse, rather than the centre of a circular orbit as once thought.

2. Each planet moves so that a line connecting the planet and the Sun sweeps out equal areas of space in equal periods of time. In other words, a planet moves more quickly in its orbit when it is closer to the Sun. Kepler came upon this law after painstakingly calculating Mars' distance from the Sun at every degree of its orbit. He used Tycho Brache's meticulously recorded observations for this work. From his calculations, Kepler deduced that Mars couldn't possibly revolve

around the Sun in a circular orbit. Instead, the planet must revolve around the Sun in an orbit shaped like an ellipse. Thus, the first law of motion was born. (Kepler himself never numbered the laws.)

3. The square of a planet's period of orbit around the sun is directly proportional to the cube of a planet's average distance from the Sun.

From the top of the Signal de Lure, ski lifts are strung across mountainside, a more modest attendance of trees, the ground cleared for the snow crowd, a snowplough sits idle, a Bar boarded up, possibly open in winter but with that utilitarian aspect of the merely functional, no thought of trying to blend into the countryside, scabby buildings like barrack ablution blocks, further on, the Refuge de Lure set back, blending rather better with its surroundings.

By a picture of stag, wild boar, deer and a hunter with hounds, a sign addresses:

'Amis utilisateurs de Nature Chasse en cours aujourd'hui soyez vigilants'

Nature lovers, hunters are out today, keep your eyes peeled.

The Abbaye and Oratoire of Notre Dame de Lure 9 kilometres from the summit was founded in 1165 and the oaks and limes in front of its chapel are, reputedly, centuries old.

Saint-Etienne-les-Orgues was once well-known for the distilling and preparation of herbal remedies from simples and aromatic plants.

3. LIGURIA

According to the 6th century BC travel writer Hecataeus, the Ligurians were the indigenous neighbours of the Greeks at Massalia [modern Marseille, see RIVIERA]. What he said deserves to be listened to for, in one of his books, on myth, he advertised himself as a cool observer of things as they go: 'I write what I believe to be the truth, for the Greeks have many stories which, it seems to me, are absurd.' During the 3rd century BC, the Romans began to encroach north and westwards out of Italy into territories of what they knew as Gallia (Gaul). They annexed the lands north of the river Rubicon up to Mediolanum (Milan) as the province of Cisalpine Gaul (that is Gaul on the nearer, i.e. the Italian, side of the Alps), then pushed further west into the landmass they knew as Transalpine Gaul. At the time, the Ligurians were allies of the Celts, the principal ethnic bloc of central Gaul, and occupied lands along the Mediterranean coast from the river Rhône to the river Arno (on whose banks is built Florence) and inland as far as the Durance and the mountains south of the river Po, which traverses Piedmont. (The Arno, Tuscany's principal river, flows into the Ligurian Sea, south of Pisa.)

A series of Roman campaigns between 238 and 117 BC reduced to submission the Ligurian tribes in this southern part of Gaul. The Romans had had them in their sights for a long time. After the first Roman incursions, these tribes had supported Mago, brother of Rome's formidable enemy Hannibal, who, amongst other bellicose activities, invaded the Balearic Isles where his name is preserved in Minorca's principal town, Mahon. Mago was defeated by the Romans in 203 BC and the Ligurians' strength was sapped. They intermarried with the Celts and, their blood diluted by miscegenation, they gradually lost their separate identity. Accordingly, the Greek historian-geographer Strabo, writing in the late 1st century BC and early 1 AD, refers to the people living round Massilia (the Roman spelling) as Celto-Ligurian or simply Celts.

Their virtual disappearance as a distinct people may, perhaps, inform the choice of Liguria as the title of one of the 11 *regiones* into which the first Emperor Augustus divided Italy, probably as a basis for the census, in 7 BC. This Liguria stretched from Lucca in

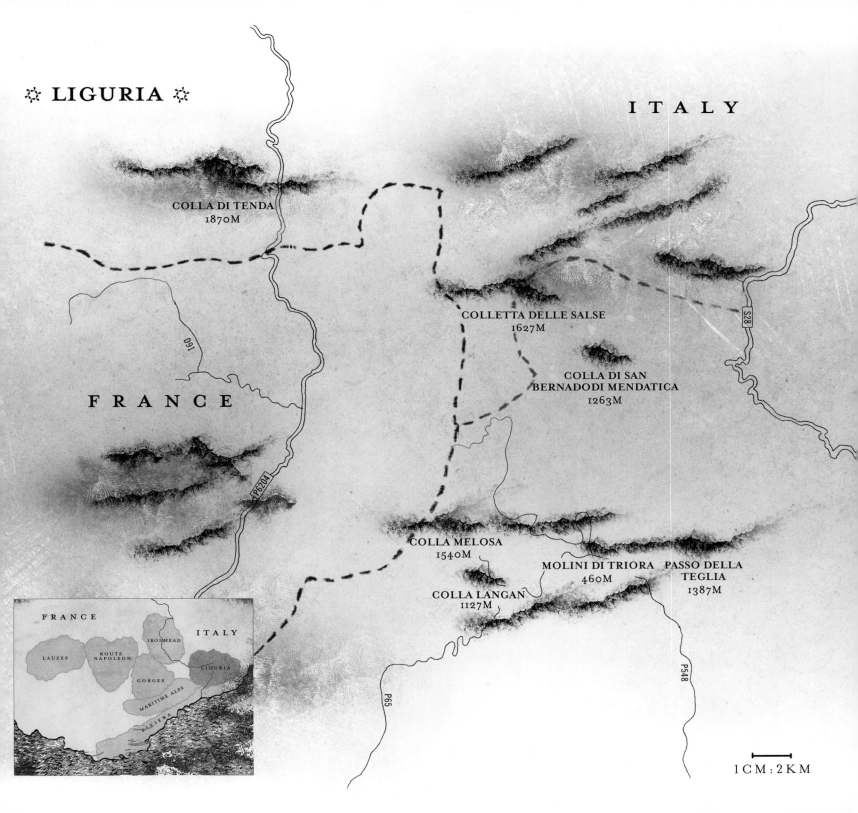

✧ LIGURIA ✧

ITALY

FRANCE

COLLA DI TENDA
1870M

COLLETTA DELLE SALSE
1627M

COLLA DI SAN
BERNADODI MENDATICA
1263M

D91

P6204

S28

COLLA MELOSA
1540M

COLLA LANGAN
1127M

MOLINI DI TRIORA
460M

PASSO DELLA
TEGLIA
1387M

P65

P548

FRANCE

ITALY

LAUZES

ROUTE
NAPOLEON

IRONHEAD

GORGES

MARITIME ALPS

LIGURIA

RIVIERA

1CM:2KM

Tuscany, past Genoa to just west of Nicaea (Nice). Modern Liguria, a reduced version of the Augustan region, lies wholly in Italy and stops at the French border. Our sector concentrates on its western end, *Liguria ponente…* 'Liguria of the setting sun'.

The orator Cicero referred to the mountain peoples of Liguria as 'physically and mentally tough men of the soil', the historian Livy praised their fighting spirit, Cato, a humourless prig with the flexibility of a pair of carbon forks, wrote them off as liars, every man jack of them, while one of the poet Horace's 'favourites' came from the region as his name, Ligurinus, proclaims.

Its position, on the main coastal thoroughfare between territories east and west of the Alps, important both defensively and commercially, exposed Liguria to constant shifts of power. Caesar had his legions tramp back and forth, first to put the breeze up the Gauls (Gallic Wars), then to eradicate the opposition to his own political ambitions (Civil War). There followed, in turn, the Byzantines, the Lombards, the Franks, the Normans, the Saracens, all making themselves at home here. For a while, Genoa held sway – Simone Boccanegra, he of Verdi's opera, consolidated Genoese power for a while until the feuds between the powerful families tore the city republic apart. The Visconti of Milan moved into the vacuum, then the French, then the Milanese again, then the French again, seesaw, seesaw, then the Austrian Hapsburgs, eventually driven out by Napoleon. After Napoleon's abdication and removal to the principality of Elba with a guard of 800 men, the Congress of Vienna agreed to annex Liguria to Sardinia, part of the kingdom of Savoy. The Genoese didn't like it. In 1821 they rebelled and were bloodily stamped on. Bitter resentment lingered. It is no surprise, therefore, that four of the leaders of the Risorgimento, the uprising to free Italy from the foreign yoke in the mid-nineteenth century, were born in Liguria: Giuseppe Mazzini (the politician who first stirred patriots in exile to insurrection), Giuseppe Garibaldi (the great inspirer and military leader of the uprising), the writer and musician Goffredo Mameli (who wrote the Italian national anthem, first heard in 1847) and the patriot and solider Nino Bixio (one of Garibaldi's captains). The Risorgimento is another – and gripping – story but no space for it here, though its famous Ligurian quartet leads us to conclude that perhaps Cicero was right in his estimation of these people.

Molini di Triora 460m to Il Pin 1393m

Superstition and culture

LENGTH:	35KM
HEIGHT GAIN:	933M
MAXIMUM GRADIENT:	11%

We generally eschew dead-ends, unless they have iconic status – the ski station at Pra Loup, for example (q.v.). However, this ride from one of the hubs of our Ligurian sector to just below the ridge along which runs the frontier with France makes a fine ride, and it does have that virtue of being long enough and taxing enough to make a pleasant excursion should you want a lighter day's effort. There and back in time for lunch, why not? For the Albergo Santo Spirito in Molini is a fine place for lunch – menu del giorno – and it also has good, clean rooms.

Molini di Triora, sited at the confluence of two rivers, and a thriving industrial centre during the middle ages, is called after the 23 watermills (*molini*) which once were at work there, serving the surrounding and outlying communities. The Piemontese destroyed them in the 17th century in the course of a savage investment of the area. Triora itself, in a better defended position up the valley, held out against two sieges in that grim period. (Latin *tria ora*, 'three mouths', from the three streams which flow down the hillside there to swell the waters of the Argentina before it reaches Molini. Playing on this, the municipal coat of arms shows an image of the three-headed dog Cerberus who guarded the entry to the Underworld in Greek myth.) German reprisals hit Triora hard during the dying throes of their retreat in 1944 when the Italian resistance began to fight back.

The ride up to Triora, some 5 kilometres, gives a lovely view of mountains all round. The road is narrow, it climbs steadily, the surface is pretty good, broken here and there, the inter-knitting valleys are densely cloaked with trees. A sign shows Corte and a Palestra

Centro Madonna de Ciastreo. In the ancient world a *palaestra* was a low building with a central courtyard whose floor was dressed with fine sand. Here schoolboys were taught how to wrestle. According to the poet Horace, the god Mercury polished the rough manners of newly-created men with the gift of speech and the handsome shaping of their bodies in the *palaestra* (Odes I, x). In Italian, *palaestra* is a gym. Should you be inclined, there is a twiddler's road that winds up from Corte into the heights and a sanctuary to the Madonna. Since it is dubbed a *via crucis* brace yourself for a short bout of penitential suffering.

This area contains a number of interlocking loops of climbs and rides. From one road as it climbs, you look across an intervening valley to another road as it climbs. The receding perspective rinses out the colour paler and ever paler, so that the furthest band of green is a thin wash of the dark foreground. Small towns hover in this still life – Molini nestled on the side of the mountain, its church tower standing up proud from the roofs of the houses like a sentinel marmot up on its hind legs scouting the territory and, further up the mountainside, Ardagna and its church. You are looking at the same kind of scenery which characterises the Italian landscape painting of the quattrocento.

About 3 kilometres out of Molini a damp and streaked concrete side wall to the right on a spacious left hairpin is adorned, in somewhat faded chromes, with four witches, a fly agaric (hallucigenic) mushroom – the hookah-smoking Caterpillar whom Alice meets in Wonderland sits on one – and a pumpkin-headed demon, all about 6 feet high, painted under drainage spouts (by accident or design?) and pretty perished with weather, in garish acrylic colours. A Halloween cartoon? Now we must speak of the Triora witches.

The Triora witch trials of 1588 came in the wake of a concerted, often furious, Catholic riposte to the Protestant Reformation that convulsed Europe.

The Catholic church exercised absolute control over every aspect of human activity, the split in the church compromised this dominion, and the Holy Office or Inquisition, which investigated and punished the contamination of heresy – thought and action – in all its manifestations, pursued witchcraft with especial venom. It was the work of the devil. Joan of Arc, remember, was (nominally) burned as a witch.

By the autumn of 1587, after the failure of two successive harvests, Triora was crippled by famine, a not uncommon occurrence in communities which relied utterly on a fairly sparse agri- and horticulture, although the loss of two growing seasons in a row was particularly severe. At a meeting of the town's council one of the citizens pointed the accusatory finger at a group of women who consorted together in a small shack in the country between Triora and Molini, the *Ca 'botin*, 'rustic hut'. (A stone building immediately outside the city walls of Triora, called the *Cabotina*, is now undergoing restoration.) These women were known for their skill in herbal medicine, their salves and decoctions. They helped women in childbirth and were, almost certainly, both able and ready to conduct abortions. They were, in short, living on the margins of pious society. What we might term their alternative approach to healing could be considered an offence to legitimate (if unsound) medical practice. Such heterodoxy at a time of public calamity made them obvious targets for blame. To a primitive imagination inflamed with superstition, harried by fear of divine wrath at human error and miscreance, it was a short leap from women plying the healing juices of plants from meadow and hedgerow and covert dabbling in obstetrics to witches' covens, spells and potions, Satanism, the black arts and impious compacts with diabolic forces. A popular local saying, still in use, hints at their dark powers: '*Quando u ciöve c'u sue, e bàgiure i fan l'amùe*' (If it rains when the sun is out, witches are making love. An alternative telling has it that 'the Devil is beating his wife').

The thirteen women, four young girls and a boy who frequented the Cabotina were arrested on the order of the Podestà, the provincial governor in Genoa, as *bàgiure* (Ligurian for witches) and, in October, put to trial – without the sanction of the Inquisition in Rome – by two priests, one from Albenga, the other attached to the Inquisitor of Genoa, one Giulio Scribani, roving Commissary of the Genoese republic and a witch-finder of extreme sanguinary temper. All Europe was convulsed with a frenzy of witch-hunting and the hapless women of Triora who were fingered by Scribani were dealt with summarily – strung up alive over a tree bough, with a fire lit under them. The luckless prisoners were accused of witchcraft, drunkenness, unnatural practices, and of cavorting round the *Ca 'botin* by night among the walnut and chestnut trees, tossing about like balls infants stolen from their cots. The inquisitors resorted to torture, but in January the elders of Triora protested at their inhumanity and petitioned for an end to the trial. The process dragged on, however, and was transferred to Genoa after a visit of its Inquisitor in May. A decision was sought from the Vatican but the Vatican deferred until August 1589 by which time five of the women had died in prison. The rest were set free and the priests who had initiated the trial were excommunicated.

Triora today is a classic Italian hill town: narrow, winding cobbled streets within the circumvallation, covered stone alleys, churches squeezed into tiny *piazze*, tourist shops, a fine stone arcade under the walls skirting the main street and portal, the old wood-fired town's bread oven with costumed mannequins in attendance. (Triora's bread is celebrated: it keeps fresh for a week and is therefore ideal to pack in napsacks for men heading off for long stints of labour away

from town.) And, of course, much about the famous *streghe* (witches). In Triora's Palaeographic museum, they get their place in the basement: mannequins, one tied to a wooden bed, feet and hands – over head – stretched by a windlass, a fire lit under the bed. Even more poignant, somehow, a young, blonde-haired woman in a cotton shift sits forlornly on a low wooden bench in a tiny cell, straw on the floor, a metal grille across the whole width and height of the aperture on the other side of which stands a Franciscan friar by a small wooden table on which a book, papers, pen... the inquisitor and his wretched prisoner.

In the glass cases in rooms adjacent are countless books about witches in general and these witches in particular. One case holds vellum-covered volumes containing reports of the Holy Office. Halloween is celebrated big time hereabouts.

Out of Triora the road descends into the valley for around 15 kilometres, the massif dominating the skyline ahead. A pleasing company of deciduous trees, acer, ash, sweet chestnut, beech, oak, many of the trunks clad with ivy string vests. At a junction with a road to Loretto (642m) across a little bridge stands a shrine inscribed with an elegiac couplet: '*nullius hoc fructus pereunt sub culmine voti hac nullius hominum tristis ab arce redit*' (No food perishes beneath this roof-ridge, no man leaves this refuge disappointed in his prayers). A pleasing motto for a round-the-clock drink and eatery, *non pensi?*

Alongside it is a memorial to a commander of the 2nd division of the Garibaldi killed in 1917 and another to the *Martiri della Liberta della Valle Argentina* killed in the Second World War. One man was *fucilato* (shot) in 1944, another in 1945... '*chiusero gli occhi per que altri li aprisero alla luce della liberta*' (they closed their eyes so that others might open theirs in the light of liberty).

Continue towards Realdo. One kilometre from the bridge, the hillside ahead is a veritable corduroy of small terraces overgrown with grass, possibly

constructed for the planting of single lines of trees, every cultivable square metre of land put to use. There are, though, some very spindly trees, evidence of poor soil, lack of moisture and sun, scant attention of their owners? They look starved, like that witch in the cell, thin-sticked trunks barely thicker than small branches.

A sign into Creppo (820m), 3.4 kilometres from the bridge, forbids the picking of mushrooms, for *funghi* abound in these forests. Mushroom hunting is a serious enterprise and we do well to remember that the French word *amateur* and Italian *dilettante* (notions at which we sneer in English) signify love and delight. No bad thing, even in a professional. The true mushroom hunter has to know exactly where to search, under this bush or that tree, and it's almost a psychological game of hide-and-seek they play, the fungi being so elusive, so secretive. And what excitement when a real prize finally appears – the dark colour, the smell, the firm meat: the *amanita* known as Caesar's mushroom... the precious (and very expensive) Italian white truffle... the black and autumnal *porcino* (piglet) which is what Italians call the cep and we call 'penny bun'. . . Finding a cache in forests of chestnut, oak, birch, beech – pines exude acids which the fungi shun – they will pick them and carry them off before cleaning them, as the scrapings leave evidence of treasure trove and rivals must be decoyed. And they never, ever, reveal where the mushrooms come from.

Of Realdo (1060m) 6 kilometres on, the poet Cravét said it is '*un nido d'aquila posata sull' una roche*' (an eagle's nest on a rock) which it is, and this road up to and beyond it might be the terrestrial equivalent of a big raptor's riding of the thermals in long sweeps of the aerial contours, a quiet exuberance of movement in a lovely tract of these joyous couplings of mountains and valleys, splayed eminences and hollows between.

Casale Borniga (1300m) is a little community planted on a spur of rock and we learn that these houses were occupied only in spring and summer seasons by some people but by herdsmen all year round, their survival dependent on flocks of sheep and goats and the cultivation of chestnuts – for flour – potatoes and cereals. The sturdy houses have one ground floor, a *ballatoio* (a wooden gallery or balcony) and stone slates on the roof.[12] A 1st century AD bronze bracelet was unearthed near here, unique in western Liguria, Celtic for sure, made of eight torques twisted round a sheath of bronze, happily preserved.

And so to Il Pin (1393m) in the loom of the sheer cliffs and high rock which screen the end of the Argentine valley and along which runs the Via Alpina and the border with France. Mountain bikers ride it and many of them come to this area because the off-road riding is splendid. For the racing bike, however, the ride finishes here on asphalt fusing with a dirt track. The view is fantastic and, that late evening in November of my visit, a ghostly white *mer de nuages* (sea of clouds) rose up from the valley as if to bask in the pink glow of the sun as it sank out of a nacreous blue sky.

I talked to a very friendly man who was busy measuring the levels in his two cisterns. He was quite firm about his ownership of his water. (Two cylinders, a stone outer skin round a cement lining.) *'Per la verdura* (vegetables),' he tells me. He smiles and explains that up here, they cultivate, as they have always cultivated, wheat, barley, oats, onions, barley, potatoes, beans, tomatoes, olives and chick peas (*cicer* in Latin and Cicero made a self-deprecatory joke of it), leeks, turnips, garlic, the staples of the *cucina bianca*, 'white cuisine'. (A *'strada della cucina bianca'* encircles this larger area in the mountain communities in which people subsisted

on a singularly pallid diet: cereal starch, milk and cheese, potatoes, leeks, onions, turnips, garlic. They probably became see-through with age.) My friendly informant tells me that there hasn't been much rain this year as his nondescript dog and a husky, both friendly, come up to greet me. His hound dog, who is *timido*, hangs back.

He says: 'When you see that red car, that means I am at home, stop for coffee.' Riding a horse he took the flocks down the day before (20 November) and explains that the second phase of the *transhumanza* will happen, according to the weather, any time in November. This season, as the trees change colour, the racing green warming to deep reds, russets, salmon pink, amber, orange, ginger, a friend of his says to him: 'All you have to do is look out of your window and you have one of the best sights in the world.'

The Albergho Santo Spirito in Molini celebrates over a century of cheery culinary excellence – '*Da 100 anni fantasia in cucina*' – and lodging. The cooking is indeed superb and cheap. The chickpea soup declares local interest and the *aperitivo della casa* – martini rosso, gin, campari soda, vino bianco – is sensational. They serve wine made at a nearby vineyard and their cheeses celebrate the best of Italian tastes: *gorgonzola, suola* (means 'sole', thus the shape), *pecorino mare mano, pecorino sardo*, (i.e. from Sardinia) *ricotta salata…*

As a digestif I am offered grappa or the home-brewed *myrtillo*, whose constituent fruit is picked up on the Melosa at 1540m, and I choose this, of course: it is a beautiful pale tea-rose pink in colour and has a toothsome, sweet spirituous flavour. The growing at high altitude, where the temperature is so markedly cooler, brings to mind Prince von Metternich's vintner's

accidental discovery of *Eiswein*. The Austrian statesman was chairing the Congress of Vienna, September 1814 to June 1815, a gathering of ambassadors whose objective was to redraw the continent's political map after Napoleon's abdication. Delayed in the capital during the first sessions, Metternich did not return to his estates till much later than the vintage would normally have been taken in. His steward had not dared to pick the grapes without permission but, once picked and fermented, those frosted, icy-cheeked little fruits produced the first *Eiswein*. Hurray.

The walls of the dining room are hung with a hotchpotch of old tools, copper jelly moulds, pans – deep small skillets, a bucket long- and side-handled, a tiny bed warmer and flat pizza and *ensaïmada* pans. There are radios of various sizes dotted about and behind my table a big old radiogram in a veneer cabinet, its dial offering tuning to a broad band of stations evoking an earlier age of radio – from BBC to Baden-Baden, Sottens to Stuttgart, Munich to Monte Carlo, Athlone to Athènes and that great stalwart of independent broadcasting before the offshore pirate stations came in, Hilversum.

There are also old plates, an ancient map, and photographs of Molini before a bomb hit it in the latter stages of the war, when the village was disembowelled, eviscerated, and the main piazza destroyed – yet another example of the ruthless vindictiveness of the retreating German armies, a wholly pointless bombardment, as in France during the Germans' retreat in 1918. There are remnants of what must be the original masonry below the *Centro Storico*, 'historic centre', next to the street which climbs up into the old part of town, and a commendation from HM Britannic Majesty's government for the fortitude exhibited by the Mamma of the present owners during the war. Molini also boasts an excellent, well-stocked *Alimentari*, 'grocer and greengrocer', open 07h00 to 19h30.

12 *L'ardessia* (slate) is a characteristic element of the Ligurian geology and this province of Imperia particularly. Its composition lends it impermeability, high resistance to changes of temperature and strength and has been widely used since the middle ages for roofs and walls exposed to the north, where more friable materials would deteriorate, as well as in the towns of the Valle Argentina in paving, window surrounds, architraves, lintels, doorways and quite frequently elaborately carved and engraved.

Passo della Teglia 1387m

Take the SP17 just out of Molini (460m) on the south side

LENGTH: 10.2KM	
HEIGHT GAIN: 927M	
MAXIMUM GRADIENT: 10%	

Quite a steep climb away from town (8–9%), past the outlying houses and on into trees. A series of ample hairpins, gracious as the landings on a palatial main staircase, and up you step a nice metreage. By one such hairpin stands a magnificent larch like a palace guardsman and, past another, a wall on which is painted '*VAI AMO*'. (This is odd. Is someone called Amo being encouraged – *vai...* go – or is the author of the message, in a desperate tangle of emotions, beseeching the object of his love to 'get out of here'?) Gaze up at the battlements of crests, overhead the butte of the mountain and the road slicing up its flank like the strait and narrow to the promised land. Do you find the sight of the road you must ride daunting or is it an encouragement?

See, too, Andagna, the town above Molini, its church high on a promontory. The first of a succession of signs gives 2km 730m, and 500 metres on is a wee Capella di San Bernardo overlooking the empty space of the valley. There are frescoes inside from 1436 depicting the Passion and the Seven Virtues and Seven Deadly Sins. Keith Richard, when asked if he thought that original sin was responsible for all the wrongdoing and nastiness in the world, replied: 'If I knew what original sin was I'd try it and

let you know.' (You know the sins, naturally, but in case you are hazy on the virtues, they are faith, hope, charity (love), justice, fortitude, prudence and temperance. Not a very inspiring list, I must say. Compiled by a deep-dyed killjoy?)

3km 850m, therefore the kilometre up from Ardagna is 10% and then, on a sinuous road – this descent is tortuous, very technical – it slackens and, for no obvious reason, dips down a ways. How depressing: all those metres won and now scattered like rain spray through your spokes. Sweet chestnuts and oaks line the road, stout timber to be had from both, almost unbreakable across the grain, easily split in smooth planks down the grain, much used in furniture-making and roof structure. Oh, this climb is fine, the road moving all the way – a real exultancy in it.

The ledge of road grows twisty, its far-extended self visible across the gap of the valley and 4km 950m bespeaks 10%, although that does not feel so. Here another chapel, this to Santa Brigid and an appeal: '*prega per nos*' (pray for us). Good timing. The climb looks hard from here. The saintly woman was Irish, revered as the 'Mary of the Gael', so God knows what she is doing dispensing her spiritual largesse up here.

Suddenly, a foreshortened and intimidating view of a rack of exposed hairpins. Optical illusion: they look far worse than they turn out to be. And *graffiti* (we *are* in Italy) on the road: '*Arrivo*' then '*cambio a piedi*' (I'm getting off to walk). Don't. You are on a bike. You came here to ride, to enjoy yourself. If

you had intended to walk you would have come equipped with boots and long socks.[13]

5km 1010m, under the beetling slab of the ridge, striated rock and, through the trees, a cheering view of the road you have ridden, of San Bernardo's chapel and of Ardagna. (San Bernardo, patron saint of mountaineers and alpinists, served in the cathedral at Aosta, on Italy's northern alpine border with France.)

6km 1090m, 7km 1150m, and a shrine to Nostra Signora di Drego. Drego is the name of a tiny deserted village a bit further on, now a tumbled-down gathering of stone hovels once used by shepherds, one cabin just about standing and serviceable, the rest nobbut piles of collapsed masonry. Two black and white striped barriers and written in red: '*portare di alpio presto serve un morel in pietra*'.[14] 9km 1300m, and a real shelf here to 10km 1390m. Look down and there is the bridge at Loretto, afar off, beneath a broad panorama of distant heights.

Our anonymous cicerone has got back on his bike, now, for his instructions in white paint on the road, fading, as perhaps he was (you are?) at this point, read: *Tiene fidale* (it ought, surely, to be *fedele*), 'stay true' which we may take as Italian for *tiens bon*, which is French for 'stick to it'. A few more minutes and the col. *Teglia* means 'baking pan' but there is no clear link between this gentle hummock of a *paso* and its lovely expansive view and a pie dish. A board depicts a Neolithic settlement of sheep byres in an area of much pastoral farming. From the milk of the

---

13 The only rider to wear long socks is the Frenchman, Christophe Moreau, who displayed them in the 2008 Tour. This caused some merriment before he quit the race because of a bad back, about which, to then, he had kept very quiet. Word is he went before he was asked to leave.

14 This linguistic enigma has, alas, proved undecipherable, despite exhaustive reference to a number of experts in many aspects of the Italian language as well as Ligurians from the immediate vicinity. Here is how I fathom it. 'Un morel means 'strawberry' in Ligurian dialect and pietra is Italian for 'stone' so that, putting aside all professional scrutiny, we may have something as simple as a local individual – illiterate but enthusiastic – advising us to bring the alpine strawberry down as fast as possible (presto) and serve it on a boulder, for want of a plate, to make sure it is enjoyed fresh.'

great plethora of flocks and herds brought up to the summer encampments in the *transhumanza* the shepherds made cheese and *bruzzo,* a sort of ricotta (the word means 'cooked again'). The watery whey left after the squeezing out of the creamy milk's curd for harder cheese is left to ferment awhile to produce the necessary acids, then boiled. The resulting soft curd is separated from the liquid by filtering through a cloth and, lo, ricotta.

On down through woods, observing fingerboards for walks off to higher places inaccessible by bike. This north-facing side is quite thickly wooded most of the way. About 1 kilometre down, in a brief treeless stretch past a gathering of unattractive buildings and animal sheds, a sizeable chunk of road has fallen away leaving only just enough space for a car to get through. Back into a closer attendance of thick-trunked poplars and open sight of the road ahead snaking away. The surface is poor, but there is more shade. This is another quite hairy descent, no barriers to speak of – which always makes a road feel that much more exposed – and a lot of bends. A pair of black and white striped barriers publicises the 50 San Remo WRC. This is the 50th edition of the Rallye di San Remo in 2008, a race in the World Rallye Championship first held in 1928. (There was a gap between 1929 and 1961.) Someone not so enthusiastic about high-powered saloon cars screeching up these narrow mountain roads shattering the rustic tranquillity to hell has added, in gold and red, '*e uno scandalo*', 'is a scandal'. 3.5 kilometres down, a T junction: left to Rezzo, right to San Bernardo di Cunio and 2 kilometres on, at a fork, turn right for the COLLE DI OGGIA (1245m).

A pleasant 1.6 kilometres from the fork to the shallow pass below Monte Grande (1418m) and a pleasant view over rolling countryside. About 1 kilometre down, fringed by an avenue of mature silvestris pines, lies the seven-hectare estate of *Prati Piani* (flat fields) once owned by the Agnesi family, makers of pasta since 1824 – the Agnesi brand still commands attention – its three main buildings, including the original villa (which became the Albergo Agnesi in 1948) and workers' house offering accommodation for corporate or holiday lets. This road, up from Carpasio to San Bernardo, was built by the military in 1935.

Two kilometres on at 1115m there was, that day, a car parked by the side of road with its boot open and a black and white water spaniel, possibly a truffle hound, standing there, ears pricked for the command from its owner, eager to get on with its foraging sniff and snuffle.

Carpasio (715m, 4.5km) from the pass is twinned with Saorge, a fortified village, pretty well due west just over the border in the French Maritime Alps.

A board in Carpasio lists the fauna which frisk in the woods and fields hereabouts: *capriole* – goats, *volpi* – foxes, *tassi* – badgers (*tasso* also means 'yew'), *pernici* – partridge. (Not mentioned, although it should be, is *cinghiale* – wild boar.) As for flora, it singles out *quercia* – oak, *castagno* – horse chestnut (whereas *castagna* is that other species of chestnut tree known as 'sweet' or 'Spanish'), *pino* – pine. It also speaks of the Antica Strada Marenca linking Cuneo in the north to the coast at Imperia by way of the Valle Vermenagna past Limone Piemonte and on across the Oggia. Once a mule track, this 'old Marenca road' certainly dates back to the Roman era although documents referring to it exist only from 1207. An important and ancient communication between two sections of these alps, it was used principally for the transport of oil and salt.

The Rallye San Remo comes through here on its way to the Teglia in October as does the Rallye Valle Imperiese in September/October.

4.3 kilometres on Montalto Ligure (315m), and another 2 kilometres to Badalucco (179m) where this road joins the main valley road from Arma di Taggia on the coast up to Molini.

Passo della Teglia *continued*

Southern approach to the Oggia

LENGTH: 11KM	
HEIGHT GAIN: 889M	
MAXIMUM GRADIENT: 9%	

First records of the commune of Montalto Ligure date from the 11th century and the story goes that it was founded by some newly-weds who took exception to the Count of Badalucco's insistence on exercising his feudal right of bedding every virgin bride [see also Dolceacqua, page 161]. Half of Badalucco joined them, in solidarity against the aristocratic slob's ruthless insistence on hymen-bagging. Some time later, the Count, having seen a big chunk of his feudal revenues and a majority of his able-bodied workers vanish up the hill, invited the secessionists to a banquet of reconciliation. However, the desertion had robbed him of fresh harvest and he had nought but old-season chestnuts to offer them. The Montaltani, however, accepted his invitation and came down the hillside with the provisions for a sumptuous feast from *their* bumper harvest, enjoyed a slap-up, then went back home and stayed there. Reconciled? More triumphant if not triumphalist, like as not.

In Montalto there is a piazza named for one Rossi Marco Dino Fuoco who died on 9 September 1944 aged 22. He was awarded a gold medal of honour posthumously. The gradient kicks up out of the village – note the sanctuary on a promontory off to the left. There is 'LOEB' graffitoed aplenty, referring not to the publishers of that most useful tome, the Loeb edition of classical authors – Greek or Latin on one page and a crib translation on the facing page – but to the Frenchman Sébastien Loeb, world champion rally driver. One kilometre on from the top of town at 430m (around 9% therefore) begins a gentler climb up the valley of the Carpasina,

tree-clad slopes gradually pinching in. A pleasant, fairly shady ramble on a good surface at around 6% as the next marker– 490m – shows. Then 555m by a road dropping away to Costa and a plea: *'TI AMO TORNA DA ME TITO'* (I love you Tito, come up and see me some time) in red on the tarmac.

Another kilometre shows 629m, and another 700m and into Carpasio. Stop in the café/bar by the turn – right leads into the centre of this tiny village – and a friendly woman will serve you a good cup of coffee (take it Americano, else it comes so punishingly strong it will give you heartburn and dental neuralgia) and a fruit croissant to restore you.

The ride out of Carpasio is around 8–9% for a kilometre to 780m. Vines grow in rows above the village and you will see up to the col, the yoke of the hills dipping to the pass on either side. The gradient may appear to slacken for a way but it maintains a steady 7–8% to 1030m where the road starts to fall away as if it has suddenly gone shy and shrunk into itself, head down, hoping not to be seen for some 400 metres before it recovers itself, striding boldly once more through a sort of gateway of two shoulders of rock to the other side – as it were onto the stage – where it stands up again and grasps the attitude nettle to 1240m and the col itself.

Look across to the hillside opposite where a long scar of road traces down from San Bernardo: a long haul of a climb but a most agreeable descent.

In San Bernardo a plaque marks the tenth anniversary of what the Garibaldini – a local anti-German partisan group – boldly dubbed a second Risorgimento on 5 December 1944. In a battle on Montegrande, they inflicted a heavy defeat ('humiliation') on the Nazis – the almost invariable appellation of the German forces in these memorial inscriptions. The word used is *cacciandone* from *cacciare* which means 'to hunt', a nod at the pastime,

crucial to the filling of their pantry, of the local men. Another plaque commemorates partisans whose names were lost:

Non vi abbiamo dimenticato:
in nella nostra fede il vostro e sempio,
in nella nostra lotta la vostra vita,
in nella nostra speranza il vostro ricordo,
in nella nostra liberta il vostro nome

We have not forgotten you:
your example sustains our faith,
your life [meaning the sacrifice of it]
encourages our struggle,
your memory lives in our hopes,
your name lives on in our liberty

There is also a little water trough, one large and one smaller basin adjacent above which someone has stuck a cardboard notice: '*Signori Ciclisti questo non e un pisciatoio*'. A *pisciatoio* is exactly what it sounds like, a urinal. Hateful to think such combination necessary.

From San Bernardo (1055m – 986m on the map) the 9 kilometres to COLLE SAN BARTOLOMEO (621m), the beginning of which looked steep from across the valley, are in fact a steady ascent of easy gradient and a very happy descent, trees, a small community or town, a good long view off to the right. The Colle San Bartolomeo is made much of in these parts – signs for it here there and everywhere, but no obvious reason for its pre-eminence. Turn left at its junction and cut on down towards Pieve de Teco and thence up the same road to COLLE DI NAVA (934m).

From Imperia on the coast, the SS (i.e. *Strada Statale*, 'state highway') 28 goes north to the Colle di Nava at 33.8km, not a bad ride and it does give access to the next loop which is a gem. The road does carry traffic, of course, but generally not too heavy, the slope is of that sort to stimulate a steady rhythm and beyond Pieve di Teco (formerly a Byzantine fortress, τειχος – *teichos* is Greek for 'city wall') the surroundings are more conducive… fields of lavender worked by bees to produce the famous local blend of honey. The Colle di Nava is a slight dome and on the promontory to the immediate east stands the exceedingly gloomy Forti di Nava, built for a garrison of 200 men between 1870 and 1890, to guard the main route between the coast and Piedmont and the Po valley.

Northern approach to the Passo della Teglia along the Giara di Rezzo starting at 320m

LENGTH: 18.5KM

(*Giara* means 'jar', here the neck of the river Rezzo.) The road off the SS 28 to Pieve di Teco is a trifle elusive: follow the sign to Rezzo.

This is a confined wee valley, adorned with a rich mix of deciduous trees, olive terraces, signs of brisk cultivation, a number of churches set back from the road, often one in the heart of the village for everyday pieties, another set apart, loftily placed above it, quite aloof, a dedicated sanctuary, maybe, for the more particular appeals of mercy and votive apostrophe. The standard form of the churches hereabouts: a long nave and open belfry on a solid pinnacle tower, the roof steeply raked. One church off to the left has a rounded apse and a pineapple-shaped cupola on its belfry, but, stuck to its side wall, like a bleb in a tyre, a goitre on a neck, the swelling of a bee sting, a chapel built on after the main body, perhaps, or an outhouse for the sacristan's liturgical frocks and gear.

Rezzo's church (563m, 6km) boasts an onion-shaped belfry dome, bulging round with a kinked-in waist like those familiar in Russia. There is also what looks like a good restaurant *Al Fine.* Journey's end? Otherwise, *vino e panino* in a bar. A fairly substantial wood yard packed with timber in stacks and a lot of reclaimed timber. A *Municipio* (town hall) with 'RETIUM' written on the side of it, presumably the community's original Latin name, meaning 'net' which, given the proliferation of nets under the olive trees at harvest time, is apt. (Olives are not picked. They are left to fall – sometimes, as is the case with walnuts, the branches are beaten to encourage them – and then gathered.) Rezzo's second highpoint church is a 15th century Santuario della Madonna Bambina.

Just above Rezzo a water fountain is inscribed, '*AQUA RA CAUSA GAIORDA*'. This presents another linguistic enigma which the Italian department of the University of Reading hunted with alacrity but which, like the elusive unicorn, could not, finally, be run to earth. However, it may be a mixture (macaronic) of Latin and Ligurian dialect: *aqua* and *causa* are Latin, 'water' and 'cause', *ra* is how the Ligurians pronounce *la*, i.e. 'the', and *gaiorda* means 'courageous' in central Italy. Therefore – and if there is egg on the face it splats upon my own cheek – we may hazard at some kind of encouragement, albeit ungrammatical and deficient in syntax, to drink water, Adam's ale, for it is the source of a strong heart and spirit.

As the houses thin out towards the head of the valley, the road pinches in (not so long since it was no more than a track), the wooded slopes look quite desolate, the trace of a hut in a clearing way up to the left in what is emphatically cattle and flocks territory, now. Rocks jut from the side of the road like commissaries pouncing out of secret controls. Trees overhang, the eager spectators of an epochal bike race, metamorphosed, like Philemon and Baucis of Greek myth, a devoted elderly couple, she into a linden, he into an oak, their trunks entwined. The road swishes around quite a lot, flings itself incautiously here and there at a bend, gets sudden vertigo when it sees the drop and goes back to hug the mountainside close as ivy. Some stretches look rather makeshift, as if they'd been crudely hacked out of the stone bed and some make-do of a surface slapped on top.

A curious stone-built obelisk with three projecting sawn-off buttresses commemorates three partisans killed in 1944.

There are plenty of intervals of rest on this climb, long as it may be. The last section of the climb through woodland up to the junction with the road leading off left to San Bernardo is harder work, but breaking clear of the trees onto the Teglia and the vista laid out far beyond and below is an uplifting moment.

COLLETTA DELLE SALSE 1627M *and Colla di san Bernardo di Mendatica 1263m, Colla di Piano 1242m, Colla dei Boschetti 1229m*

From Ponte di Nava 800m

LENGTH: 25.3KM	
HEIGHT GAIN: 827M	
MAXIMUM GRADIENT: 12%	

This describes a big loop over the Salse and back to Colle di Nava so that the height gained does not take into account a number of intermediate descents and ascents which make the ride interesting but tougher.

Ponte di Nava, 2.8 kilometres north of the Colle di Nava, sits on both sides of the river Tanaro, which flows along the boundary between Liguria and Piedmont. It's a dangerous junction, so be careful when you turn left onto the SP 154 in the direction of Viezone/Upega. The valley road runs very close to the river into a narrow gorge – naked rock and a line of ridges on the horizon beyond. There is a succession of altitude signs with names, the first, Rocca Tombaa, showing 896m 2.47% over the next 3km and 17.6km to a mysterious Ponte del Girairetto, which appears on no map I have seen nor any ground I have traversed.

The road drops away, larches on the left, to join the river and the next sign reads 970m 7.22% over 3km. After a brief encounter, the road climbs quite hard away from the green-blue river up through trees on a bumpy surface, cliffs muscling in and a bullying presence of buttress.

A vigorous little road, this, nosing into a deep pocket of these burly Ligurian alps, a road that was, in its youth, no more than a track for mules plodding down from the remote outposts of habitation for people who would have as little truck with *citadini*, 'city folk', as possible.

Six kilometres from Ponte di Nava, Viozene 1186m 3.8% over 3km. An old water wheel at the side of the road by a bend seems to be wooden, the timber worn and polished till it gleams like wet iron, a number of millstones grouped by it. Should you stop at a small café/bar opposite the church, you may encounter a compulsive singer-talker who mooches in wait for an audience. He will insist on bending your ear, more or less tunefully, with broken English and snatches more of *can belto* than *bel canto,* an insistence that grows tiresome. A poster inside the bar will tell you of the presence hereabouts of cyclamen, gentian, saxifrage, poppy, peony, aquilegia, pulsatilla, anemone,

delphinium, aconite, clematis and dianthus. Of trees: hornbeam, walnut, hazel, elm, oak, ash, beech, alder, willow, poplar, lime, wild cherry, chestnut.

Le Pianche 1300m 2.9% 3km. The road falls away to the river, down the inlet of a torrent feeding the main flow dancing and leaping over boulders, and a small bridge over it on the cusp of the bend. A sign bids '*Ormea Arriverderci*' – Ormea being a municipality whose eponymous mediaeval town lies on the SS 28 north of Ponte di Nava.

The road creeps round a big overhang, on through a very narrow hole in the cliff face and then down, down, down, clasping the limestone wall to a set of snow tunnels made of girders, no more than 4-5 metres long and thereon into a veritable gorge, a mature gorge after the very tentative novice cuts further back.

The conjunction of the chalk with layers of impermeable rock has led to the formation of a number of grottoes and canyons in this region. The minerals caught in these substrata, combined with a favourable climate, has produced a remarkably rich flora. Early pioneer botanists in

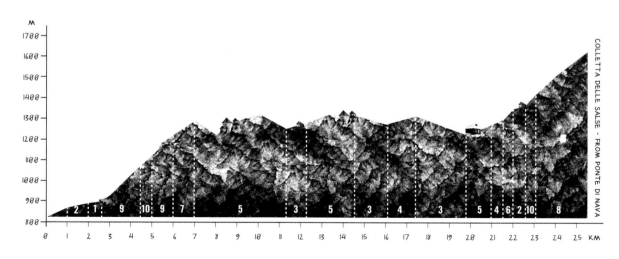

the 19th century identified no fewer than 1500 species in the area of what is now a designated natural park. All Italy is reckoned to contain no more than 6000 species in toto.

The road strikes out, quite visible, far ahead, a dramatic image of intrepid early journeys through inhospitable territory, the Alta Valle Pesio e Tanaro, now a *Parco Naturale*. A sign, 'Colletto Carnino 1213m 3.35% 2km', names a *Paso Fascetto* – a track over the Cima Cantalupo overhead– and this ravine is called the Gola ('throat') delle Fascette.

A couple of kilometres out of the gorge and its fierce overhang – note some caves in the rock over to the left, troglodyte apartments – along a balcony road and into Upega, a small community with a memorial to partisans killed in 1944 and a round wooden cabin with a peaked cap, a ligneous yurt which is the shower-block for a campsite. Cannondales (American racing bikes) for rent in the reception/shop.

First sign out of Upega on a road which has shrunk to scarcely a car's width: 1280m 7.52% 1km. At the end of that kilometre, standing back from the road, a wayside station dedicated to our ever-present spiritual vigilante, with supplementary portfolio of climate and travel assurance – a Sanctuario Madonna delle Neve looking like one of those old Baptist chapels or a Non-conformist reading room. She gives her name to the immediate sign: 1355m 8.3% 1km. Then, Rio Corvo 1435m 9.85% 1km, and a very steep haul – probably around 12% in parts– up into woods, a hairpin acting like a slap on the bum to send you up onto it, no argument, and a gauntlet of dark woods pressing in on both sides.

Bosco delle Navette 1533m 8.7% 6km, past a picnic area, and here is the col with a sign that does not mention Salse. Instead it indicates the Bosco delle Navette, the forest planted across the height above it. A dramatic view, far and wide from what is the anonymous Colletta.

The descent into a much broader valley towards Salse is more exposed, the trees by the roadside sparser, the gradient quite as steep and tough as on the north side, pretty well 9+% the whole way.

Below Le Salse (1350m, 4.4km), the road widens, like a river out of its first headlong rush, into woods and deeper woods. The gradient is milder, the bends less taut. At Valcona Sottana (1235m, 7.2km, Lower Volcano... the upper village, Volcana Soprana, like the singer, is high above) trees thin out, bridges span torrents supplying the main stream and we say farewell to Imperia province and on into Cuneo as the gradient lifts into a gentle up.

Houses become more frequent, like a paper-chase leading to a string of communities lower down the mountain and here is the commune of Briga Alta and a town, Piaggia (1310m, 9.7km), one of a group of settlements serving the ski station above Monesi di Triora – pistes from the crest of the Cima Valletta della Punta (part of what they call the 'Little Dolomites') along which runs the Alta Via dei Monti Liguri. Dotted with alpine refuges, this high path courses the whole sweep of the Ligurian mountains between Ventimiglia and Ceparana (above La Spezia) – 440km.[15] On the ridge above Monesi, a great amphitheatre of rock, sits the Paso di Garlenda (2110m), one of the main crossings of the high ridge in this part of the Ligurian alps.

Monesi di Triora (1400m), at the dead-end of a snake of hairpins, has all the charm of an out-of-

15 'A long green way' and worth investigation: www.altaviadeimontiliguri.it

season ski station – none: ski lifts, edifices falling down, abandoned, disused, various snow-folk emporia *but...* persist in your delving and you will light upon two restaurants. That in which I lunch – the further of the two – one Saturday afternoon in late November has a clientele largely composed of working men and a couple of families. A big wood-burning stove, cheery *padrona* serving a hearty *menu del giorno. Buon appetito.*

A signboard says that it's possible to ski over the ridge and onto the much larger piste network out of Limone Piemonte just north of the Colle di Tenda, one of the larger Franco-Italian crossings, its road now replaced by a long tunnel.

The houses below the ski station itself look forlorn, bleak, uncared for, but presumably they come alive in winter. They are a chapter in a story of small mountain communities which once were pastoral farm communities and now eke out a new living by catering to people coming up the short way from the coast to disport on the ski slopes. They were originally built by people fleeing that same coast for safe refuge in the interior during the 8th and 9th centuries, when the Ligurian seaboard was terrorised by Saracen pirates. Mendatica comes from the Ligurian dialect word *Mendàiga*, that is *manda acqua*, 'circulation of water' from the abundance of springs in the area.

Leaving Monesi, the road falls away via Monesi di Mendatica (1310m) for about 3 kilometres to the COLLA DI SAN BERNARDO DI MENDATICA (1263m). An Italian expression '*la salsa di San Bernardo*' means 'to have a good appetite', but it was Saint Basil who is quoted by an English writer in 1649 as saying, 'Fasting sauceth best the use of meats', so who knows? Basil was a great scourge of the wealthy.

This is wonderful terrain, a landscape blessed with the attractions of its own separateness and solitudes and the very road seems to enjoy being there, shimmying through it, trees – larch, beech, Scots pine, alpine laburnum and hazel, sacred to poets – and pastures and rocks and all, with a sweet view of the valley spilling out below to the left, it's grand. There is a shrine up to the right and, for sure, there is much wayside devotion hereabouts, the blessing of the traveller's path always at hand.

Many of the houses round here are roofed with brightly-coloured graceless metal sheeting, of no aesthetic appeal but evidently very practical, against snow which will melt on the stove-warmed covering and slide off, one supposes.

The Colla di San Bernardo di Mendatica, not much of a col as cols go, straddles a crossroads, a lonely place, nothing open, nothing at all and some of it looking abandoned, a bar/restaurant, a couple of houses.

To the right: a fine descent round 16 *tornanti* (hairpins) into Mendatica (743m) thence left to Cosio d'Arroscia (721m), 5 kilometres from the colle. Another 2.5 kilometres for a drop of 75m brings you to the SS28 just south of the Colle di Nava.

To the left, an up-and-down road crosses the Poggio la Croce (1332m) then the Poggio San Martino (1402m) on its way to the Colla di Fieno (1242m) and the Colla dei Boschetti (1229m), none of them named, and on to the road at Nava (850m) just north of its colle .

Just below the Colle di Nava, someone has written '*SCUSA*', ten times on a metal barrier. What kind of guilt trip is that?

Colla Langan 1127m & Colla Melosa 1540m

Psychological bridges

LANGAN – LENGTH:	12.8KM
HEIGHT GAIN:	856M
MAXIMUM GRADIENT:	10%

MELOSA – LENGTH:	6.6KM
HEIGHT GAIN:	408M
MAXIMUM GRADIENT:	10%

The Langan marks the top of the 33 kilometre-long climb north into these most rideable quarters from the coast near Ventimiglia up the Valle Nervia.

The descent from the Langan is pleasurable, an open road slicing across a sun-beaten hillside, sparse vegetation winding round at 1.5km into trees on a narrow cut. At 6.6km the tarmac suddenly broadens like a singer filling his or her lungs to rhapsodise upon valley prospects, ramparts of rock, layered bands of colour stretching into the distance, stock elements of quattrocento. The gradient applies a descant of tough percentage for those coming the other way.

At 13km, the village of Pigna (280m), whose Trattoria la Posta on the main (narrow) thoroughfare offers excellent restorative fare and a goodly, cheap *menu del giorno*. Fifteen kilometres beyond that, Dolceacqua with its magnificent bridge, spanning the Torrente Nervio and joining the new town with the old and its imposing *castello*. The old town, immured below the 12th century fortress, is a network of interwoven, stone-paved, vaulted alleys, archways opening into tiny landings, house doors set into side walls like safes, shadowy cellar-like vennels (passages), sudden spillage of light from open sky overhead where thin stone bridges span between towering side walls as flying buttresses.

I am a great devotee of bridges for psychological reasons which I have explored in some intimate detail but really need no airing here and hail the cambered Dolceacqua bridge, with a single arched span of 333 metres, as a splendid example of pontine architecture, gracious in dimension, bold in structure, majestic in its effortless strength, a portal to the old town at once elegant in style and high-backed to challenge passage up and over it. Built in the second half of the 15th century, it was described by Claude Monet, who painted it in 1884, as 'a jewel of lightness'.

During the 14th century, the Marquis of Dolceacqua, Imperiale Doria, was an enthusiastic invoker of his feudal dues, including the infamous *ius primae noctis*, which gave him power to deflower his female vassals on their wedding night. (This crude facet of aristocratic privilege is satirized in Beaumarchais' play *Le Mariage de Figaro*, turned into an opera by Mozart and Da Ponte and banned, as seditious, by Louis XVI before the French Revolution.) A local couple, Lucrezia and Basso, newly wed, baulked at this. The Marquis sent his guards to bring Lucrezia in by force. She refused to surrender her virginity. He sent her to the *castello* dungeons where she starved to death. Basso, armed with a dagger, hid in a bale of hay and was carried inside the keep on the back of a mule. He confronted the tyrant and demanded the abrogation of this vile ancient right. He may have used a coarser word than abrogation. The Marquis bowed to the demand and published an edict of renunciation next day. The virgins in town rejoiced and the town celebrates the event every year on 16 August with dancing and lavish imbibing of the excellent local Rossesse wine (at least 12.5° and, when it reaches 13°, labelled '*superiore*'), fermented from a vine unique to this area. It bears a coveted *Denominazione di Origine Controllata* (DOC) classification.[16] The town bakeries also produce the *michietta*, a tasty two-bite-sized, stubby, sugared finger of soft, sweet dough. This is coyly described as being 'in the shape of a woman's pudendum'. In fact it evokes the clitoris and, during the August festivities, boys importune the girls they fancy to hand over their *michietta*. Right.

The local extra virgin olive oil is highly prized – there is clearly an added premium on virginity per se, in and around Dolceacqua – horticulture thrives, roses, mimosa, brooms and decorative green plants supply the San Remo flower markets and on Italy's Liberation Day, 25 April, Dolceacqua celebrates a traditional spring festival of *Carugi in fiore* by decking the tunnels of the old town with bouquets. (*Carruggio* is a narrow alley-way or vennel.)

16 Below DOC comes IGT (*Indicazione di Geografica Tipica*), that is wines grown in a specific geographic region, and slumming it at the bottom, simple *vino da tavola* (table wine).

Colla Langan & Colla Melosa *continued*

Approach to Colla Langan from Molini di Triora 460m

LENGTH: 11KM	
HEIGHT GAIN: 667M	
MAXIMUM GRADIENT: 8%	

Leave Molini on the P65, a short drop into the channel worn by the Argentina, across a bridge and turn right past a few houses, a deserted bar/ristorante/pizzeria very shabby, very shut. A sign spells out altitude, kilometrage, average gradient: 500m 1km 4.2%. A bosky lane, most attractive, Ardagna up on its height across the valley, Molini nicely tucked up below. Signs shift to kilometrage, altitude: 2km 600m… 3km 690m, and a sudden jolt of quite steep onto a more open stretch, fruit trees netted below. Hairpins begin and, in the tight crook of the first, an elaborate grille on a shrine to John the Baptist. Perhaps in deference to the holy man– though he was, in truth, a certifiable weirdo, distinctly marginal, of unsociable personal hygiene, erratic behaviour and very queer dietary proclivities – the road levels for around 250 metres to another pin, as is so often the pattern in these mountains. The gradient settles at around 7-8%. 6km 760m, more flat and even a dip. 7km 850m, a big right-hand bend, the surface intermittently bad. 8km 920m, 9km 1000m, 10km 1080m and, at a crossroads, a sign points to Monte Ceppo up the Strada del Monte Ceppo, the peak overlooking PASSO SAN BERNARDO.

Now some 800 metres past 11km 1120m, trees still in attendance, the col sidles up like someone you don't recognise claiming acquaintance. The road to the COLLA MELOSA (1540m) leading off the Langan is a dead end – a stony track for hardy trekkers winds up to the frontier ridge – though cyclists do ride it for the extra 7 or so kilometres

and the wide views on offer on the descent – the artificial Lago Tenarda immediately below and the ring of peaks above. A refuge with a rather grumpy aubergiste stands at the foot of the track.

Strada del Monte Ceppo to Croce di Praesto 1513m and over the Passo San Bernardo 1135m

LENGTH: 11.5KM	
HEIGHT GAIN: 598M	
MAXIMUM GRADIENT: 10%	

Should you ride this at a weekend, there will probably be hunters roaming with their hound dogs to flush out the prey, open cages in the back of the cars, a lugubrious accompaniment of hunters hallooing. They are after whatever they can get, but principally *cinghiale* (wild boar).

Signs indicate mountain bike trails off to the right up through the pines and the MTB fraternity is much drawn to the area.

The narrow road winds all round the wooded mountainside, brushing the side wall in places, past a shrine at 1240m to San Giovanni dei Prati – Saint John of the Fields. An odd place to plonk that, one might surmise, this high, in a forest, but there is a direct and natural correlation between altitude and sanctity in most religions. Appropriately, perhaps, the etymology of our English 'heaven' is unknown although 'heavens' in the Bible translates Hebrew *shamayim*, 'the skies'.

A number of other buildings and cabins, summer hideaways, dotted about as deciduous trees – beech, sweet chestnut, oak etc. – take over the ground. Towards the top this narrow by-way broadens out markedly, but then tightens again onto what is assuredly a col that is not noted here and only registered on the map as a height – 1513m – marked

Croce di Praesto. The road crosses in a clearing in a glade of trees on a right-hand bend and slips away towards the Ghimbegna.

I asked a hunter that day in November, thick snow on the road, whether it was *cinghiale* they were after, and it was indeed. There were not so many around this year, he said, compared to last year but they do eat them, and lower down I passed a circle of hunters standing round a crackling fire. Their guns propped up against a wall, their glance suspicious, they looked at me warily with close-set eyes as black as Bakelite as I beaded them in what I hoped was innocent 'hi, fellas'. Taking a wild boar on the point of a short spear was the stoutest test of mettle before firearms came to the chase. Those critturs are mean of temper, fearless and violent and their hide tough to pierce. They are very powerful, compact of form, they charge straight for their quarry at all-out speed, their tusks lowered for the goring, so that standing one's ground to meet them head on, steady of nerve and muscle for the late stabbing thrust of the blade into the boar's more vulnerable chest below the shoulders and ribs was a heavy call.

Just below the col, past a section of bare mountainside up to the right and a patch of meadow – thank you San Giovanni, on the case, I see – suddenly we look way out over the sea and the coastline between San Remo and Imperia. Glorious.

1.5 kilometres from the top, 1470m, the road loses its bodyguard of trees. Three kilometres down it develops long straights with kinks which makes it easier to descend, and houses begin to pop up in a number of tiny communities enjoying, too, the prospect of the sea. And so over the (unmarked) Passo San Bernardo (1135m) at around 8.5 kilometres from the true pass.

Two kilometres on, a T-junction(1040m) offers left to Vignai and Badalucco. Right joins the Ghimbegna [see RIVIERA].

From Badalucco 254m

LENGTH: 18KM
HEIGHT GAIN: 806M
MAXIMUM GRADIENT: 10%

A narrow and steep descent. I pass a cyclist, out of the saddle, suffering. Kilometres marked on the way up, a plaque to a Sergeant Major (Serg Magg), killed in fighting with the Nazi Fascisti, 9 Nov 1944.

From the main Argentina valley road, ride up the SP54 through a profusion of olive trees. The first 5 kilometres of the climb are fairly testing – partly because of the changes of rhythm: at 2km, 360m, i.e. 5%, then 3km, 440m, so a sudden 8%. However, the slope eases for a stretch, finding its way, searching out the contours, the permanent mark of human travel, people on foot with donkeys and mules finding the best way around or over the mountains, the natural line of least resistance. Near a turn-off left a Colla dei Morti and right to yet another hilltop sanctuary to Our Lady of the Snows. Perhaps she is a stern incarnation of her multi-faceted genus, a Florence Nightingale type, for the gradient stiffens under her distant gaze – ah, but little escapes her notice – and continues at a constant 6–7% to Pallara, home of another of the Madonna's chapels. (In the Argentina valley in the vicinity of Badalucco there is a shrine to Madonna degli Angeli, not far from a Madonna dell'Acqua Santa, not so far distant from a Madonna di Santa Croce, a Madonna del Buon Consiglio and, just by Molini, a Madonna del Buon Viaggio. (Angels, Holy Water, Holy Cross, Good Counsel, and Safe Journey.) And Florence Nightingale who, when she overheard some men vapouring about the celestial delights of heaven in store for the faithful, snapped disapprovingly: 'Actually, I think heaven will be rather *rigorous*,' her clipped tone suggesting that if it wasn't rigorous *before* she arrived, she'd bloody well make sure it was *afterwards*.)

There is lots of movement which always makes for a pleasant ride. The V of the valley is formed by two parallel spurs like causeway heights which meet at the bottom to make an angled trench, the crest of the ridge to the right topped with a single line of trees, each with its full bonnet like models in hats in a line… like beach umbrellas. There's a clear and open view of the mountain we are climbing, its flanks creased and corrugated with interfolded fingers forming the V of the valley. The land is energetically cultivated, that's obvious, and the terraces abound with plants.

At 7km, 590m, look back at an equilateral triangle of turquoise sea, like a mermaid's quim, and a bit further note a tiny plantation of eucalyptus. It looks experimental or a souvenir of the home country to cheer an exile. 8km, 640m.

How did the people who lived here originally survive? Scratched a living out of the earth, needing so little of what we need habitually today, the chestnut so vital, their staple, growing all round in bounty providing essential carbohydrates. The flocks made do with what they could graze and everything to hand got used – stone and timber for houses in plentiful supply.

In Argallo (640m) there is a grove with stone revetments, a grassy precinct enclosing the entrance to what might be a crypt with a green door and solid round column topped by a large globe with metal figures attached – 1884-1934 – but no indication as to who its inhabitant was. 9km 690m, 10km 710m, 11km 730m and Zerni. I am hard put to say of what Zerni consists. The two widely separated houses? The road is pretty flat here. At 12km, 750m, the road gets wider into Vignai (765m, 14km). This ushers in a harder 7–8%.

A sign on a house with caramel-pink-brown walls claims to be, at 740m above sea level, flying recklessly in the face of reality. Another sign indicates the *chiesetta* (chapel) tenanted by the Madonna della Grazie. 13km, 780m, and into trees. 14km, 840m, off to the left, a stone obelisk and another structure with an infangthief ball (signifying an area of local feudal jurisdiction) on top of a short column with collar, possibly a tomb. The obelisk is dated 1884–1934 but no rubric of explanation.

Beyond that an unlit tunnel but you can see end to end and it's only 50 metres long.

Through woods and out onto a wider balcony stretch and a final blast of out-of-the-saddle steepness. 15km, 900m, and immediately through woods again, 16km, 980m, on a pretty good surface, past the T-junction and on to the Ghimbegna, 18km, 1060m. Here the road divides: both branches head south – that to the west through San Romolo to San Remo, that to the east tumbling all the way, through Ceriana, some 12 kilometres to finish in Poggio, the town on top of the famous hill [See RIVIERA]. Take your pick: rustic or urban.

Colla di Tenda (Col de Tende) 1320m

This col, on one of the main arterial routes, the Roya valley, between Nice and Cuneo and a major trade route first exploited by the Phoenicians, has been included in the Tour de France twice – 1953 and 1961 – but is excluded here because it carries so much traffic. I did see a man on a recumbent shooting off the lower slopes on the French side with a juggernaut up his rear tyre but, as a way to pass the time, that seemed to me foolish, if bold.

The tunnel under the col, just over 3 kilometres long, opened in 1882 – the original road survives. The southern and northern sections of the early track, heavily utilised by mule trains, were paved to take carts in 1591 and the entire length opened to four-wheeled vehicles in 1788, the first such route in the Alps. (The paved road over the Grand Saint-Bernard opened in 1810.)

The 1953 Giro d'Italia finished badly for the French national team: only two riders made it to Milan, Raphaël Géminiani and Roger Pontet. Louison Bobet abandoned in snow on the penultimate stage, but had been in a bad way all through – a hardening of the tissue of his scrotum caused by his forceful style of riding, it's said. 'An ordinary man wouldn't even be able to tolerate sitting on a saddle,' said Marcel Bidot, the directeur sportif. 'Bobet has just ridden 4,000 kilometres.' There was grave doubt as to whether he'd be able to start the Tour and, days before the start in Strasbourg, Bobet still hadn't decided. He came back from a training ride – 150 kilometres in the Chevreuse valley – and reported fit. He rode to his first of three consecutive victories and it was his fellow Breton, the 1953 winner Jean Robic, riding for a regional team, who crossed the Tende (on the stage between Monaco and Gap) first. That same year the great climbers Charly Gaul of Luxemburg and Jesus Lorono of Spain (who won the mountains prize), the great rouleur André Darrigade, the surprise winner in 1956 Roger Walkowiak, made their debut in the Tour and the first-ever green (sprinters') jersey went to the Swiss, Fritz Schaer.

4. Route Napoleon

The Route Napoléon is marked by commemorative plaques adorned with the image of a soaring eagle, inspired by Bonaparte's boast that 'The eagle will fly from steeple to steeple until he reaches the towers of Notre Dame'. The Emperor had adopted the eagle as a finial for the regimental banners of his armies, inspired by the Roman legionary *aquilae* in their myth, the bird of Jupiter, father of the gods. A sacred eagle, emblematic of courage, strength, the sun and everlasting life, was released above the funeral pyre of an emperor to symbolize the flight of his soul to join the immortal pantheon.

Napoleon escaped from exile on the island of Elba – 12 miles off the coast of Tuscany in the Ligurian Sea – on 26 February 1815. On 1 March, the first of what became the Hundred Days which ended at Waterloo, he, together with the 800-strong bodyguard he'd been allowed on Elba, landed at the Golfe Juan, the westerly indentation of Cap d'Antibes, and after a brief stop in Cannes set out at 2 o'clock in the morning by the light of the moon. The route which he and his growing army of followers took, avoiding the Rhone valley which he knew would be heavily guarded, is marked by the line of the old Route Nationale 85, now the D5085, via Grasse, Saint-Vallier-de-Thiey, Castellane, Digne-les-Bains, Sisteron and Gap to what was later called La Prairie de la Rencontre (The meeting meadow) near the Grand Lac de Laffrey on the Côte de Laffrey, just south of Grenoble where a battalion of the 5th regiment confronted them. Napoleon famously unbuttoned his greatcoat and, walking alone towards them, cried: 'Soldiers, this is your Emperor. If any of you wishes to kill his general, here I am.' The young officer in charge of the troops gave the order to fire but the men broke ranks and ran, cheering, to mob him, 'Vive l'Empéreur.' The march became a triumphal progress all the way to Paris.

The Route Napoléon winds jovially through lush green valleys, dips and dives and sashays up an enjoyable series of rocky hillsides across a string of cols offering a diversion which might interest the cyclist with a sense of history. The route is, after all, a route *away* from the sun just as the Paris–Nice is the race *to* the sun. Thus: Col du Pilon (780m), north-west of Grasse, Pas de la Faye (981m), Col d Valferrière (1169m), Col de Luens (1054m), Col des Leques (1148m), then the long valley of the Durance and finally

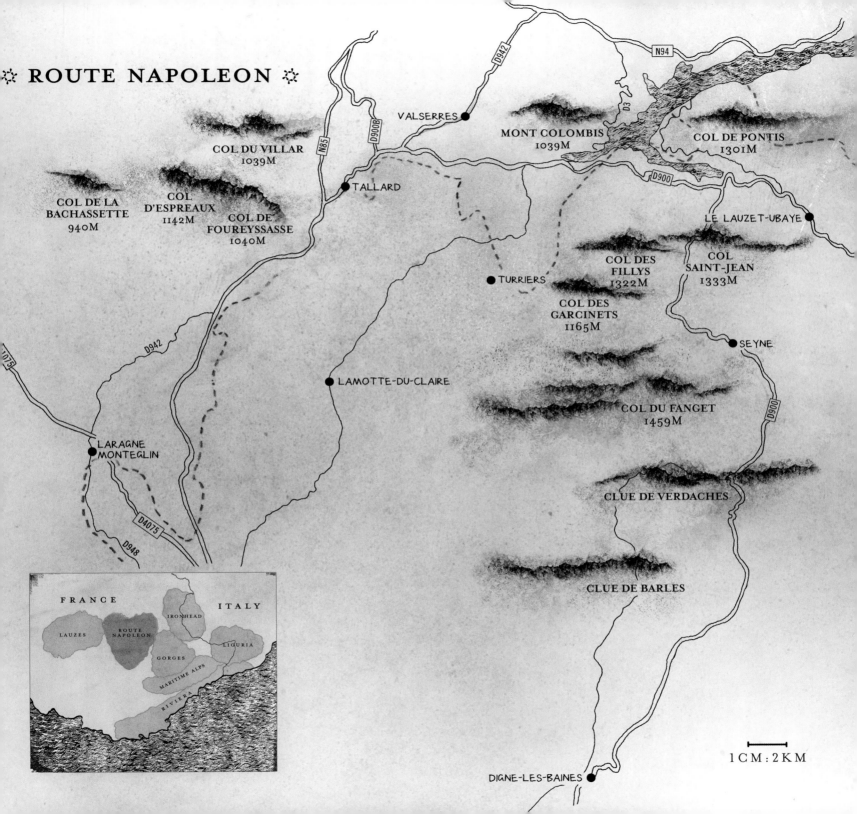

✸ ROUTE NAPOLEON ✸

COL DU VILLAR
1039M

COL DE LA
BACHASSETTE
940M

COL
D'ESPREAUX
1142M

COL DE
FOUREYSSASSE
1040M

VALSERRES

MONT COLOMBIS
1039M

COL DE PONTIS
1301M

TALLARD

LE LAUZET-UBAYE

COL DES
FILLYS
1322M

COL
SAINT-JEAN
1333M

COL DES
GARCINETS
1165M

TURRIERS

SEYNE

LAMOTTE-DU-CLAIRE

COL DU FANGET
1459M

LARAGNE
MONTEGLIN

CLUE DE VERDACHES

CLUE DE BARLES

D942

D4075

D948

FRANCE   ITALY

IRONHEAD

LAUZES   ROUTE
NAPOLEON

LIGURIA

GORGES

MARITIME ALPS

RIVIERA

1 CM : 2 KM

DIGNE-LES-BAINES

the Col Bayard (1248m) north of Gap. Pursue the road to Sisteron, a good town to stop and entrée, west, to the climbs of LAUZES, east to this sector.

The sector divides into a northern area and a southern. The northern centres on Les Demoiselles Coiffées.

These bonneted rock stacks – 'coiffed ladies', 'capped maidens' – sometimes called *'cheminées de fees'* (fairies' chimnneys), were made by a combination of climatic and geological factors over some 30,000 years. The landscape is morainic, a moraine being an accumulation of debris accumulated and carried down a mountainside by glaciers. The consequence was a soil composed largely of clays studded with strata of rocks, like layers of currants in a suet duff. Through a long process of crystallisation of the rock and erosion by rainfall of the less stable elements, the stone became exposed as the clay above it was washed away. What remained dried out through evaporation and locked the stone in place. More infiltration of rain and erosion left the stone layer completely exposed and, slowly, the clay layers underneath were also worn away leaving tall chimneys capped by the larger stones from the rock layer. Thus over 30,000 years' worth of natural sculpting the column grew taller as the ground sank, leaving the Giacometti-like figures of the lanky, spindly-trunked ladies – think Ottoline Morrell, Virginia Woolf, Nefertiti – with extravagantly bobbed hairstyles. And were the stone cap to fall, the vulnerable pillar would soon succumb as well.

The Colombis and the Pontis both have examples of this strange phenomenon. There are other outcrops dotted about the region – on the western (French side) approach to the Colle d'Agnello, for example.

Geology

The geology of the region south of Gap, including the territory covered in Demoiselles Coiffées is worth noting. Where rock strata incline downwards they are called synclinal, where upwards, anticlinal. When two sets of opposed synclinal slopes meet they form a valley, and where anticlinal folds meet they form a dome or ridge. Through the aeons of successive geological eras and the cataclysmic shifting of strata, the clash of anticlines and synclines leaves a landscape stippled with heights and hollows, basins and cliffs, concavities and convexities. As erosion wears away the softer interlayers of the surface, so the folds of the strata became exposed to present the corrugations, the *millefeuille* striations commonly seen in these mountains and most particularly in the Gapençais, the area round Gap. The Dôme de Remollon incorporating Mont Colombis and a number of summits and basins in the vicinity is one such example of the process of these folds and erosion – the Demoiselles Coiffées themselves arose as part of that process – and the area south-south-west of Gap between it and La Saulce, some 18 kilometres along the Route Napoleon is another. Its dominating feature is the Montagne de Céüse.

Cuisine

Since I speak hereunder of a fine eating place, I infiltrate here a note about Provençal cuisine. *A la provençale* means lots of garlic and parsley, olive oil as the staple and the herbs which grow so abundantly in the fertile soil of the region are a constant in the recipes – rosemary, thyme, basil, bay, sage… I once asked an Italian woman from the Italian lakes near Milan about the marriage of tomatoes with basil. 'Essential,' she said. *Tomates à la provençale*, large tomatoes split across their girth, the soft pulp impregnated with slivers of garlic and then cooked in a slow, slow oven until they are almost falling apart with gratitude that you have chosen to consume them is simply a triumph of the culinary art. And true ratatouille is much more than an oily vegetable ragout.

Garlic and onions combine to add flavour to what the Provençals call a dish cooked in an ovenproof pot, a *tian*, and more subtle than your routine *gratin.* Black olives stud the onion tart called *pissaladière* the sweetness of the onions countered by the salty anchovies – hence the name, from *poisson salé* (salt fish). Anchovies and olives form the base of another speciality known as the *tapenade* which, with capers, makes a perfect appetizer with that essential of any bumper lunch or supper, the *apéritif.* Fish feature in a number of celebrated entries in the Provençal cook-book, from the Bouillabaisse so closely associated with Marseille, a variant on the fish soup – more like a stew – of Genoa, recipes rooted in the culture of fish quays and the using up of remnants of the day's assorted catch which had not sold. The traditional *bourride* (from Provençal *bourri*, in French *bouilli*, 'boiled') is another form of the dish using white fish, only – monkfish, sea bass, whiting – seasoned with thyme, bay and the liquorice savour of fennel and aïoli sauce (garlic, egg yolk, olive oil and lemon juice). Sardines, tuna, conger eel, sea bream, prawns, dorade, the teeming *foison* (abundance) of the sea, even if it ain't quite so teeming these days, amply fills the table. And *fruits de mer*… well, now, seek out the chance to regale yourself with shellfish, seize it immediately and order from the cornucopia on offer of: oysters of bewildering descriptive nicety – is there room to expatiate here, of *Fines de Claire,* of *Creuses de Bouzigues,* of… ? Probably not – and *moules, amandes de mer* (dog cockles), *palourdes sauvages* (small clams with white, yellow or light brown shell), clams (larger), *praires* (the warty venus rose pink of shell), *crevettes, tourteau* (the large Atlantic crab, much prized), *homard* (which is properly lobster), langoustine (which is not lobster at all though called a Norwegian lobster, but closer related to a crab and is scampi), *bulot* (whelk), *bigorneaux* (winkle), *écrévisse* (crayfish). They will come lounging on pale white mattresses of crushed ice, like Olympe, naked on her chaise longue. Call, then, for crisp white wine if you have not already done so.

Nice's eponymous salad never fails to delight with that very delicious tandem of fish and hard boiled egg and we haven't even got to pudding. (It is infra dig to speak of dessert. Say pudding, say sweet if you must but eschew the *faux poli* 'dessert'. Dessert is quite as vulgar as the inept, supposed courtesy of 'I' in an accusative e.g. 'our friends gave my wife and I a lot of support'. Pooh. Remove 'my wife' and would you say 'our friends gave *I* a lot of support'? No. Then don't use it in a pairing.) Isidorus, the bishop of Seville in the early 7th century AD wrote on a wide range of subjects, including cooking, and he speaks of *panis focacius,* a flat bread baked in the ashes of the hearth (*focus* in Latin). This is the ancestor of Italian *focaccia,* called *fugassa* in Liguria and *fougasse* in Provence where it is generally enlivened with olives, cheese, anchovies etc. or, as *fougassettes,* small figure-of-eight shaped rolls scented with saffron and orange water. Almond tart, apple and pine-nut tart, *ganses* (the word means 'the crook of a hairpin'), which are carnival doughnut hoops steeped in rum and orange flower water… get stuck in.

The rosé wines of Provence are the perfect adjunct to a baking hot day at a table under ample shade and the low-fat *tomme* cheeses produced from the skimmed milk after the cream has been removed to produce butter and richer cheeses, native to the Alps but widely sold in Provence, sit well in that sun-drenched, dry hot climate.

Col
D'ESPREAUX
Altitude: 1160^m

Mont Colombis 1734m

From Remollon 668m

LENGTH: 12KM

HEIGHT GAIN: 1066M

MAXIMUM GRADIENT: 13%

This is a real leg-breaker, relentless and unforgiving but there are three things to commend it: the view at the top, the Salle du Bal des Demoiselles Coiffées at around halfway and, at your start point, one of the best little bar/restaurants in the area – Rêves d'Ailleurs Route des 3 Alpes tel: 04.92.54.68.26. Fabrice and Laurence are *bon accueil* in person, the menu is varied and exceptionally toothsome, full of the flavour of the warm south – she is from Provence and the cuisine speaks volumes… the fish ragout… the *moules* (from Chile – I asked)… the steak… As you tuck in, try not to think about the small community called Piégut across the river.

At 0.5km along the D900B east, turn onto the D53. This part of the Durance valley running east to west towards the Gorges du Verdon is known as the Route des Fruits: a superabundance of market gardens with netted orchards and giant cloches housing fruit trees – apples and pears, cherries, apricots, as well as soft fruits and tomatoes. Camp sites aplenty, too.

Cherries abound and line the first section of the climb at a kindly gradient. Be warned: at around 3.5km, 860m, the kick is muleish, to 11+% up into Theus, a wickedly steep, sharp bend and hard climbing past the graveyard (left) and the church (right). Overwhelmed by these stark reminders of your mortality, as if they were needed at this point, you may feel like stopping. Resist. There is a slackening of the punishment back out into high meadows and the generosities of nature herself. The concrete emplacement and graded steps down through and over which funnels the Torrent du Vallauria is not very attractive but it is vital to the ecology and the preservation of the geological phenomenon you are about to witness in canalising the brutal onrush of winter off-mountain water and melted snow.

Ignore the turning left on the D53 at 6.2km, 1154m, and ride on to a viewing platform to take in the wonderment of the curious rock formations alluded to previously, 'The dance-floor of the girls with hats'.

From the Demoiselles (and there is a board giving a full explanation of this remarkable geological evolution) the 5.8 kilometres to the top of the Mont Colombis is a tough assault of up to 13%. Should you have the desire and the legs, another 350 metres leads to the Croix Choureille and an orientation table from which you can spot the peaks in the chiaroscuro of the middle and far distance all around.

COL DES GARCINETS 1165M

Northern approach from Espinasses 647m

LENGTH: C.18KM	
HEIGHT GAIN: 518M	
MAXIMUM GRADIENT: 7%	

From Espinasses, take the D900B right to the junction with the D900C where you turn right. The first 11 kilometres follows the gorge of the Blanche River, arid canyon country, easy climbing, exposed, a good leg-stretcher to the D1, right turn, c.1010m, in open meadows fringed with trees. The road loses some height but eventually cuts through bare slabs of pinkish, chocolate-brown-blancmange rock as if it were traversing a quarry. At the road's edge you will see splinters of eroded stone known as *frites* gathered in heaps at the foot of the slab. Now you are riding a balcony, the dry gulch of the gorge way off below to the right. It feels high but is actually no more than around 1040m on this long ledge. The surface is a tad uneven but this adds to the rugged aspect of the ascent. At 15km, 1150m, you pass briefly into the shade of trees and then out again round the rock of the mountainside. Broom grows on the slopes below. Long hairpins mete out the gradient. The col sneaks up unannounced and is a satisfying place to be, even if the climb is not very tough. So what? It is a quiet pocket of this most cycling-friendly terrain. The col sign reads 1250m, my altimeter tells me 1190m. It's a mystery but not one to detain us. Besides, another rider has tut-tutted and marked '1185m' on the col in resistant ink.

On the descent north, at both 500 metres and 1km below the col, 'GPM' (Grand Prix de la Montagne) inscribed on the tarmac indicates a race. (Another graffito on the way up, 4 kilometres from the col, exhorts 'GUYS GO'.) Just beyond that graffito, the road forges into wide open country, farmland and houses dotted about. At 2.4km a bridge and the road flattens out onto a welcome pacey, fast-rolling, high-gear flat-out descent. At 4km, 1140m, (my reading) a hamlet, Les Dorats, a short way beyond that a bridge and then the junction with the D951 which swings fast back to Espinasses.

Southern approach from Selonnet c.1010m

LENGTH: 11KM	
MAXIMUM GRADIENT: 7%	

The D1 is a narrow lane out of the village nosing at once into fields and open leas with a border of spinneys, a sweet rustic bywater. At 1km a row of pines shaped like café umbrellas and a short descent to the junction with the road up from the gorge of the Blanche River.

COL DES FILLYS 1322M

Out of Espinasses

LENGTH: 13.5KM	
HEIGHT GAIN: 657 M	
MAXIMUM GRADIENT: 10%	

Linked with the Garcinets, the ascent and descent of the Fillys explores similar territory, adding to the number of climbs in this relatively unknown pocket. The scenery is canyonesque, the ground quite arid in summer when the waters of the Durance's tributaries slow to little more than a trickle, and the road tranquil, largely unharried by traffic. Once more out of Espinasses (665m), follow the D900B past the right turn on the D900C up the gorge to La Bréole for a steady climb of 5 kilometres at around 4–5.5% and turn right on the D7. A good kick of 8%, 9.5% and 7% to an intermediate summit (1242m, 11.7km) then a kilometre drop into the hollow where sits Eygave. Another 1.8 kilometres hops up to the col and the descent into Selonnet on the south side is 6.4 kilometres of gay abandon.

Col de Pontis 1301m

Northern approach from Savines-le-Lac 790m

LENGTH: 9KM

HEIGHT GAIN: 511M

MAXIMUM GRADIENT: 11%

This is a cracker – wild, off-the-beaten track, extremely hard, superb.

The first 4.5 kilometres sidle westwards along the D954 beside the gleaming sapphire-blue waters of the Lac de Serre Ponçon. The river Durance which flows into it from the north-east, was always prone to unleashing torrential flooding when the snows on the high mountains melted and flushed down off the land into the valley. Work on the dam to contain the danger began in 1955, although two years later it could not contain the massive deluge from the swollen Durance and the valley was inundated. Now the Barrage de Serre-Ponçon[17] holds the waters, and the artificial lake, formed in 1960, is one of the biggest reservoirs in Europe. As a consequence of this, the community of Savines-le-Lac was inundated and subsequently rebuilt.

The way is flat for 3 kilometres or so to a bridge over the Torrent des Vernes (803m), where the slope lifts to 4.5 and then 6%. At 4.8km, 910m, turn left onto the D7. The gradient bites tighter, so here is the start of the real work, though the view of the water receding into a postcard perspective must surely lift you. A steep and, the gradient apart, soothing excursion into woodland and interspersed meadow – Le Pré d'Emeraude ('the emerald lea') speaks for itself. Grassy banks, a fine deciduous wood and, 2 kilometres from the turn, through Pontis (1114m, 6.8km). A small church, wash-day basin and slanting slab for bashing the linen, and a sundial which tells us: '*Les sourires données nous reviennent toujours.*' Now, I don't want to spoil the gnomic party, here, but that is a sentiment I do question. Smiles given always come back to you?... but sometimes as a smack in the mouth. There are times when the inexhaustible sunbeam gormless grin of a nincompoop, happy-clappy smiler, gets, well, exhausting. So too, times when being told to 'cheer up' makes you want to slap the irrepressibly chirpy git. Even Cistercians, the sunniest of individuals, are, on apt occasion, sombre.

Open meadows follow the level through the village past a rock wall, a passage of rough surface onto an open balcony, edged with a few twisted pines which offer some shade as you take in a long view of the lake. The slope is fierce, a crank of 10–11% but the crest is not far and the last of the two kilometres left softens to a cheery 6.5%, at whose smile you will not bridle.

Southern approach from Ubaye 800m

LENGTH: 5.3KM

HEIGHT GAIN: 501M

MAXIMUM GRADIENT: 12%

Wow, what a belter. Right steep, narrow, a chancy surface, great views, wild honeysuckle twining round branches in the cordon of trees from whose branches drip clumps of pale, viscid mistletoe, in glorious country far from people and noise, a way not friendly to cars, either. Enjoy. Sweat, strain, curse your decision to probe it but, ultimately, enjoy.

The hairpins are tight, the gradient does not slacken below a punishing 9% and tops that most of the way. The verges fuse with the confining rock and make the ride very exposed – a very nervy descent, for sure. However, if Rapha were to develop a sliding scale of *sauvagerie* this climb would score high on it. As the man Goncourt said: 'Wildness [i.e. as opposed to civilisation] is essential, every four or five hundred years to revitalise the world.'

The view from the top adds to the exhilaration by being somewhat understated, a place of tranquillity where to absorb the suffusion of your pleasure at taking on and beating the challenge this day... a sweet spot, like an unexpected sun-filled glade in a forest, a mossy moot by a sparkling river, the sight of a café or bar just when you need one.

---

17 Curiously, the construction of the dam at the western end of the lake has affinities with the *demoiselles coiffées*. The barrage, the largest in Europe, formed in 1960, was constructed on an American model – an impervious core of clay dredged from the riverbed covered with compacted earth and clad in concrete.

COL SAINT-JEAN 1333M

Gentle preambles

LENGTH:	20.4KM
HEIGHT GAIN:	668M
MAXIMUM GRADIENT:	6%

The D900 flips over this col at a regular and undemanding gradient, never much more than 6%, and is included here as a footnote: the scenery is agreeable, the road wide and well-surfaced. 17.6 kilometres further south along this fast road from the Durance valley, for the cyclist in a hurry to get to the flesh-pots of Digne-les-Bains, stands the COL DE MAURE (1346m), little more than a pimple with gradients no more severe than an airport walkway, and, a further 10.5km, the COL DU LABOURET (1240m) with a stiff neck of around 8% for a bare kilometre on either side of its top.

COL DU FANGET 1459M, CLUE DE VERDACHES, CLUE DE BARLES

Impressive clues

LENGTH:	34KM
HEIGHT GAIN:	367M
MAXIMUM GRADIENT:	6%

From Seynes, on the D900 11.8 kilometres south of the Col Saint-Jean, take the D7 into a *clue*, a narrow defile. A bare 5 kilometres of riding to the col from which there is a wonderful panorama north to the valley of the Blanche – that gorge which the easterly route to the Garcinets follows – between the summit of the Dormillouse and the Montagne de la Blanche off to the east and the high ranges flanking Gap to the north. From the summit, a short but very steep drop into a hamlet called Infernet, thus called (presumably) before the emotive link between 'hell' and 'lack of broadband' became common currency for some of us. The slope eases on the 10 kilometres from the col to Auzet and another 3 kilometres to the T-junction with the D900A (1067m). Turn right into the Clue des Verdaches, a verdant alleyway into Barles (998m) 3 kilometres on.[18]

The Clue de Barles is impressive indeed – the road squeezed in with barely room to move. Look up to what Oscar Wilde, in the confines of his cell in Reading Gaol, called 'that little tent of blue, the sky' and the sharp dark outline of the upper lip of the *clue* against it. The rock sides are marked with traces of water currents when the defile was no more than a shallow crack.

About 8 kilometres south of Barles, off to the east, a walk up to the ruins of the village of Esclangon and a remarkable rock formation – a deep bowl in the mountainside lined with striated layers of stone, known as the Vélodrôme, formed by successive folding of layers of sandstone coupled with constant erosion.

Another 8 kilometres bring you to the junction with the D103 and a museum on the site of a discovery of a fossilized Icthyosaurus, a prehistoric fish-lizard 5 metres long, which swam in the sea which once covered this entire region.

18 Verdacho in Provençal signifies the white mullein. Under the dominion of Saturn, according to the great herbalist Nicholas Culpeper (1616–1654), the white mullein has a number of curative properties, in various decoctions applicable to gout, rough warts, inflammations, cramps and colic etc.

Cols du Villar 1039m, de Foureyssasse 1040m, d'Espreaux 1142m, de la Bachassette 940m

A glorious loop

LENGTH: 50KM

HEIGHT GAIN: 204M

MAXIMUM GRADIENT: 8%

Turn off the D994 west of Gap (the D994 between Serres and Gap has a cycle lane on both sides) onto the D19 at Freissinousse for a loop of around 50 kilometres over some glorious country to rejoin the D994 near Veynes. The early climbing is easy, the middle section (Espréaux) is hard, the final section a gentle pat on the back for having endured.

Through Freissinousse (976m) and on a charming country road towards Pelleautier and, off to the right, the Montagne de Céüse rears up out of the plain like a massive fortress, its mighty keep a massive ring of rock, a curtain wall towering above the sloping skirts of a natural glacis. Seen from above, it describes a huge horseshoe ring of peaks, the Céüse, Petite Céüse, La Manche and the Sommet des Marseillais, which enclose a deep bowl in the shape of a wash-basin, the *cuvette structurale*.

Pelleautier boasts a lake given over to water sports, its far bank lined with holiday chalets. From there into trees for a short stretch and after 6.5 kilometres over the insignificant Col du Villar (1039m) into Villar hamlet, a broad smooth road rambling onwards under your wheels, an easy rustic ride. Les Courtes musters a few houses off to the side and thence downhill into Sigoyer at 9.5km. A stuffed dummy wearing a bee-keeper's veil slumps on a chair by a house on the minimal pavement, advertising honey. Out of the village past the *déchetterie* (public rubbish tip) and onto open road which flattens out and then dips away to the Pont de Baudon, a new bridge, on through trees and out into the open again. An undulating broad expanse of farmland grassy meadows and an untaxing climb to the

Foureyssasse (1040m, 14.3km), and thence down, down, down into a wide ravine, trees poking up out of the scree. To the south the line of the Canal de Ventavon, which follows the course of the Durance River, part of an EDF hydro-electric system.

Turn right out of Lardier-et-Valença at 17.5km onto the D420 and, still descending, ride into a basin of farmland, neatly laid out with fields, up a way and on down to a bridge over le Briançon and then up and along to Vitrolles and so towards the rocky interior, bare country, heathland and Les Faysses village. Very narrow, down again and quite steep to a stone bridge over le Déoule, followed by a hard climb up into Barcilonnette – a narrow street winds through. Barcilonnette (population 104 at the last count) also gives its name to the canton including Vitrolles (pop.139) and Esparron (pop.27) which is the smallest in France. The canton, a post-revolution administrative division corresponding to the parish of the *ancien régime*, is the one-but lowest tier of French local government.

France is divided into 94 *départements* formed arbitrarily in 1790 out of the old provinces or military governorships and, with a few exceptions, named after a natural feature, often a river. Each *département* is governed by a *préfet* appointed by the President of the Republic and assisted by a *conseil-général* (general council) sitting in the chief town of the *préfecture*. *Départements* are sub-divided into *arrondissements* (also the name of the administrative divisions of the cities of Paris, Lyon and Marseille) each with its *sous-préfet* and *sous-préfecture*. The canton, a subdivision of the *arrondissement*, is the judicial unit, under a *juge de paix* (literally 'judge of peace' whose principal function was mostly settling disputes in civil cases, hence the ascription of mountains as the '*juges de paix*' of the Tour de France… the arbitration judges). Each canton sends one representative elected by

direct vote to the *conseil-général* and another to the *conseil d'arrondissement*, but it is not, otherwise, an administrative entity and has no budgetary powers. The canton includes a number of communes (sometimes called parishes). The commune, presided over by a *maire*, is the administrative unit of local government. Barcilonnette, therefore, has status far outweighing its tiny size.

Barcilonnette is one of a ring of *villages perchés* in the area. Perching on crags and outcrops of the limestone which dominates the geology of Provence, the 'perched villages', some tiny, others of more substantial size, were built as strongholds in lawless times. Brigandage, a perennial threat in remote districts when the protection of royal or princely force was scant and erratic, drove communities to wall themselves in on sites from which unwelcome if not violent intrusion might more readily be resisted. Suspicion of strangers, including the inhabitants of other communities, was a constant theme. Marcel Pagnol, a native of Provence, explored this theme of rivalrous fear in his novels (made into films, first in versions by him) *Jean de Florette* and *Manon des Sources*. The quaint little Provençal villages seated on ledges and cliff-tops, vantage points from which they could monitor all approaches, often with imposing gateways cut in their curtain walls, speak of a time when hospitality to travellers was not always prompt and the threat – perceived or real – of pillage constant.

In fact, perched villages are to be found all across Provence, whether designated by local tourist offices for publicity purposes or not. The Gapençais tourist board is clearly eager to promote interest in its area and will seize on any excuse to turn anonymity into celebrity. So, you are riding the *Villages Perchés* route.

Out of Barcilonnette signs begin with 1km 855m 6%, as the road strides out onto mountain slopes reaching for the open space above the houses like an unwelcome visitor stamping the dust of an unfriendly town off his shoes... or a traveller who has found rest, shelter and nourishment in a friendly village after long and weary wandering. '2k 910m 5%', then '3k 960m 6%', and so into Esparron, where a Bar du Tourisme snack and restaurant may be open – and friendly – or shut, and, therefore, a miserable disappointment. For, as Dr Johnson said: 'There is nothing which has yet been contrived by man, by which so much happiness is produced as by a good tavern or inn.' There is also a 'phone box: use it, should the bar be closed, to call the proprietor so as to remonstrate.

Beyond Esparron begins the wild country, a step-up into the final lifts of the Espréaux. Aptly: *esparro* means 'the rung of a ladder' or 'traverse' or 'vine prop'. 1015m 6%, on a good surface as the way becomes narrow. At 1075m 8%, the mountainside below the road has furrows and mounds, dinted and pitted, like pumice which, as you will know, is petrified lava. The thin ribbon of tarmac mosies round the convexities and concavities of the rock flanks like the folds of solid drapery, so you have a view that swings across each gulf of the cut line of the road to the bluff opposite. 1130m 3%, and round the inner side of a shallow re-entrant (the cleft in a mountainside formed by a stream or torrent, flanked by two projecting salients or spurs) to a concrete booth on the lip of a sheer drop, next to it a rusting gantry for a telegraph cable and on *down* to a sign indicating 1155m. Is this descent an optical illusion? A queer transport of reality? I have, have I not, waxed upon the unreliability of signs and their ilk? The road curls on at about the same height on the high ledge of this bare mountainside to the col sign (1160m but 1142m on the map),

7.6 kilometres from Barcilonnette. The view into the parched canyon below, a no man's land, a trackless waste of sun-flayed rock and minimal vegetation, adds to the remoteness of this stony Espréaux pass surrounded by the Céüse's family of peaks. Streams there will be flowing in grooves of the chiselled valley sides when winter's rains supply them. In summer, they are empty and the place is desiccated, dusty and arid, like that place in the midst of which Ezekiel was set down by the hand of God in chapter 37, a 'valley which was full of bones', and, as the spiritual says, 'dem bones, dem bones, dem dry bones, now hear the word of the Lord'.

The road goes on through what might be a tufa quarry. At 1150m a house and a barn herald the Hameau d'Espréaux and its church. (Incidentally the Basques, another mountain people, have no word for God: to them he is the 'lord of the high places' and you may muse on this as you pass wee Espréaux's house of worship.)

Down to Isnards (1105m) and into a tight ravine, its side of bleached stone to the left, layered at an angle like a stone baklava. Another kilometre to 1045m, then 970m and a tiny stone cabin set into the side of the mountain, then a bridge. Was the cabin perhaps the home of the dwarf who guarded the crossing? Ah, there are myths, a powerful body of myths, in the Celtic world, across Europe, hinging on bridges and their precarious nature, the narrow span that hovers in mid-air above the burly stream or the yawning gorge, and the perils attendant on crossing water – the inherent danger and nastiness that may, only *may*, uncertainty being part of the riddle and risk, that may lie in store on *the other side*, do you see? And of malevolent creatures, hideous of aspect, lurking in wait for the unwary pilgrim... and unlikely schemes - fairy godmothers, princes

disguised as frogs, providential AA patrolmen and the like – for bypassing the menace.

At 945m the road straightens out a way into a settlement of three houses. 920m and a junction with the D20a towards Chateauneuf d'Ozes and the COL DES VERNIERS (945m). This is a pleasant doddle of 2.6 kilometres at 4% over a narrow col that might have been cut out by a junior Titan in a single afternoon. It is of no great majesty but an integral part of this splendid loop. And here is another burgeoning of the Route des Fruits – a generous quantity of well-managed and extensive netted pear orchards, poplars in abundance, the nursery garden of Saint-Auban d'Oze. A sign indicates 'COL DE LA BACHASSETTE'.

7.4 kilometres on, again no real gradient and at 940m a line across the road and 'GPM'. Be heartened. They race in these parts and, at some stage in a long, hard and fast ride, this apparently innocuous Bachassette will seem like a real pig of a climb. Quite a steep descent, the grey wrinkled stone of the rock like elephant's hide. Into a canyon and a long view of Veynes in the Petit Buëch valley. The troubadour poet Guilhem de Canestanh (in French, Guillaume de Cabestang) may have been born in Veynes although the Cabestany - spelling was not fixed – with which he is associated is in the Roussillon, near Perpignan on the far side of this huge sweep of the princedom that was Provence.[19] Troubadour poetry is rooted in the conventions of courtly love, adoration of the chosen lady, (always married), worship from afar, agonising pangs of frustration, bags of lyric desire and despair and no consummation of either. In most cases. Sometimes,

19 Named, incidentally, after the Roman *provincia* when it was the only part of Gaul, 'Gallia', that they had thus far conquered.

chosen lady acceded to the poetic importunity and, if found out, tragedy ensued.

Cabestanh's legendary *Life* records that he was the lover of one Seremonda, wife of Raimon of Castel-Rossillon. Raimon found out, had Cabestanh murdered and his heart served up as supper to the errant Seremonda. Then told her what she had just eaten. She threw herself out of the window. Fatal fall. Love, ah, love, careless love. As Cabestanh put it of the ecstatic moment of falling in love:

Aissi cum selh que baissa el fuelh,
E pren de les flors la gensor.

Like one who pulls down a twig
To pluck the loveliest blossom.

And here he is at greater, anguished, length:

En sovinensa
Tenc la cara e'l doltz ris
Vostra valensa
E'l belh cors blanc e lis,
S'ieu per crezensa
Estes vas dieu tan fis
Viusses falhensa
Intrera en paradis.
Doncx cum seria
Qu'ieu merce no i trobles
Ab vos, amia, La genser qu'anc nasques
Qu'ieu nueg e dia
De genolhs de pes
Sancta Maria
Prec Vostr'amor mi de;
...Franca res de bon aire,
Suffretz qu'ieu us bais los guans,
Que de l'als sui doptans
Guillems de Cabestanh

Can't stop thinking about your face,
your gentle smile, your lovely body,
smooth and white. If I thought as much
about God, had as pure an attachment
to him, I'd get to paradise before I
died. Maybe he'll get you to show me
some pity, darling love, most amiable
of women, me who night and day, on
my knees or on my feet, beg the Virgin
Mary to inspire you to show me some
tenderness… let me plant a kiss on those
gloves which cover your beautiful hands.
Timid as I am, it is the greatest favour
I dare ask.

You have spotted, of course, that the progenitor of such rapt pleas for aloof woman to show a little tenderness is the Roman (actually Celto-Iberian) Catullus, from Lake Garda, whose unrequiting lover's sparrow got more attention than he ever did.

COL DE FONT-BELLE 1304M

Western approach from Sisteron 465m

LENGTH: 26KM	
HEIGHT GAIN: 839M	
MAXIMUM GRADIENT: 9%	

Sisteron, the formerly walled town clustered beneath the citadel up on its flattened pinnacle of natural rock, sits in a narrow cut of the Durance valley, a corridor linking the Dauphiné with Provence.[20] High fort on one side of the river, the towering Rocher de Baume on the other, like two natural flanking stone gates. Sisteron was an important Roman legionary station, Segustero, on the Via Domitia, a very ancient route between the Rhône and Spain which the Romans paved. Named after the conqueror of Narbonese Gaul (i.e. Languedoc) Gnaeus Domitius Ahenobarbus ('bronze-' that is 'red-beard') late 2nd century BC. Their influence is written into the name of Sisteron's cathedral Notre-Dame-des-Pommiers where *pommiers* has naught to do with apples but is a survival of the Latin *pomerium*, the sacred boundary of a town or city. The Hirondelle Patisserie near the top of Rue Droite sells what may well be the best *tartes aux framboises* (raspberry tarts) in France .

The royalist regiment abandoned the fort the day before Napoleon arrived here, en route from the coast so he did the sensible thing and stopped for lunch. Did he eat that local speciality *pieds et paquets* stuffed mutton tripe fried in lard, seasoned with herbs and pepper and served with grilled sheep's feet? And did he pack some *fougasse* – an anchovy-flavoured pizza, much prized here – for the journey?

The Grand Hôtel du Cours is less pricey than its

20 The citadel was built between 1590 and 1597 during the Wars of Religion and designed by Jehan Erard, Military Engineer to Henry IV.

name suggests, the rooms and restaurant attached are excellent and it is nicely placed in town. The Saturday market is a good one and you will see baguettes with a pointed tip, known colloquially as *téton de soeur*, 'nun's tit'. We saw two young men ride through on motorbikes, guns slung over their shoulder, huntsmen, not vigilantes. Possibly.

The D948 crosses the river to a crossroads and the minor D3 heading for la Baume. The first 5 kilometres hurt, upwards of 7 and 8%, a ribbon of houses which peters out into open country and a fine vista of the citadel, now on a level with it, together with the stark shape of the gateway, blasted through by the glacier and then gnawed at by the waters of the river Durance to create the eyrie on which Sisteron's impressive donjon is built.

On up into a more rugged zone in the company of sleeping rock giants across the way to the right. At 6.4km, 815m, the road levels out for a distance, as if cowed by the sight ahead of a huge long wall of rock atop the massif. A gregarious company of houses and chalets has settled in the meadowland below.

The serpentine road hugs the stone wall as it noses into the throat of the mountain's bulk in this Réserve Géologique de Haute Provence, a narrow traverse known as La Défile de Pierre Ecrite. The waters of the Riou de Jabron chatter and chuckle over their boulder teeth down to the right. The entrance to the defile is a tight squeeze and you rather know that something is up, and something *is* up.

First, a sign at the opening of the passage dilates on '*l'histoire des Siréniens*', fossil remains of marine mammals some still extant. This reminds you that this whole region once lay under the sea, of which more later. And now the *Pierre écrite* (the inscribed stone), namely the engraved Latin inscription commemorating the exploits of one Claudius Postumus Dardanus, the Praetorian Prefect of

Gaul (that is the governor), in the early 5th century AD. The great historian of the *Decline and Fall of the Roman Empire,* Edward Gibbon, writes of this period: 'At a time when it was universally confessed that almost every man in the empire was superior in personal merit to the princes whom the accident of their birth had seated on the throne, a rapid succession of usurpers, regardless of the fate of their predecessors, still continued to arise.' (Chapter 31). One of them, Jovinus, tried his luck in 411 when he was proclaimed Emperor in Mentz, Upper Germany.

Dardanus is recorded as the only magistrate who remained loyal to the legitimate emperor, Honorius (generally acknowledged as a sort of George Bush figure, borderline idiot). Of him, the early historian, Sidonius Apollinaris, after stigmatising the *inconstancy* of Constantius, the *facility* (lack of moral strength) of Jovinus and the *perfidy* of Gerontius, other usurpers, states that '*all* the vices of these tyrants were united in the person of Dardanus'. Howsoever that may be, after his defeat in 413, Jovinus fled to Valence, in the Drôme. He was captured and taken to Narbo (modern Narbonne) where Dardanus had him executed. His head was sent to Honorius who commanded it to be mounted on the walls of the imperial city of Ravenna along with the heads of four other usurpers. Dardanus subsequently converted to Christianity and struck up a correspondence with Augustine (later saint) of Hippo and was, it is said, so inspired by Augutine's seminal book *Civitas Dei* (City of God) that he determined to set up his own terrestrial version, calling it Theopolis (the same name in Greek, Θεοπολις). The inscription proclaims that, contrary to report, he was a man of noble and patrician character. It lists his various offices, praises his 'illustrious wife, mother of his children' and relates how the two of them ordered and oversaw the work of cutting through these rocks to fashion stone gates and walls as an entrance-way into the quietude of the valley beyond. There they built a community on land belonging to Dardanus (who, as a Roman magistrate, had accumulated considerable wealth by early process of 'supplementary income' i.e. perks and bungs), with the help of his brother Claudius Lepidus. The stone was inscribed so that, as the Latin puts it, 'their zeal for the safety of all and recognition for their devotion to their fellow citizens might be put on record'.

Through Dardanus' gates spreads a plateau, the heights of the Montagne de Gache to the left, and, some way along, the small village of Chardavon (1046m, 12.7km). Imagine what those Gallo-Romans must have felt when they'd broken through the rock, or else inched their way along the minute cleft cut by the Riou de Jabron to find this flat green sward. Did they have prior intelligence that it was there, that secret, hidden place? It must have seemed like a patch of the promised land, protected by the Gache's natural rampart of rock. Ruined walls and buildings of what may have been this Theopolis have been found between Chardavon and Saint-Geniez (1105m, 15.3km), yet there is no written record of its existence, nothing but the aspiration expressed in Dardanus' letters to Augustine.

An avenue of trees lines the approach into Saint-Geniez and a restaurant offers *haut-débit* (broadband) internet connection.

Just beyond Saint-Geniez, in a bowl of the broadening valley down to the right, the remains of a chapel are planted on a knuckle of rising ground. This is the hamlet of Chabert, reached by a side-road spliced into the main road below the Rocher de Dromon. Built in the 11th century, two

of its original naves have fallen away and been lost – or else demolished by locals wanting building materials, the more likely explanation. The base core of the building is Roman and may, therefore, be part of Theopolis or what legend wants us to believe was Theopolis.

A lesser Briançon (1210m, 20.2km) sits off the road to the left as the slope tops a rise at 1235m and sidles downhill for a way to a belvedere at 20.5km with an information board about the geology. Tectonic shifts cause one area of terrain to ride up over and cover another and this whole area exemplifies the resulting mix and interlayering of different forms of rock, gypsum and marls in a great pudding laced with various minerals, including galena – native lead sulphide or 'lead-glance', the common lead ore, often containing traces of silver, iron or zinc – and barites, a native sulphate of barium, an alkaline earth distinguished by its great weight. Its medicinal properties as a muscle stimulant in low doses were certainly known from the late 18th century. (Because it is highly insoluble in water, all traces of it are expelled from the digestive tract.) Through the action of different pressures and relative buoyancy, certain other deposits also appear. This process is known as diapirism (from the Greek διαπείρειν – *diapeirein*, to pierce or thrust through). Diapirs commonly intrude vertically upward along fractures or zones of structural weakness through denser overlying rocks because of the contrast between a less dense, lower rock mass and overlying denser rocks. The density contrast manifests as a force of buoyancy which propels the diapir upwards like a ball released under water. In the process, segments of the existing strata can be disconnected and pushed upwards adding to the complexity of the geological mix at the surface. Tempting to make out of the clash and batter of

tectonic plates that mythic war of the Titans from ancient Greek mythology.

From this belvedere, on clear days you can see the Durance valley, the peculiar rock formation known as Les Pénitents des Mées as well as the silhouette of Mont Sainte-Victoire and the twinkling waters of the sea not so far beyond it. The gaunt rock outcrop of Mont Sainte-Victoire (1011m), dominating the horizon east of Aix-en-Provence and painted almost obsessively by Paul Cézanne, is regarded as much a symbol of Provence as are Mont Ventoux and the Sainte Baume massif further on near the coast, east of Aubagne.[21]

Cézanne, a Post-Impressionist painter, stated as his core aesthetic the desire to make Impressionism 'something solid and durable, like the art of the museums' and, in a conscious effort to draw art back from a colourful vagary into the reality of nature, evoked the 'cylinder, sphere and the cone' as the basic – the intrinsic – shapes of artistic form. In 1881 his brother-in-law bought a house outside Aix-en-Provence with a long view of Mont Sainte-Victoire, a mountain to the east, of striking form, like the slope of a recumbent woman's breast with ample nipple. Captivated by the force of the mountain's shapely bulk, Cézanne painted it a reported sixty times. Indeed, it offered a subject through which to explore in the bold application of paint which characterizes his work all that he saw wanting in Impressionism – a three-dimensional, tangible reality with discernible body and weight. *'Peindre non la chose'*, wrote the poet Mallarmé, voicing the central Impressionist doctrine, *'mais l'effet qu'elle produit'* (Paint not the thing but

21 Sainte-Baume was thrown up by the same folding process which produced the Pyrenees. See the introduction to my *Great Road Climbs of the Pyrenees*.

the effect it produces [on you]).

The Penitents des Mées, a striking rock formation near the village of Mées further south in the Durance valley, are a giant bas-relief of a line of conical pillars, bulbous in the waist, standing close together, some separated by thin crevices cut deep round and behind their projecting bodies. They stand up to 100 metres high and the full parade of them is 2 kilometres long. The columns stand ankle-deep in a sea of vegetation. They do, indeed, resemble a huddle of hooded monks, their heads bowed in shame. The legend says that they were the monks from a community on the Signal de Lure [see LAUZES – page 130] who were turned into stone by the hermit and martyr Saint Donat. He was infuriated at their malleable attitude to the vow of celibacy occasioned by the arrival in the vicinity of a number of beautiful Moorish women, captured by a local lord as booty on a 'thump-the -foreigners' (in this case Saracens) expedition. Saint Donat was probably a troglodyte, like Sainte Baume, and his was a humourless, nay vindictive, response to human frailty. He should have got out more: it might have improved his temper.

In a crook of the road stands Andy Goldsworthy's egg-like stone cairn, shaped of finely interlocked, chosen thin stones, a serene object of surpassing fine form, emblematic of rebirth, the rich plenty of nature, the love of wildness and beauty in natural materials which characterize all Goldsworthy's remarkable work. This cairn spells out in hinted acronym and is dedicated to the Centre d'Art Informel de Recherche sur la Nature based in Digne-les-Bains 'for the development of contemporary art in their region. The 200,000 hectares of the Geological Reserve of Haute-Provence have, thereby, become a working studio used by a number of major contemporary artists.'

A placard hints at the fusion of natural beauty and the implanting of works of art – 'here the marls of the soil produce a landscape which is poetic and fragile' – and, indeed, the effect of the cairn is to emphasise the joy of passing through such wild places, the silent worship of all nature.

In the hamlet of Authon (1132m, 22.5km) at the bottom of the dip where the ascent begins again, a gîte by the river also offers internet access. The whole area is, therefore, wired as well as wild.

A quiet, woodland road crosses a narrow meadow past the Forêt de Mélan and at 24.7km it kicks up onto the maximum of this whole trajectory, a big grunt of 9%. Trees on either side, a fairly wide road, large bends and hairpins for 2.4 kilometres and, on final slopes of a mere 3% or so, the col arrives.

Continue down through trees, still. Gradually, on what is a very steep ascent from this side the view beyond opens up and, at 29.5km, 1236m, the COL D'HYSOPE.

'Purge me with hyssop,' sang the psalmist in Psalm 51 'and I shall be clean: wash me and I shall be whiter than the snow.' Sadly this col lacks any facility which would neither get you close to such a state of purity nor, yet, nourish the physical being, so you will have to content yourself with drinking in of the fresh mountain air and a fine panorama. (The ancient Herbews used a hyssop twig to sprinkle water – an *aspergillum* therefore – in ceremonies of ritual purification.)

From the col, a walk would take you up to the Circuit des Brigands (I told you) and the Tidalite Site, 'where nature has recorded the rhythm of the tides along a beach several million years old when part of the region lay under the sea'.

This landscape – incorporating the *chevauchement* or overlap of the famous Nappe de Digne – was formed during the terminal phase of raising the

Alps. The Digne *nappe*, or sheet, is a massive slab of rock, like a giant flagstone some 5000 metres thick overall which curves round the north-west of Digne-les-Bains. Several pinnacles rise up out of the depression south-west of the *nappe*, including the Dôme de Remollon [see page 169].

New tarmac, no barriers, at 30.8km the descent merges with a stretch of flat which then rises gently up again to 31.4km and a wooden building, *Les Feux Nouveaux*, a Scouts and Guides of France Accueil centre. They have a camp site further down.

A side road leads to Le Castellard-Mélan, about which I know nothing at all, and here filter in houses, sheep, a collie dog taking a break from sheep, a twisting road through grassland, more houses with rabbit hutches – pot, not pets – and the beginning of a more concentrated settlement. A farm or two whose out-buildings show that they are of long date.

At Le Planas (37.9km, 740m) Le Café Glacier serves pizzas etc. and a road leads off to Thoard set up on a hill, its church visible and prominent.

Lavender fields fill a generally flat valley towards the PAS DE BONNET over the Ravin de Saint Pierre, a stony, dried torrent bed. At 43.3km the road begins lazily to climb for a couple of kilometres to a flat stretch which then *descends* to the Pas de Bonnet (986m). This dipping down to the col is an oddity a number of times repeated in this area and quite baffling. A topographical *trompe-l'oeil*.

A board tells you that the village of Champtercier, just below the Pas, is the birthplace of that Pierre Gassendi (1592–1655) of whom I have spoken elsewhere. Clever little beggar, and multi-talented: mathematician, astronomer, philosopher, naturalist, geologist, priest and theologian. Mind you, there can have been little else to do in the Champtercier of those days but bone up on scientific observation and the abstractions of the eternal verities. Gassendi published the first data on the transit of Mercury in 1631, when the planet Mercury passes between the earth and the sun and is seen as a black dot passing across the sun's face. He named the Aurora Borealis, has a lunar crater named after him and is made much of in Digne – a college named for him and a memorial.

At 55.3km, this D3 which has wound all the way from Sisteron meets the main road into Digne. This constitutes a marvellous long ride in either direction, and is manageable from a base in either Sisteron or Digne.

Digne-les-Bains, gateway into the Route Napoléon sector, was known for its waters in antiquity. Napoleon arrived here on 4 March 1815. That same year, the engineer Alphonse Beau de Rochas (died 1893) was born in Digne. He worked on a telegraph line between France and England in the 1850s and also proposed the construction of a metal tunnel under what he called La Manche and we call the Channel. Alexandra David-Néel (1868–1969), the first woman to enter Lhasa, the capital of Tibet (in 1924), settled in Digne in 1927 and bequeathed her house and anthropological collection to the town.

5. Gorges

The Spanish word is *cañon* (tube, pipe or gun barrel) and was first Anglicised as 'canyon' to describe that particular feature of the deserts of America's southern states. The French use the word as well and apply it, for example, to a spectacular section of the Verdon River south-west of Castellane, the Grand Canyon du Verdon and its Corniche Sublime which many will – or must – consider a shameful omission from this book. There is no worthy answer and I offer no excuse. The best views of the river as it twists through the rocky defile are from the pinnacles and crags high up on the Corniche Sublime and the annual invasion of tourists to this scenic feast is colossal.

Locals used to harvest wild honey and the much sought-after and therefore costly boxwood from the bottom of the Verdon Canyon This involved sitting astride planks lowered down the cliff-sides or else shinning up a succession of poles fitted with crossbars and even inching out along the sheer flanks of the rock on metal spikes driven into crevices, forerunner of the modern rock-climber's pitons.

The gorges of the sector's title are two of a number which cut through the landscape like deep crevasses, an ascription harking back to their glacial origin.[22] The word *gorge* itself is French, meaning 'throat', although the possibility of any connexion with Latin *gurges* (a whirlpool) is very doubtful. From it stems 'gorgeous', which the OED defines as 'adorned with rich or brilliant colours' as of opulent necklaces and jewelled, precious metal gorgets encircling the throat, also for a greedy stuffing with food, a gorge… 'Nor would his slaughter'd army now have lain on Africk's sands… To gorge the wolves and Vultures of Numidia' wrote Thomas Addison in his poem about Cato. [For whom, see introduction to LIGURIA.] Another French word for the chasm or ravine is *gave* (from a Gaulish pre-Latin *gaba*) and *gaver* (to stuff) is used for the process of force-feeding –

---

22 For the geology of the gorges, see Introduction.

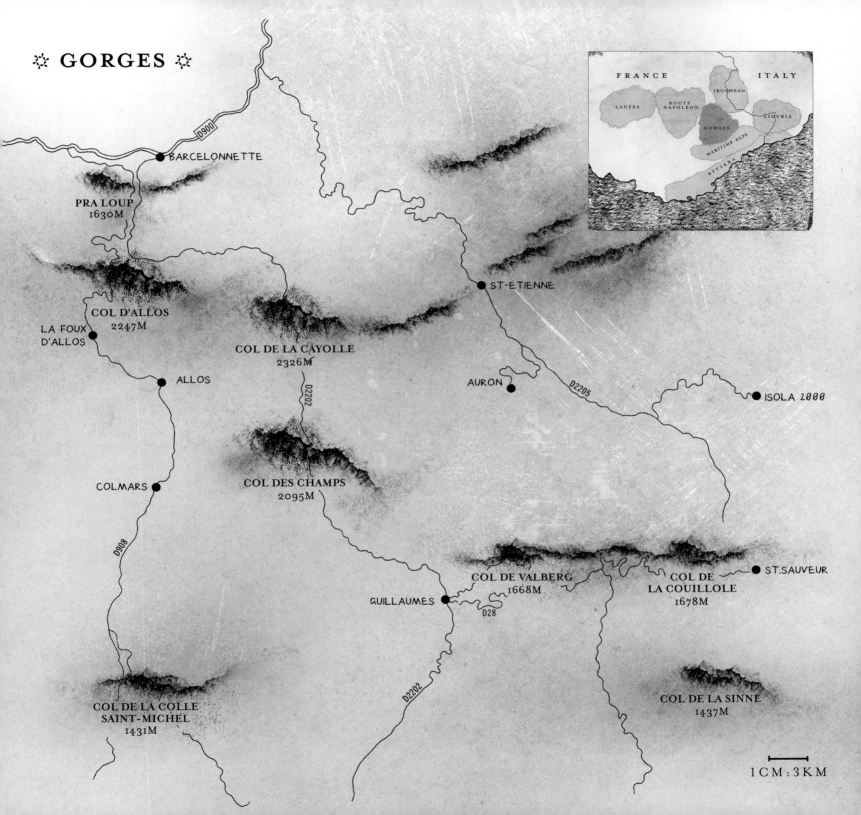

✤ GORGES ✤

FRANCE   ITALY

LAUZES   ROUTE NAPOLEON   IRONHEAD
                                    GORGES   LIGURIA
                    MARITIME ALPS
                              RIVIERA

BARCELONNETTE

D900

PRA LOUP
1630M

COL D'ALLOS
2247M

LA FOUX
D'ALLOS

ALLOS

COL DE LA CAYOLLE
2326M

D2202

COLMARS

D908

COL DES CHAMPS
2095M

ST-ETIENNE

AURON

D2205

ISOLA 2000

COL DE VALBERG
1668M

COL DE
LA COUILLOLE
1678M

ST.SAUVEUR

GUILLAUMES

D28

D2202

COL DE LA COLLE
SAINT-MICHEL
1431M

COL DE LA SINNE
1437M

1 CM : 3 KM

gorging – geese with corn grains to make their liver plump and rich, thus *gras*, for *pâté de foie*.

Peculiar to this part of Provence and unique in Europe is the red of the schist-laden earth, in places a dull brownish red-like maroon, in others quite vivid. This is due to the *pélite*, a rock composed of broken fragments of other granular rock which was originally sand or silt to make a fine-grained compound of mud or clay (Greek πηλός – *pelos*: clay), here rich in iron oxide, whence the russet coloration. The Gorges du Cians and the Gorges de Daluis [see below] exhibit this curiosity of soil type rather well.

Col de la Colle Saint-Michel 1431m

Southern approach from Les Scaffarels 655m

LENGTH: 18.5KM	
HEIGHT GAIN: 776M	
MAXIMUM GRADIENT: 6%	

The road (D908) was built some time before 1906 in which year it was described by one writer as 'interesting', if only because it was one of very few in the area. The Digne–Nice railway which follows its course and that of the river Vaire was under construction at the time. Known as the 'Train des Pignes' after the pinecones once used for tinder to start the engines, this one-metre gauge steam line has been described as 'a showpiece of civil engineering skills'. The 151 kilometre journey beside fast-flowing rivers along steep-sided mountain valleys is certainly picturesque. It takes about three hours and the stations are period pieces.

The first 2.2 kilometres along the D908 follow a pretty flat valley road into Annot (700m), a sizeable town, once a way station on the Roman road, now the RN202. Observe the striking rock formations hereabouts known as *grès* (sandstone) *d'Annot*, sculpted by wind and rain into weird shapes and natural arches. They make a fascinating subject for pencil, watercolour and oils, and thanks to their draw, Annot has been described as 'the painters' paradise'. Steep, twisting lanes, arcades and vaulted alleyways, the Cours Provençal, an avenue of fine mature plane trees, a Romanesque church with an elevated east end doubling both as defensive redoubt and watch-tower, together with another of those communal ovens at the end of the rue Capone. I resist punning aside. *Capone* means 'thickhead, blockhead' or 'large mask'.

The road undulates somewhat for a while out of town, the railway appears on an elevated track and, off to the left near Bontes, a short viaduct with two small bridges under which the road passes before slipping gently downhill again.

Le Fugeret (820m, 7.7km) has a narrow main street and here the railway ducks under the mountain to gain height. The gradient now asserts itself and continues at around 5–6% for the remaining 10-plus kilometres to the col. At 3.3km, a second junction with the D210 which swings off (right) on its way round and up towards Méailles squatting high up on a long limestone ridge.

Walnut, sweet chestnut and pine trees abound and the keynote Provençal lavender, too. Bees flock to it.

The col road follows a large left-hand bend leading to a big right-hander, a small bridge over a lateral stream and at 10.5km, 950m, a commanding view of Méailles on its rocky butt away to the right. This is dandy riding, plenty to look at, a good surface, sweeping bends, the company of the railway across the valley, the impressive perch of old Méailles, a patchwork of fields behind and beside the town, the long loping zigzag of the road leading up to it, the bare escarpment on which it sits and the extending stone supporting wall of the plateau which gives it its foundation.

At 14.5km the road flattens onto a ledge and at 15km, 1200m, look down into a wide, V-shaped crevice which looks as if it has been gouged by a giant's mattocks. The gradient bites from here, a health-giving workout of 6% towards Saint-Michel-Peyresq. Because of its lofty position at 1380m, the views it commanded at the head of this important through-route valley and its eminent defensibility, in 1232, the Count of Provence, Raymond Béranger V, chose the site to replace the old *castrum* of La Colle Saint-Michel. In 1388, this fortified village known then as Perets became a frontier post between Savoy and France and remained so until the cession of Savoy in 1860. The line of the original frontier was marked by boundary stones bearing the cross of Savoy and fleur-de-lys, and ran through Colmars, Lac Lignin and Entrevaux. By 1932, only 17 people still lived in Peyresq, the village school had shut down, abandoned houses fell into decay, untended roofs caved in under the weight of snow, winter moved in. In 1952 a Belgian academic, Georges Lambeau, came to a near-derelict village inhabited only by the mayor, his wife and one of his daughters, a handful of sheep and as many goats. So began the miraculous restoration of Peyresq by Lambeau and a succession of Belgian students. The village is rebuilt and now houses a Foyer d'Humanisme, a centre for artistic, academic and cultural study. Hurrah.

The col (1431m – there is no sign) looks out over pastureland and meadow, a fine, airy spot. The descent of 8 kilometres is mild, between 4 and 5%, with one large sweeping bend at 1km, 1410m, a patchy surface, wooded slopes to either side, a big vista of the Verdon valley ahead, and the little town of Thorame-Haute nestling in it. The road narrows here and there as the rock wall to the right muscles in and, to the left, an outcrop of dead, dessicated, bony-branched trees… they might be ossified. Take care on this stretch, there are no barriers to speak of and there is no divining the potential malicious hex an ossified tree may cast upon you.

The junction with the main road (which, heading for the major Col d'Allos, takes this lesser road's number, thus reinforcing its primary importance in the matter of linking valleys) arrives at 1130m, 8 kilometres from the col.

The town is on the line of the Train des Pignes and the station, on the fringe of town, is an outdoor picnic area, with wooden benches and tables shaded by giant sequoias, firs and pines, some well over a hundred years old.

COL DES CHAMPS 2095M

Western approach from Colmars 1235m

LENGTH: 11.8KM	
HEIGHT GAIN: 860M	
MAXIMUM GRADIENT: 10%	

Colmars is named after an ancient temple to the Roman god of war, Mars, which stood on the rising ground, hence collis Martis – 'hill of Mars'. Aptly, the old town has a belligerent aspect, having been encircled by fortress walls, first in the 14th century and strengthened by Francis I in 1528. When the Duke of Savoy declared war on France in 1690, a French army pitched up to garrison Colmars, after which the forces of Savoy besieged the stronghold and nearly took it. Vauban – inevitably – redesigned the fortifications as well as drawing up the plans for a second fort – the Fort de Savoie – just to the north.

Colmars within the walls is rather a pokey affair, a number of antique shops, a post office and a gloomy air of neglect or, more to the point, of the gaol it once did double service as.

North 0.8km out of Colmars up the Allos valley (there's a fine stone bridge a bit further on), take the D2 right on a very narrow road setting off through trees on new tarmac round some very tight hairpins for around 0.7km where the road pinches even closer (there's a warning sign), the surface alternating rough and smooth, past a small water chute to the left and, at 1.5km, 1385m (do the math), a splendid view of Colmars down below, always a moment of satisfaction to register the distance of the slope you have just surmounted.

These hairpins are *steep*. It's real climbing business: even if the gradient is not actually savage, it feels so and that is, most often, what counts. However, it's a bosky little venture – some of the bends do swish rather than snap – and attractive. At 3.4km, 1545m, comes a wee meadow, flower-sprinkled grass, in the top corner of the field a small stone-built bothy with a wooden upper storey looking very sorry for itself, neglected and slowly shedding, like an orphan's tears, morsels of its fabric, alas.

There is plenty of shade down here and the woods house a chapel, perhaps, to Saint-Jean Colette at 4km, 1560m. A kilometre on, with a short dip in the ascent, the road spills onto a large parking area in front of a wooden chalet which is a *restaurant/buvette* (bar) and the centre for the Ratery *ski du fond* (cross-country skiing) station at 1660m.

Away from civilization once more, grass-covered banks, the trees grown to more mature height and size, dropping-branched larch in abundance, a succession of traffic-calming bumps marking the hollowed course of a torrent flowing off the mountainside across the tarmac. At 8km, 1860m, a view of the attendant mountains off to the north opens up, one rumpled section of green slope that looks as velvety soft as moss, moulded, squeezed, crimped, indented, stroked into the image of a velour scarf let fall as it will, lit and shaded.

A cattle grid, another torrent groove, a slight dip of gradient, the opening out of the sky and mountainside giving, as ever, that growing sense of altitude and remoteness. At 9.4km the road becomes a ledge, loose shale fragments bestrew the slope to the right and then arrives a stark shaping of this bit of the geology: the road hacked out of soot-black rock like a sickle-shaped scar round to a spline of living stone, a DIY-hacked shelf of a road without railings, no trees below now, as if the barren rock had parched them brittle and the drifting scree had swept them away. Glance down at the interlocked knuckles of the mountain slopes, across at the pleated ridge that shows itself, now, as part of the line of the crest on which the col sits and at 11.8km, here it is, on the bumpy line of the ridge we saw from way down the climb. A windswept, bleak, lonely place on the border with Alpes-Maritimes, and the road climbs *higher* than the marked col, which is indeed the neck between the shoulders

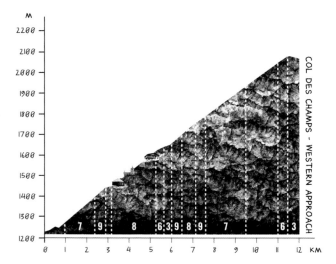

of this massif and, below the actual summit, the onward road, snaking like a Scalextric track, the ground to either side a smooth, grassy sward with a heavy acne rash of protruding boulders. New tarmac, no barriers, a big swish of road spinning off into open air and a benign landing on free-range, sheep-nibbled lawn.

Eastern approach from Saint-Martin-d'Entraunes 1010m

LENGTH:	16.7KM
HEIGHT GAIN:	1085M
MAXIMUM GRADIENT:	10%

The Tour de France has crossed this col only once: in 1975, when Eddy Merckx, under mounting pressure from the apparently unflappable Bernard Thévenet, attacked without thought of sparing himself energy – niggardly caution was not in his temperament – on the way to the finish, and collapse, on Pra Loup. He crossed the Col des Champs, from this eastern approach, in the lead.

The sundial on the church in Saint-Martin tells the passer-by: 'My guide is the sun, yours is your pastor'. Inside there is a splendid altarpiece, La Vierge de la Miséricorde ('The Virgin of Mercy') painted by François Bréa (c.1555). It shows the Virgin Mary in a gold embroidered gown with gilded green cloak – green in religious symbolism signifies the gladness of the faithful and the resurrection of the just. She is attended by two angels with high cheekbones and pointed chins – one somewhat stern, the other chubby-cheeked and gamine – who touch the high brim of her gilt halo in gestures of blessing.

The climb begins on a long, whippy straight with mild kinks and hairpins at a punchy pace of between 8 and 9%, trees to either side. A good view of the stony bed of the wide-banked Var in the valley below, the bouldered and pebbled banks scarcely above the flow of the water.

At 1.8km there is a junction with the D278 (a detour via Le Mounard which later rejoins, at 5.8km) and the gradient slackens to around 6% before cranking up to another kilometre of 9%. This continues to around 7km near the hamlet of Pra Pelet and a Chapelle de Saint-Jean where there is relief, a slight dip, a bridge over water… 5.5% and flat.

Away to the left looms the peak of the Aiguilles de Pelens, its slopes used by the ski crowd for whom the Auberge des Aiguilles waits at 8.4km. The road ahead sways and bends, like a skier's hips in an easy glide, at around 6–7%, the brooding presence of mighty bastions of scored and pitted rock over to the left. The trees begin to lose both heart and foothold at around 11km where the road is newly surfaced and begins its Scalextric imitation at 8.5km followed by a tooth-skinning 10%. The final 2 kilometres ease off to a soft 3.5% and then hand you almost gently, after such needless punishment, onto the col.

There are many cols of which the following summation of our need to address natural wildness is apt, but let us place it here:

And although this beauty seems, at first, in its wildness, inconsistent with the service of man, it is in fact more necessary to his happy existence than all the level and easily subdued land which he rejoices to possess.

John Ruskin, *Modern Painters* vol. 4, 1885.

COL DE LA CAYOLLE 2326M

Southern approach from Saint-Martin-d'Entraunes 1010m

LENGTH: 20.5KM	
HEIGHT GAIN: 1316M	
MAXIMUM GRADIENT: 9%	

A posse of cyclists, peeling off into a bar for restorative hot chocolate and coffee, inform us that they are from Thonon-les-Bains riding south over the cols de Saisies, Aravis, Roselend, Izoard, Cayolle… a week of Grandes Alpes.

The 6 kilometres to Entraunes, at the confluence of the rivers Bourdoux and Var (the longest river in the Alpes-Maritimes) are fairly easy, no more than 4.5% and mostly less on a lightly curvaceous road. The surface is good, across the narrowing ravine the mighty rock cliff of the Crêtes de la Voya rears up like a curtain wall, cascades in spate crash down its slab. The church in Entraunes has an asymmetrical bell-tower as if reminding the parishioners of the unpredictability of fate.

Out of Entraunes (1250m)… beware: 9%, oh yes, and a narrow twisty little road that seems to feel the pain of it and tries to shake it off. An angry fling of bends just north of the town almost does the trick and, after 3 or so kilometres to 1480m, the gradient eases slightly. Two short tunnels, more like railway bridges, intervene, the stone of the mountain wall to the right striated with slantwise crevices, while over to the left the cliff has become the Grandes Tours du Lac. Into Pont-Saint-Roch where a bridge hops left over the river and at 13.5km, 1750m arrives Estenc, a small town built on a glacial ridge below the (signposted) source of the Var, meadows and a chalet/auberge. Estenc's grandiose claim is premature, however: the Var itself disputes it [see below].

Hereon, the road braces itself for the main work of the day: grimping up to the high fastness of the col round the steeper and steeper sides of the mountain. The goldfinches which flew ahead of us may not be there every day and what do they care about gradients? They flit and swoop in endless search for insects on the wing, adding brilliant flashes of vivid colour from their own plumage to the variegated buttons of flora which spangle the ripening hay.

At 15km, 1900m, a stone bridge with low parapets spans a stream battering its way past a drift of large boulders from the Pas du Lausson up near the Sommet des Garrets where the chamois gambol.

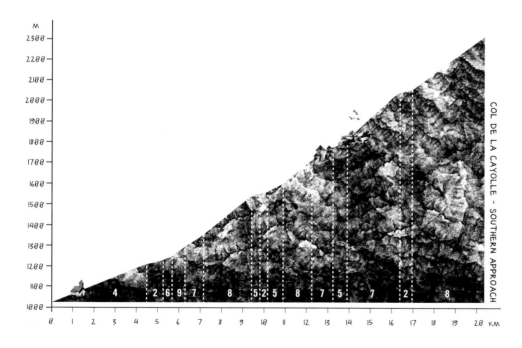

Half a kilometre on (1920m), a meadow littered with boulders, fringed with trees, the river flowing below to the right, still some distance from where it actually rises.

The way gets lonely but there is the drama, as always, of solitude, that loneliness much beloved of smugglers, poachers, brigands and wayfarers sick of towns. At around 17km, 2020m, the road creeps gingerly into a tunnel, feeling its age and the stress of thinning air. You will sympathise, maybe, but here, no more than 800 metres from the summit, arrives a tiny pond and then the stone, the stone marking as high as this one gets.

Until the mid-19th century, the Cayolle marked the border between France and the Italian kingdom of Piedmont-Sardinia. Provocatively, the French engraved the frontier stones with a carved fleur-de-lys, royal symbol of France and, in 1860, added the region to the *hexagone* (metropolitan France).[23] Even some while after that, the two valleys, Haut Var to the south, Ubaye to the north, were joined only by mule tracks for the passage of grain and livestock and the road was not build until late in the 19th century. This was part of a more ambitious project 'La Route des Grandes Alpes', linking Thonon-les-Bains with Nice via Barcelonnette (in the Ubaye valley) and Entraunes at the southern foot of the Cayolle. Begun in 1900 near Barcelonnette, the road didn't reach Bayasse, 16 kilometres south, until 1908. The French President Raymond Poincaré had hoped to cut the ribbon on the Cayolle in 1914, but the war intervened and delayed the opening until 1919.

23 From the perceived outline shape of France as a rough hexagon.

Northern approach from Barcelonnette 1130m

LENGTH:	29.4KM
HEIGHT GAIN:	1196M
MAXIMUM GRADIENT:	7%

The first 4.5 kilometres of the D902 from Barcelonnette to Uvernet-Fours (1183m) make no great gradient and, a slight crank in slope over a bridge and through the village apart, the next 3 kilometres even out again into the Gorges du Bachelard, where the river has cut a tight ravine into the mountainside. I note stone ribbed like corduroy, a ridged form of velvet described by the *Evening Standard* of 28 August 1884 as 'the coming material', which is popularly reckoned to be *corde du roy (roi)*, i.e. the king's cord. Not so. It is an indisputably English fabric and the name may be connected with a family name, Corderoy. Further than that the Oxford English Dictionary will not go, although it is worth mentioning that weary travellers worn to a frazzle of exasperation by the jolts of coaches on the rough highways of 19th century Britain refer – biliously – to 'these abominable corduroy roads'.

At 8km the climbing proper begins: over a bridge and a large bend to the left, a steady 5–5.5% into Le Villard d'Abas (1530m 12.8km) and on for another 3-plus kilometres. These canyons somehow iron out gradient, however: perhaps it is a trick of perspective, the narrowness of the defile subtracting from any real kick of the road. Illusion it may be; but if you are fooled, then enjoy the folly of perceived ease and leave your practical conscience to its own futile battles.

There is an excellent *menu du jour* in the tiny, modest-seeming restaurant in Les Longs and as the gorge sinks behind you, the road noses onto the narrows of the valley, the rock bastions more apparent at a distance to either side. From the open balcony of the road, observe the stream flowing in an irregular snaggle like liquid metal in a simple earth mould of shingle. Out of Bayasse (1780m, 20.5km) there is an injection of spite, 6.5% for a kilometre or so and then a truce for a couple of kilometres at around 4% before the last 5.4 kilometres into the real business of the high pass at upwards of 7%. At 20km, 2050m a bridge and a thumping cascade to the left as the broad shallow V of the valley starts to spread into the bleak grassy moorland of the upper reaches, a borderless road, occasional lanes of trees, boulders.

A refuge stands 1 kilometre from the col at 2250m.

Total Collapse

The Col de la Cayolle has featured in only three Tours de France – 1950, '55 and '73 – and this Snapshot centres on a rider who did not make it, in 1950. For the first time, a team from North Africa was included, among them Abd-el-Kader Zaaf. (Born in Algeria, 1917, he turned professional in 1946, retired in 1955, took 27 victories, rode in the Tour four times – abandoned twice – and died in 1986.)

In the furnace heat of the stage into Nîmes, Abd-el-Kader wobbled off the road under the shade of a tree and collapsed with heat exhaustion. He woke up after some time and, in his dizzy state, set off again, in the wrong direction. The sag wagon (a support vehicle) scooped him up and conveyed him to the finish. Sick with disappointment, he was all for riding the next day, protesting that he would go back and ride the kilometres he had missed out. The *commissaires* (officials) refused. There were popular – malicious – rumours that he had, in fact, been drunk and the coma had been wine-induced. However, the man was a devout Muslim, he'd never even sipped a drop of alcohol in his life and the story went that locals, in this region of vineyards, had tried to arouse him from his deep slumber by spraying him with the local red, or else that some malicious nitwit had handed him a bidon containing wine.

And the Col de la Cayolle? The veteran and 1947 winner Jean Robic led over the first crossing but his teammate (in name only, they were constantly at loggerheads) Raphaël Géminiani won the stage into Gap.

Col d'Allos 2247m

Northern approach from Barcelonnette 1130m

LENGTH: 19KM	
HEIGHT GAIN: 1117M	
MAXIMUM GRADIENT: 9%	

Turn off the D902 2.5km out of Barcelonnette onto the D908. Narrow, well-surfaced, hedged with trees, past the right turn at 4.5km, 1218m, up to Pra Loup. This is where you feel the climb should begin. There's a very big mountain up there somewhere, out of sight, 15.5km away. The road is barely two cars wide, a bridge at 6.5km, 1350m and, for the next 5km the gradient is fairly disagreeable, up to 9% in parts. At around 7.5km, 1430m, there is a long, long view of the dip in the ridge where the col must be and, to the left, a sheer drop into the gorge. Half a kilometre on, a sudden cavity scooped out of the Naples-yellow rock – why? how? – and the road begins to cling to the side wall like a timid infant, shrinking from the giddy height into the ravine, a spasm vertigo, which puts me in mind of Shakespeare's *King Lear* [Act IV, sc. vi] where blind Gloucester is duped by his loving son Edgar (the story too complicated to tell in full but Edgar is pukkah) into believing that he is standing atop the beetling cliffs at Dover:

> *How fearful*
> *And dizzy 'tis to cast one's eyes so low.*
> *The crows and choughs that wing the midway air*
> *Show scarce so gross as beetles…*

The slopes are clad with trees, at 9km the slope draws breath at around 4% for 3km to a bridge where it gets steep again and stays so, if no more than 7%. The gaze may stray left across to an open pasture on the slope and muse upon its smooth greenness. Water tumbles off the mountain to supply the torrent below, the road is still very narrow kneading the contours with shallow bends.

Around 13.5km, 1750m, a pleasant leafiness comes upon the road like a friendly umbrella proffered by a boon companion. The final 6km have no such profit of shade: they twist and turn, panting to be up there, on the top, done with this climbing thing… So now, perhaps, you may muse upon that day in 1975 when Merckx came over that top and down this way towards Pra Loup.

Pra Loup 1630m

Curious melancholy

LENGTH: 21KM	
HEIGHT GAIN: 1117M	
MAXIMUM GRADIENT: 9%	

We do not usually include cul de sacs or ski stations in our guides but sometimes they are made indispensible by beauty or racing history. The climb to Pra loup is 6.4 kilometres of smooth, broad, featureless road with wide bends and a final 4 kilometres of around 9–9.5%. Should you wish to make a pilgrimage to this otherwise anonymous tract of tarmac where Merckx cracked, then you will submerge your spirit in a curious melancholy. Here (overleaf) is how it happened:

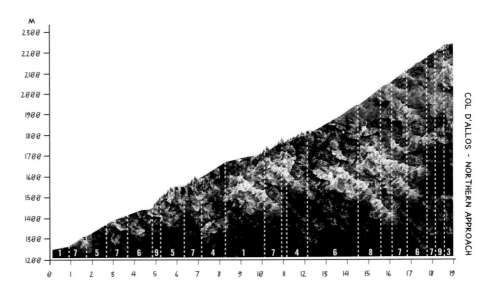

COL D'ALLOS – NORTHERN APPROACH

The End of the Cannibal

On the Col des Champs, Thévenet (58 seconds behind Merckx on general classification) attacked six times, withering bursts of acceleration which the Belgian matched instantly. As soon as he caught up, Thévenet went again. Merckx crossed the col in the lead but this was going to be a real duel. On the descent, Thévenet punctured, Merckx, ahead, knew nothing of that and was coursing on at reckless speed. Thévenet, new wheel taken from the car, set off in pursuit and rejoined him on the lower slopes of the Allos. Nearing the col, Merckx attacked and took 50 metres straight away. Thévenet responded, chased hard but blew up 500 metres from the top. Merckx crossed alone and launched into the descent, but, according to Thévenet, was already showing the strain, visible symptoms of the growing weakness which cost him the day. Nonetheless, when he topped the col, a brief glimpse of Merckx only, flying round the hairpins, and then he was out of sight.

The temperature was fierce, the tar had liquefied in places. The 1965 winner Felice Gimondi was out in front somewhere, closely followed by his *Directeur Sportif*, Giancarlo Ferretti, in the Bianchi team car. The car took a bend too sharply, the surface was loose, the motor skidded into the metal barrier, cut through and toppled 80 metres over the side. Luckily, both Ferretti and the team mechanic Lunga were thrown clear. Ferretti, blood streaming from his head, staggered back up to the road. Lunga, his leg broken, was unconscious. Merckx flew past, his team car came up and tried to follow but Jacques Goddet, the course director, intervened on *Radio Tour*: 'No, you can't go past. This is a bike race, not the wall of death.'

Merckx, a famously reckless descender, was slicing the corners tight, almost brushing the side wall, in the grip, one imagines, of a furious desire not so much to beat off for good the man who had attacked him so boldly but to *win*. That was ever his motivation and if the result of that desire, the ceaseless crushing of rivals, inevitably came with the manner of his winning, it was not the prime impulse. On that descent, he was clocked at around 100kph. Behind him, Thévenet, no great descender knew, this day, that Merckx was vulnerable, and stuck to the business. However, told he was losing a lot of time, he began to think his chance of overall victory was slipping away.

At the foot of the Allos, 6.5 kilometres from the finish at Pra Loup, Merckx had a 1min 10sec advantage. Then, in the opening kilometres, with sickening finality, his strength went almost completely. There can be no doubting that his willpower howled *work* at every feeble turn of the pedals, but there was nothing left. Thévenet hit the slope and, as he rode up, spectators yelled out that he was gaining. It spurred him on and, 2 kilometres from the top, he saw Merckx up ahead. He came up behind him, out of the saddle, sprinting, speed more speed, to get past. He didn't look at the Belgian hunched in agony over the bars, his face livid with effort, his features torn with dismay at this calamity happening to him. The melting tar clung to his wheels as if even this French road had joined in the conspiracy to slow him down. Thévenet, accelerating still, rode on at maximum effort to put as much time into Merckx as there was to be taken on these final metres of the day. He caught Gimondi, who had surely believed victory was his, and, flat out, went for the line.

When Merckx eventually came in, he had ceded 1min 56sec and, by what may have seemed at the time an ominous coincidence, Thévenet now led him by 58 seconds. In those last 2 kilometres he had gained nearly 2 minutes.

Merckx stopped to felicitate Thévenet on his win *and* his yellow jersey then went off to his hotel. The crowd applauded him as they had rarely applauded him before: he had shown grace and courage in the manner of this day's defeat. As far as he was concerned, however, the verdict was more sober: 'I tried everything and I lost. I don't believe I will win this Tour. It's over.'

Except that with Merckx, it was never over and there is no satisfaction in an easy victory. As intense as his desire to win was his refusal ever to give up: nothing is over till it's over. 'As long as the blood flows there is hope,' he once said and, as Thévenet put it to me, 58 seconds on Merckx was *un grain de suie*, 'a speck of soot'.

It emerged later that Merckx had suffered extreme pain and discomfort in his back on the descent of the Col des Champs, a consequence of the terrible fall on the track at Blois (his Derny driver died) in 1969.[24]

(For the story's outcome, see my *Tour de France: The history, The legend, The riders*.)[25]

24 Derny: a custom-built, two-stroke pacing moped behind which racers ride in certain events on the vélodrome track.

25 Mainstream, Edinburgh, 1999. Latest updated edition, p/back, 2008.

COL DE VALBERG 1668M

Western approach from Guillaumes 792m

LENGTH: 12.3KM	
HEIGHT GAIN: 876M	
MAXIMUM GRADIENT: 8%	

The D2202 along the Gorges de Daluis makes a pleasant 20 kilometre approach to Guillaumes at the start of the climb. It continues on north to the Cayolle. Here you'll see the chestnut dull brownish red of the schist [see the introduction to the sector] and here begins the climb.

Just beyond the rather elegant Pont de Berthéou over the river Var, an information board indicates the Sentier du Point Sublime – the words really means 'the footpath under the lintel of heaven' and, therefore, lofty, raised up.

The walk promises oaks, *pinus silvestris, cigales* (those crickets whose stridulation fills the air of Provence with a seething hum), and a sight, off the cliffs nearby, of *aigle royal* – Golden Eagle, *faucon pélégrin* – Peregrine Falcon and *grand-duc* – Eagle Owl. The red *pélite* (clay compound) in this dry soil favours aromatic herbs for cooking and a wide diversity of birds and insects. This path follows a route used for the transhumance from ancient times, droving the sheep of Basse Provence to the pasturage of the high valley of the Var. Ancient roads and tracks such as this path were first opened up and either paved or rendered more passable by the Romans in the 2nd and 3rd centuries AD and supplied the only link between Guillaumes and the south before the construction of the road along this gorge in 1878. Mining for copper and other rare minerals hereabouts goes back to the prehistoric era.

Tucked under the glass (how?) of the information board, is a photograph of a naked woman sitting cross-legged on a bed and her presumed opinion written beneath: '*Je trouve que la photo de nu est un art à part entière*' (In my view, photography of the nude is

an entirely distinct art). You may depend that your photographer, whose interest in the matter was wholly technical and any that I evinced rooted only in support of lively discussion on that wide range of topics and divagations thrown up in the compiling of a volume such as this, and I discussed this at some length though without, I must say, any firm or even pertinent conclusion.

A short way from the bridge, the Tête de Femme (841m) – a rock which wind and rain has carved into the shape of a woman's head – stands by the road at the entrance to a very tight defile leading to a succession of tunnels. A stele commemorates patriots of Haut Var and the Maquis de Beuil who fought the Germans here in July 1944 – three men who died are named.

The Gorges draw fishermen and canoeists, although at the fag end of summer the water tends to be rather too low to support either activity.

There are some 16 tunnels, all quite short – the longest only 839m – and unlit but straight so that you can see the far end. Several are twinned in parallel and one-way. The Pont de la Mariée (787m) leads across the gorge to a road on the other side and the village of Tiré-Boeuf. It is much used for bungee jumping, a macabre reminder of the origin of the bridge's name. After a particularly boozy wedding celebration some time in 1924, the revellers wandered onto the bridge, at that time a crossing for tramcars. The bride, (*la Mariée*) who must have stumbled over the rails or, in some crazy act of ostentation, decided to walk the parapet, fell off the bridge, fatally down into the gorge.

A long straight out of the gorge arrives at Guillaumes (792m) and the D28 to the Col de Valberg, 13 kilometres distant.

It's a steady climb of a constant 6-7% pretty well all the way. The view of the gorge opens up ahead, the road traverses a number of bridges and at 3km, 994m, enters an arid zone – parched rock with scrubby

vegetation clinging to the steep sides. The Pont des Vallières is one-way, the tarmac is new and a stele remembers one Alex Massaferro '*une randonée en vélo un vallon et la vie se termine à 62 ans. Pour nous tu es toujours présent. 1994.*' (A cycle tourist, one hill too many and, aged 62, he bought it but, say his friends, he is ever present.)

At 4km, 1074m, pastureland and 5km, 1147m, a side road (dead end) to Veynas and Cardenas. 7km, 1290m, bring a grand perspective of mountains from a wide road with a good surface. Saint-Brés (8km, 1361m) consists of a few houses, a church, a bar/restaurant, while 11km, 1585m offers the Déchetterie des Charmes beside a wooden cabin and works site on a right-hand corner. 'Rubbish Dump of Charms' does rather beg a question, don't you think? Certainly the man guarding it when we went by did not look as if he were over-endowed with captivating bonhomie – he glowered – but, well, you never can tell.

The Aire du Vasson viewpoint – a scrubby unmetalled stony pull-off – affords long sight across the Mercantour national park ringed by mountains and some very high peaks like a cordon along the northern skyline. A large chalet overhead and opposite calls itself the Résidence du Col and then a sign for the Col de Valberg (1627m) as the Valberg hoves into view. A cycle lane takes you down the leafy approach to town – a skiing nowhere-anywhere.

The ride up is fine, though, so just ride on straight through Valberg or stop for coffee and then f**k-offee down the commonplace broad ski highway – a fast descent, of course – and, once shot of the buildings and lifts and other ski junk, the road essays the greener valley through Les Launes and Beuil, attractive mountain villages set amid green pastureland in what is a summer holiday resort, a '*station verte de vacances*' and so on over the Col de le Couillolle.

For a description of the southern approach, from Port de Cians, see Col de la Couillole which follows.

COL DE LA COUILLOLE 1678M

Eastern approach from Saint-Sauveur-sur-Tinée 510m

LENGTH: 16.5KM	
HEIGHT GAIN: 1168M	
MAXIMUM GRADIENT: 8%	

The river Vionène flows down the gorge below, the first few kilometres of the road are tight, twisty, smooth of surface, hasty of height-gain, a more or less relentless 8% to the top with occasional pauses to snatch a breath at a little under 7% – but this is tough riding, with fine, airy views across the open cleft in the mulberry-red schist much in evidence hereabouts. The dusty-pink crystalline, fissile schist is interlayered with grubby cream clays.

About 2.5 kilometres on, the flex of the hairpins gives way to a longer, serpentine stretch. A succession of short tunnels emphasise, somehow, the sense that the road has been built against the dam wall of the mountainside. If you are lucky, you will see a newly-reintroduced bearded vulture plying the thermals overhead on the beady *qui vive* (look-out) for dead sheep or chamois. Known as 'the bone breaker', this carrion bird will strip large bones from a carcass, fly to a height and let them plummet onto rocks to smash them open so as to make the juicy marrow accessible.

At about 8km, the gradient unchanged, the road gets fretful again, hairpins hoisting you up to the mediaeval village of Roubion, (1300m, 12km) perched up on a cliff, digging its 12th century fortified masonry toes into the living rock. A white-chevronned red sign warns '*Risque d'attente*' referring to the possibility of hold-ups due to rock-falls but, remember, *attente* also means 'ambush'. So it comes that, 4 kilometres from the col, the road opens out wide for 1.5 kilometres to lull the unsuspecting traveller into false hope before snapping its jaws once more.

Hamlets and stony vacancy follow and the col itself sits on a broad hummock of heathland. A gîte, La Fripounière, by the col has a very youth-hostel air (don't get me started) and, perhaps unjustly, evokes *fripon* which means 'crook'. We came, we saw – an intent coven of the guests cross-legged on a rise close by, some kind of group experience *en plein air* – we cleared off.

Southern approach from Pont-de-Cians 338m

LENGTH: 29.5KM	
HEIGHT GAIN: 1340M	
MAXIMUM GRADIENT: 10%	

A long haul on the D28 up the Gorges du Cians, limestone at the bottom, schist at the top, a narrow cleft cut deep into towering, sheer cliffs. There are a number of tunnels en route but paths (of indifferent surface) to allow you to circumvent them. The two clues (Provencal for 'bottlenecks') are narrower stretches where the road has been hewn out of the living rock.

From kilometres 8 to 13 the gradient kicks up from a fairly gentle approach, with minor blips of around 6%, to a fiercer 8, 9.5 and 9 with viitations of 10%. At the Petite Clue (980m, 13km) the slope eases and does not repeat that bristling steepness.

Just below the Grande Clue tunnel (1095m, 15km), a plaque indicates the Casemate du Raton – a *casemate* (probably from the Sicilian *casa matta*, 'dark house') – a vaulted chamber built in the thickness of the ramparts of a fortress, in this instance in the depth of the cliff. This, we learn, was constructed 1939–40 as a 'second line of resistance' in the Alpes Maritimes against possible invasion by the Italian army over the Cols de Crous and Moulines, both existing fortified works just north of the Gorges on the ranges above the border with north-western Italy. The Alpine Line extended the

COL DE LA COUILLOLE *continued*

French defensive Maginot Line south-eastwards to the coast.

The view all the way is fine indeed, a real canyon, a goodly torrent flowing in the close-hemmed channel below, trees by the roadside much of the way and, for the first 8 kilometres or so, not much to trouble the legs or lungs. A nice warm-up, indeed, to prepare for a long stretch, some 9 kilometres of a variable steepness, as the upper heights crowd the skyline ahead. Here come some nasty injections of as much as 10% and less of a toll on 5.5 and 6%, before the slope grows weary of its aggression at around 17km and doddles quite gently up to the junction with the D30 leading to the col.

Beuil, at the junction (1450m), began as a Roman fort and was, for centuries, a stronghold commanding ingress and egress to and from this much-disputed territory. Guillaume Rostang, a man of bellicose and cruel disposition who called the shots from 1285 to 1315, reasserted the *droit de cuissage* which had, in his view most regrettably, fallen into desuetude. This allowed a seigneur to 'put his leg' (legalistic euphemism, compare 'get your leg over') into the bed of any female serf on the first night of her marriage – French for *ius primae noctis* in other words. The dictionary continues 'and in certain communities to pass the night with her'. The Beuillards kicked up, took an axe to the concupiscent bastard and appealed for protection to Don Andarro Grimaldi who married Rostang's daughter and kept his legs to himself, and her. Magnates of the family held it until the Duke of Savoy annexed Beuil into his County of Nice. In 1633, the old Grimaldi castle was dismantled by locals who used the stones to embellish their houses and, feeling just a bit guilty, to restore the village's Chapelle des Pénitents-Blancs. The Confraternity of White Penitents, founded by

Henri III in 1585, wore an overall burqa-style costume to stress their undyed, virtuous humility.

Condamine at the edge of the village was the *campus domini* (the seigneur's field) reserved for jousting tournaments and is now more commonly productive of wheat, potatoes and the famous Beuil lentils. In 1902, an army officer, Ferdinand Faber, flew his oversize box-kite aerial machine first 25 metres, then 50 metres from a hill overlooking Condamine.

Blood and Guts

On the 1955 Tour the French team had been sworn, by written agreement, to work for the two-time winner, Louison Bobet. That contractual unity did not suppress the near congenital predisposition of its members to bitch, bicker, spoil and rebel in their own interests rather than that of the combine. Into the Alps, Antoine Rolland held yellow and an advantage of 12 minutes over his leader, Bobet, who seemed to have found neither rhythm nor will. There was also the threat of the Luxemburger Charly Gaul, the great climber, coming onto his favoured ground. In the first Alpine stage, Gaul duly dumped the Frenchman …by 14 minutes.

The French rallied, got their act together, Bobet screwed his courage to the sticking place and south over the last of the Alps they were back in harness. The weather on that stage into Monaco was horrible but Bobet and Rolland attacked and were out in front. The torrent in the Gorges du Cians glowed red in the crimson aura of the schist rock, the narrow, twisting road, awash with water and mud, was infernally treacherous, bikes and motorbikes were going down here, there and everywhere. Gendarmes frantically waved their yellow flags to warn the riders. Géminiani, who had monitored the chase behind his leader, now broke clear. He took all manner of risks but stayed upright, rejoined the others before Nice, cut loose on the Col d'Eze still in torrential rain and, despite puncturing on the descent, won in Monaco. Back in the Gorges du Cians, Nello Lauredi, the French regional rider, had fallen and was perished with cold, his arms and legs, streaked with blood from gashes, shaking uncontrollably. 'I'm cold,' he stammered. Antoine Blondin, the writer who hated leaving his home in Paris but, every year, quit it to follow the Tour, describes what happened: 'Morvan, our driver, got him over to the car to warm him against the radiator. We opened the bonnet and he stayed there a while, a jacket over his shoulders his eyes fixed on some point in the void where his imagination tirelessly paraded images of a race where he had gone to perform, his hands lightly placed on top of the handlebars. But mechanically, his grazed hands curried his hair thick with sweat and blood, and stroked a small round bandage – like a tonsure – covering an old wound.

His pockets were empty, his bidon was empty, his stare was empty. This man had nothing left in the world but his flesh and bone visible through the torn shreds of his jersey. We said to him: "Off you go, you're warmed up again. Go steady, there are others behind you. You can't stay here." He looked round at the mad merry-go-round [of this Tour de France] which was crushing him like someone choosing a tombstone, nodded and a spot of blood added a more vivid red to the red of the rocks.'

Col de la Sinne 1437m

Eastern approach from the D2205 c.400m south of Saint-Sauveur-sur-Tinée and Isola

LENGTH: 15KM	
HEIGHT GAIN: 1037M	
MAXIMUM GRADIENT: 8.5%	

Saint-Sauveur is a pickle of higgledy-piggledy narrow streets, tall old houses and a 15th century church.[26] From the town the road down to La Bolinette courses the length of a sheer wall of the red rock through an impressive ravine cut by the Tinée River. Just past the junction with the D2565 (left) turn right onto the D59 for Irougne. It's narrow, a rare twinkler.

The hamlet of Irougne announces itself with a name plate at 1.9km, 543m, and 500 metres on the road squeezes through a *roche percée* then widens a bit. Metal barriers interspersed with dilapidated stone parapets. At 3.5km, 653m, a notice forbids *'baignade'*, presumably in the torrent flowing through. After 4km, 688m, the road flattens to allow you to take in a grand view across the yawning space beyond and below to the south and east.

Here come the jaws of what might be an unnamed col – certainly the gradient tilts down onto a flat stretch as if it were a col before climbing again through the trees of the Forêt de l'Ibac on the flanks of this chirpily named Montagne Coucouluche. By 9km, 1050m, a sign advertises 'La Domaine du Palomino Snackery'. A balcony road with a broken surface (10km, 1125m) winds into Illonse (11km, 1210m), its houses crammed together on the hillside, overlooked by the

26 There is an excellent *menu du jour* in Saint-Sauveur-sur-Tinée at an unassuming small bar/restaurant on the main street where the *ouvriers* (workers) gather. The dining room is at the back and cannot be seen from the front. The pink trout comes fresh from the Gorges du Cians. The trout in the Tinée are white.

custodian church. Leaving behind this last outpost of civilization, the road puts on its hairy tweeds and country walking boots, eschewing barriers, picking its narrow path between grass verges.

At 15km the Col de la Sinne like a saddle, marked by a brown wooden sign, a broad grassy sward off to the left. 'From ancient times' the board tells us 'this pass was deemed to occupy a strategic position, notably coveted by the Romans.'

Sheep and cattle graze and nibble, careless of their continuing place in history.

The descent is rough and steep, lightly wooded, mostly conifer and then a selvage left of blond-tipped soft grass for 500 metres. At 2.5km the surface, in the summer of 2008, got very rough and was the subject of refurbishment by the workmen of the Conseil Général des Alpes-Maritimes.

We'd essayed the western end of the climb some months prior to this visit and been prevented by a socking great caterpillar tractor, but, having just consulted the Conseil Général, I can now report the Col de la Sinne open. The improvements were not, I should point out, undertaken for the benefit of cyclists, rather for the rally cars which use the Sinne to test their skill and nerve. It is, though, on two wheels, a gem. The eastern end, from Pra d'Astier (561m) in the Gorges du Cians, follows the Vallon de Pierlas to the village of that name (c.1060m, 7km) and its shrine to Notre Dame des Carmes. She's an odd one. Provençal *carme* does refer to the Carmelite order but it also means 'money', 'a wooden clog' and – here's the cuckoo in the nest – 'a vulgar flighty woman, a coarse goer'. Never let it be said or imagined that townsfolk have the monopoly on risqué antics. An everyday story of country folk would uncover bizarreries you would scarcely believe... wholesale household swaps, close-encounter animal husbandry, werewolves...

From Pierlas, there remain some 4km to the col.

6. Maritime Alps

The Maritime Alps actually stretch as far north as the Bonette and the Maddalena passes but our sector concentrates on that part of the whole which lies just inland from the Côte d'Azur, embracing some of the Mercantour National Park.

Northwards through the Maritime Alps from the sea runs la Route du Sel (the Salt Route). The Greek author Plutarch called salt 'the noblest of provenders, the condiment par excellence'. Its uses are, and have always been, diverse: for sustaining the health of cattle, for preserving meat and fish (its most important role), as a seasoning ingredient in cooking (often to disguise the taste of tainted meat), a fixer for dyes, making soap (saponification), and a basic disinfectant. The importance of salt is marked by an array of idiomatic expressions: salt, in slang, meant 'costly, dear'… in the theatre, 'we shan't take salt' meant that box office takings would be poor… 'salting the books' means to beef up the accounts with fictional entries prior to selling a business… 'below the salt' meant being one of the lower orders sitting at tables in the lord's hall, himself and the nobs at their table on the dais, supplied with the precious condiment, salt, denied to the oiks… 'worth his salt' explains itself… 'salt of the earth', the hardy and trusted workman. . . 'Attic salt', the quality of refined wit… and, as everybody also knows who knows that Gallia was divisa into tres partes, a Roman legionary received an allowance for the purchase of salt, in Latin, the salarium, hence our word 'salary'.

Salt came from mines – a hideous fate of prisoners, to be sent to the salt mines – from draining of salt marshes or from salt pans – where seawater is left to evaporate leaving a crystalline residue of sodium nitrate, the chemical name for salt.

During the 15th century, the transport of salt, an essential staple, from the extensive salt-producing plant in Hyères, close by Toulon, as far as Piedmont marked out la Route du Sel. Inevitably, the trading of so precious a commodity was vulnerable to mischief and, during his short reign (1314–16), Louis X of France, Le Hutin (The Headstrong), ordained a system of storage in public warehouses, under tight security, from which salt could be distributed to the populace in fair portion. The finances of the French monarchy were never less than rickety and, in 1366, King Charles V, Le Sage (The Wise), badly strapped for cash, put an end to the provision of salt as a public right in favour of taking it as a royal monopoly to prop up the fiscal weal of the state. To salt was, from then on, applied the word *gabelle*, from the Arabic *qabala* (impost) adopted by the Italians in Sicily, *gabella* in Provençal. (The French for customs, *douanes*, comes from the Turkish *diwan* – our divan – the Sultan's council of state, then customs house.) The word, applied to all imposts levied on goods, including textiles and flour, at the octroi customs barrier outside every town and port, soon attached exclusively to and eponymised the hated tax on salt. People not only had to pay the tax but they were also legally obliged to buy salt in certain quantities, thus making the salt *gabelle* a sort of early income tax. Since different areas of France paid different levels of *gabelle* and some were exempted – for instance Aquitania, then in the hands of the English – smuggling was rife and punishments harsh. Contrabanders and their dogs carried the salt in thin, metal tanks moulded to their chest, the old lady of a house might be plonked in a chair under whose seat was a concealed box for contraband salt so that when the customs men arrived to search the premises – as royal decree allowed them to do – they'd find granny asleep and be chary of waking her, poor dear.

Collection of the *gabelle* was in the hands of the royal Tax Farmers, who bought their percentage of the king's gross revenues and took a cut – largely at their discretion – before passing it on to Versailles. Just before the outbreak of the Revolution, the royal Treasury received a mere tenth of the total receipts of the tax farm. Detested as this royal tax was, even the revolutionary government could not suppress it. It pulled in too much cash. Under first the Directory and then the Empire, the salt tax helped finance Napoleon's wars and, intermittently relaxed and hiked, it was not finally abolished until after the Liberation, in 1945. (Some bars, cafés and shops which sell tobacco still sport the white and blue enamelled metal lozenge indicating their licence to purvey '*sel et tabac*', two former state monopolies.)

The Cours Saleya in Nice is a relic of the passage of salt first along the coast and then on to Piedmont by a northern route avoiding the easier passage over the Tende Col into the hostile County of Tende. *Gabeliers* (merchants) bought salt in bulk to sell it on at inflated price – twelve times to the inhabitants of Nice, fourteen times to foreigners.

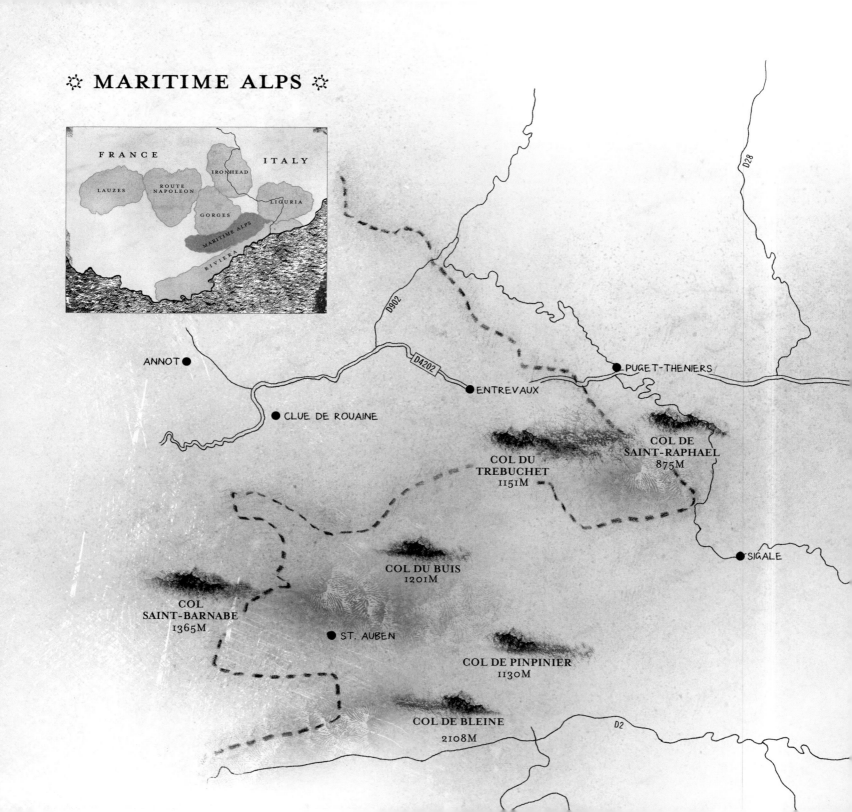

❖ MARITIME ALPS ❖

FRANCE

ITALY

LAUZES

ROUTE NAPOLEON

IRONHEAD

LIGURIA

GORGES

MARITIME ALPS

RIVIERA

D28

D902

ANNOT ●

D4202

● ENTREVAUX

● PUGET-THENIERS

● CLUE DE ROUAINE

COL DE
SAINT-RAPHAEL
875M

COL DU
TREBUCHET
1151M

● SIGALE

COL DU BUIS
1201M

COL
SAINT-BARNABE
1365M

● ST. AUBEN

COL DE PINPINIER
1130M

COL DE BLEINE
2108M

D2

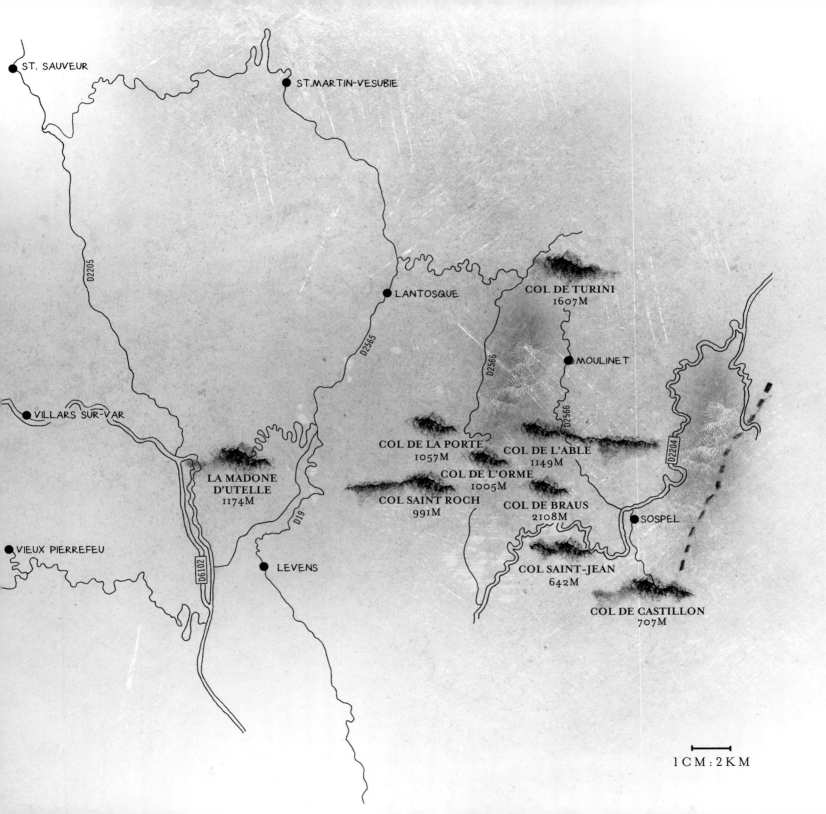

ST. SAUVEUR

ST. MARTIN-VESUBIE

D2205

LANTOSQUE

COL DE TURINI
1607M

D2565

D2566

MOULINET

D2566

VILLARS SUR-VAR

COL DE LA PORTE
1057M

COL DE L'ABLE
1149M

D2204

LA MADONE
D'UTELLE
1174M

COL DE L'ORME
1005M

COL SAINT ROCH
991M

COL DE BRAUS
2108M

SOSPEL

D19

VIEUX PIERREFEU

D6102

LEVENS

COL SAINT-JEAN
642M

COL DE CASTILLON
707M

1 CM : 2 KM

In 1433, a Nicois *gabelier* called Paganino del Pozzo whose family had originally come from Alexandria to settle in Cuneo, proposed to the Treasury of the Provençal court that he finance the construction of a road from Nice up through the Gorges de Vésubie, across the Col de Cerise (2543m) and on down to Entracque, Valdieri and, eventually, Cuneo, in return for permission to exact a toll on all those who used it. Count Amadée VIII sanctioned the deal and work began on the authority of his letters patent. The old route, via Lantosque, avoided the gorge – confined, rock-bound, impracticable – but at the cost of an extra day and lighter loads on the mules. The journey on from Saint-Martin was arduous, long and entailed crossing one of a number of passes at extreme high altitude, each prone to appallingly bad weather conditions.

Paganino prospered and lived in a fine house on the Via Roma in Cuneo's main piazza. He paid a huge outlay for the extension of his road along the valley of the Roya (in Tende county), got into debt and was slung into prison on the orders, it seems, of that same Amadée VIII (now Pope Felix V) who had smiled on him once. Paganino died, destitute and disgraced, the victim, one presumes, of envy.

The County of Tende having been subsumed by the House of Savoy, the Savoyards thereby enjoyed effective control of all the trade up and down the Roya route – salt and oil from Provence, metals from the Dauphiné, cloth and textiles from Spain and sheep from the Midi, all to the detriment of the Marquisate of Saluzzo, east of the Agnello pass. [See IRONHEAD.] The markets of Saluzzo and nearby Carmagnola depended on cross-alpine trade in their rice, flax canvas (for the naval shipyards in Toulon) and hand-woven woollen textiles. In 1480, the Marquis Ludovico II ordered the digging of a tunnel under Monte Viso by means of which traders could evade the Savoyard taxmen. Alas, the Marquisate was gobbled up by Savoy in 1588 and officially declared defunct in 1601. Thereafter, no one bothered with the tunnel and the Salt Gallery, as the tunnel was called, rapidly fell into desuetude.

In 1591 the Roya route over the Tende col was improved and opened for small carts. (Plague in Saint-Martin-Vésubie rendered the already difficult gorge route even less attractive.) Further widened and the surface cleared, the Roya salt road offered passage to four-wheel carts from 1788, the first such main road to traverse the Alps.

Col du Trebuchet 1151m

Eastern approach from Pont des Miolans 604m

| LENGTH: 17.5KM |
| HEIGHT GAIN: 547M |
| MAXIMUM GRADIENT: 7% |

Old *bornes* (kilometre stones) mark the D10. There are quite a number of houses scattered along the lower slopes and this whole area is quite populous – the coast is not so far away, so maybe this is a dormitory town.

At 3.5km, Saint Pierre has a sizeable spread of dwellings and in one field beside the road, two dark brown alpacas graze under trees. The alpaca is a South American quadruped of the camel family, although the soft wool used in textiles tends to come exclusively from the alpaca native to Peru, whence it originated.

The houses dwindle and at 5.6km the road steps out onto an open balcony by a rock wall which looks as if it could do with a mural. At 7.8km, 900m in the mountain village of La Rochette (also La Roucheto, the Provençal version) a war memorial lists ten or so names, though barely that many houses remain here now in the shadow of a church which is far too large for its moribund parish. The road passes under an imposing stone archway into the village and then on down for some 3 kilometres where it flattens out to draw breath before climbing back up to c. 900m at 12.8km. A big torrent flows under the road and from the col ride on down to the bottom of the Col de Félines road south of Entrevaux.

COL DU BUIS 1201M

Northern approach from Entrevaux 515m

LENGTH: 13.5KM

HEIGHT GAIN: 686M

MAXIMUM GRADIENT: 12%

There is a clutch of cols in the vicinity of the Buis – Félines, Trébuchet, Laval – and the roads have changed little, apart from the surfacing, since a 19th century topographist described them as difficult for the passage of carts over this remote patch of country north from the tiny village of La Serre towards the wider valleys and more accessible roads on the main trade routes. A *trébuchet* is either a bird trap, a small precision balance for weighing gold, chemical ingredients etc. or a medieval siege engine. *Félines* implies some presence of cats, therefore insinuating witches, and as for *laval* that must have to do, in general, with the valley, but for all three definitions beyond that, I cannot vouch.

Entrevaux is an impressive walled town at the foot of a high pinnacle of rock on top of which sits the citadel up and round which, recalling the pine-cone formation of La Pigna [see page 305], wind the walls and a cruelly steep, zigzag rampart walkway linking castle and town. The fortification was the work of Vauban, constructed when war broke out between France and Savoy in 1690.

The town was originally called Interrivos ('between the rivers').[27] It was fortified in the 11th century after the old town of Glandève was sacked and razed by Saracen marauders.

There is a Musée de la Moto – motorbikes of all sorts dating back to 1901 – a Musée de la Citadelle et Fortifications de la Poudrière – on Vauban himself and the geometry of military architecture and *poudre* (gunpowder) – and a wonderful view from the very top of the citadel itself loaded with a very compelling sense of the strategic importance of this fortress on the fissiparous border between France and the ancient and powerful kingdom of Savoy.

Local culinary specialities include wafer-thin sliced dried salt-beef *secca de boeuf*, comparable to the Swiss *viande des Grisons* (one of their Cantons) and Italian *bresaola*, *pain d'épice* (gingerbread) and honey imbued with the scents and flavours of Provençal flora.

The writhing climb out of town on the D610 to a lesser Mont Blanc is a killer: very, very steep, narrow and marked with triple chevrons on the Michelin map.

Other accounts of it are bland but be warned: they err. Luckily, the break-leg, crush-lung lactic acid attack lasts only about half a kilometre to just past the turn off to Bay. Here farms and outbuildings are scattered about and the road drops down into the gorge of the Chalvagne. The river off to the left, to the right a rock wall composed of broad caramel stone seams jointed with layers of grey rock, the surface of it like a rough weave – the scoring and gouging mark where it was hacked away to accommodate the road to replace the inhospitable former track.

At 2.8km, 580m, the road starts climbing again but gets bored, flattens out and drops once more to a bridge at 3.1km. Mindful of its duty at the approach to a col, however, the road ups itself again out of the Chalvagne vale, a steady 6% drawn on by a distant perspective of the remote gorge, a broad, sandy rock slope to the left patched with trees. Le Champ, a tiny gathering of houses, sits at 4.7km, 710m, and the road ascends to 780m at 5.5km, trees on either side and outlying houses, meeting the D610 to Villevieille at 6.3km. The D710 continues to Mont Blanc, falling away once more through grass and dwarf trees on a good surface. The Col du Félines (930m) arrives at 7km, modestly and almost unannounced. Just after the col, a sudden plunge down a 13% slope for 2.7 kilometres into meadows and a wide grassy bowl, fringed with trees, to a bridge (at 760m) and a turn-off into the hamlet of La Serre – this by-road continues in a loop back to Catellet-Saint-Cassien. The D911 continues on a severe ramp of gradient, an unrelenting 11–12% on the final 3.7 kilometres to the

27 Presumably the Var which runs by it and a number of confluent streams which join on the Var's bend by the town, among them the Chalvagne, whose stream used to drive the local oil and flour mills, one of which is still producing oil.

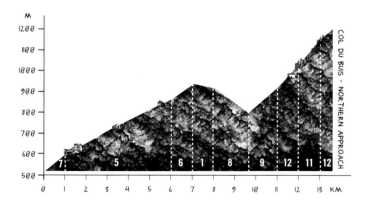

COL SAINT-BARNABE 1365M

Buis. Thus, this final assault on the col saps over 400 metres out of you. The trees thin out for some way then reassert themselves. There is no sign on the wild top of the col but from it a glorious view back down into the valley and its variegated colours: sand, grey rock, the racing green of the foliage.

Wild thyme grows on the Buis and, given that *buis* is French for 'box tree' (Latin *buxus*), these shrubby items with miniature leaves, glossy and of the texture of polished leather, must be the box, although their leaves are not so dark as the sort of box familiar to me.

We descend into a dusty wilderness and a cornice road, very exposed. At 0.6km from the col the tarmac spreads out onto a wider plan, smooth and scattered with pine cones, a vigorous descent into Briançonnet (1090m, 3km), hollyhocks growing in the verges. From your hollyhock, or wild mallow, derives a soothing lotion for aching feet or a gargle for sore throat and swollen tonsils. Pale yellow, densely-grained boxwood is much prized for chisel handles, and cabinet-makers (I was one for a time) keep bunches of box stems for inserts and repair work.

The people in the little auberge at Briançonnet were not overburdened with bonhomie but that may have been the lowering effect of a slow start to their holiday season and a preceding week of chilly rain.

Eastern approach from Pont de Miolans 605m

LENGTH: 20.6KM	
HEIGHT GAIN: 591M	
MAXIMUM GRADIENT: 6%	

An easy, if protracted, roll up a valley on the D2211A, flanked by lowish ridges, into Briançonnet, the worst steepness being the 5 kilometres after the bridge at Collongues where the intervening climb over the Col Saint Roch, 750m at 5km, turns into 6% although the last 5 kilometres into Briançonnet are all but flat.

West towards Soleilhas

LENGTH: 10.5KM	
HEIGHT GAIN: 480M	
MAXIMUM GRADIENT: 6%	

A few kilometres from Briançonnet, the D2211 enters a narrow gorge leading to that notably pinched neck in it called the Clue de Saint-Auban. There are many such *clues* – tight defiles between two opposed walls of rock – in the region, and this particular one is distinguished by a chapel with an altar set into a cavern in the rock on the west side, above the tumbling waters of the Esteron, a bare slab of cliff opposite with a lower curtain of trees, like a kick skirt. Set into the front of the altar, which stands at the centre of a broken semicircle of chairs, is a mosaic lozenge, a prominent cross whose quarters herald '*CHRIST HIER AUJOURD'HUI A JAMAIS*' (Christ yesterday, today, for ever), with a backdrop panel under the low ceiling of the rock behind the altar, depicting Her (again) and the legend '*JE TE SALUE MARIE DES EAUX VIVES*' (I hail thee, Mary of the running waters). This, it may be, is where a local wet T-shirt competition originated with a religious gloss to pacify the more recalcitrant sisters.

The gorge is sheltered, cool, alive with the splash and roar of those running waters gushing through a narrow rocky funnel, the ribbon of sky overhead, occasionally blocked out by short tunnels, adds to the visual drama of this most enjoyable pull up an even, lowly gradient into the pretty little ancient village of Saint-Auban (903m). Take the D305 west towards Soleilhas and across from the *département* of Alpes-Maritimes into Haute-Provence, up a broad, grassy valley, kempt and leafy, a perspective of low domed heights all round, swathes of the Spanish yellow of broom flowers daubed across the slopes and a spangling of smaller blooms. The gradient is not hard, around 5–6%, but it's a lovely ride into Soleilhas ('looking at the sun' – 1122m), 7.5 kilometres from Saint-Auban.

Soleilhas is tiny, a stone-built village with narrow streets for shade, one such, the rue du Four ('Oven Street'), harking back to that time when a small community could afford but one fired oven for shared use to bake daily bread and occasional roast meat.

The road continues, good surface, steady ascent, sharper gradient, easy bends with interspersed tight hairpins for the next hop up to the terracing as the col gets closer. At 1280m, 2 kilometres from the village, there is a generous view of the broad flat valley bottom and Soleilhas itself. A further kilometre on arrives the col at 1365m with another expansive view back down the valley and ahead to Vauplane, a *stade de neige* (ski station) if you've a mind to ride to a dead-end for an even longer view.

A long, 5 kilometre wiggly straight on to Demandolx, another old Provençal village, from which opens out a prospect of the Lacs de Chaudanne and de Castillon, reservoirs formed by barrages.

Col de Saint-Raphaël 875m

Northern approach from Puget-Théniers 410m

LENGTH:	8KM
HEIGHT GAIN:	465M
MAXIMUM GRADIENT:	7%

From this side, a transitional climb on a well-surfaced wide road, not outstandingly attractive save for its ingress to the country beyond. Guarding the col, a statuette of the Archangel Raphael, with enormous rabbit's ear wings and attendant ram at his feet. His name in Hebrew means 'God heals' and he is generally supposed to be that angel who stirred up the waters of the pool of Bethesda in Jerusalem: '… whosoever then first after the troubling of the water stepped in was made whole of whatsoever disease he had' (John 5:4. His healing powers are also mentioned in the Apocryphal Book of Tobias 3:25). The ram is a symbol of authority and leadership.

Southern approach from the Col de Vence

LENGTH:	57KM
HEIGHT GAIN:	875M
MAXIMUM GRADIENT:	8%

This long excursus winds up and down through canyon country and along narrow plunging defiles into close ravines porous with funnels and shafts much frequented by cavers.

The 6 kilometres of descent from the Vence to this turn-off is a joy: fast and clear into the open, past views of the valley of the Cagne below to the right. At 3.2 kilometres from the col, on the left-hand side wall, there is the expertly drawn outline of a pink pig, under a protective caul of chicken wire. Don't ask me.

Turn right on the D8 (940m) to Courségoules and through the village, past a new school with a broad balcony for the *récré* (*récréation* – play time. You may, or may not, wish to know that the French for 'I'll get

you at playtime,' is '*tu vas voir la gueule à la récré*.') The road surface is excellent, smoothly tarmacked for the passage of the school buses doing the rounds of the outlying villages, presumably. There is obviously a keen topiarist roaming the district, on the evidence of a number of neatly clipped róbinias into the shape of lollipops.

Bézaudun-les-Alpes (*dun* is an ancient Celtic word meaning 'fortress') perches up on its height, up the D208 (835m, 6km) a closeted Provençal village of stone buildings crushed together in a heap, linked by the tight, cobble-paved vennels called *calado*, plus a church in the care of Notre Dame du Peuple. Her in her demotic guise. The patent defensive aspect of these crag-top villages evokes memory of the constant hostile penetration of these parts by droves of belligerent bastards clattering down the gangplank of history: Goths and Germans, Corsair pirates, the freebooters, condottieri and hooligan, hired hatchet-men of the Late Middle Ages and Renaissance. The locals didn't have much but the marauders took it anyway.

On down into the Bouyon gorge, curving round the mountain side, lime trees in frequent attendance. Now the *bornes* give altitude: by a side road off to La Gravière near a stone bridge over a torrent 8km 758m, at 11km 700m Bouyon, and descending still, 13km 585m.

Although it feels steeper, most of this descent is at around 5%, a junior gorge heading towards the southern end of the senior Gorges de Vésubie and the Défilé de Chaudan.

At 16.5km, 610m, a view of Les Ferres up to the right on the flank of Mont Saint-Michel, the bridge across to it like a drawbridge over a moat. A blackboard at the turn notifies an auberge in the village and whether it is open or not.

18.2km, 618m, and, far ahead, another wary

hideout of a village, Conségudes, on its eyrie. At 21.5km, 600m (this stretch losing no more than 5 metres in every kilometre) a memorial to one Marc Polia of Conségudes '*mort accidentellement agé 24 ans, août 1976*'. Did the unfortunate youth, like La Mariée [see GORGES], fall into the ravine?

At the entrance to Conségudes (648m), there is a shrine to the usual pietistic suspects (Her and the babby). 22.5km into trees, 23.5km, 577m, commences a hairpinned descent into the bosky tunnel of the Clue de la Bouisse. A good surface and a steady 7%. Around 26km, note the clumps of mistletoe hanging like bee swarms to the oaks.[28]

At 27.2km, the road becomes a corniche round Roqueston and, 4 kilometres above, it, suddenly bulges like a python devouring its lunch.

---

28 French *gui* from Latin *viscum*, the parasite mistletoe, which also likes apple trees and in France tends to favour poplars, was revered by the Druids. The only plant that sprouts new leaves in winter, it was known to them as an all-heal. Virgil clearly nods at this prophylactic property – he has Aeneas cut a golden bough of mistletoe to protect him on his journey into the Underworld. (*Aeneid* bk. 6, l. 205).

Kissing under the mistletoe is an innocuous relic of these more nervy folk myths. As, too, the children's rhyme for counting out, Eena meena miny mo / Catch a nigger by his toe / If he hollers let him go / eena meena mina mo. This you chant as you point at the children standing in the circle and on the final 'mo' the child is eliminated. This was widespread in various forms across Europe and North America – the 'catch a nigger…' line is a corruption of a French Canadian version '*Cache ton poing derrière ton dos*' – and is said, by some, to have started as a Druidic incantation for the selection of sacrificial victims. My maternal grandparents once had a cat called Eeny for short – full name all the words to 'mo' – because our version began 'Eeny meeny miny mo'.

At the foot of this long descent into Roquesteron (325m), an old-fashioned, somewhat distressed metal suspension footbridge remains slung across the narrows of the gorge.

You'll find a cheery café in Roquesteron.

Up the valley on something like 8% and, just out of town, at 1.2km, 486m, sits a 15th century chapel to Notre Dame d'Entrevignes, suggesting that, amongst her many attributes and pastimes, she's either a boozer herself or likes the company of them. Note the Wedding at Cana. Wooden bars form a grille across the opening into a rather vulgar, hackwork painted vault dating from 1536. Curiously, the Madonna is shown pregnant. Chairs indicate its use as a working chapel.

Sigale is plainly visible up on its promontory ahead. Sigale (660m), a mini *bastide* (fortified town), is split by a narrow crinkum-crankum main street, its beacon-like clock-tower, atop an extravagant pinnacle of rock, built on the ruins of what was once the *donjon* or keep. The name may be pre-Roman *sik*, meaning 'a rocky spur'. In November 1793, the people of Sigale, fighting alongside Sardinians, neither much taken with the incursions upon them of revolutionary mandate and manpower from Paris, fought against but were beaten by Republican troops sent to quell opposition and the nearby chateau, built by the Counts of Provence, was destroyed, just to ram home the message of who laid down the law now.

You will find a very warm welcome in the bar/restaurant Le Village, in the shadow of both church and tower, and an excellent *menu du jour*. They also have rooms. (tel: 04 93 05 89 43). One kilometre out of Sigale (700m) and a fast drop into the Clue de Riolan, an impressive overhang hustling the road into the parapet on the left as if to force it off down into the gorge. A *roche percée*, (literally 'pierced rock' i.e. with a hole in it)

weather-shaped and smooth-polished.

Five kilometres from Sigale, the Pont des Miolans ('Mules-bridge') and a 7 kilometre climb of around 4%, with a blast of 6% midway, to the Col de Saint-Raphaël.

Eastwards from the Saint-Raphaël

LENGTH: 14.7KM

HEIGHT GAIN: 274M

MAXIMUM GRADIENT: 8%

The D27 connects this interior with the main D6202 south into Nice along the lower valley of the Var. (The Var rises just below the Col de la Cayolle, heads due south and then swings east for a long stretch past Entrevaux into the Défile du Chaudan where it again veers south.)

A short way on, a *croix de fer* (iron cross) overlooks the hamlet of La Penne with its belt and braces insurance of two churches. The altimeter count insists that this is a climb but it feels like a descent – is this the new reality? What is up or down? One man's drop is another man's hoist, depending on how willing to suspend, or elevate, belief. Seeing is believing? Don't you believe it.

Rourebel (c.1000m, 6.5km), and Ascros (1149m, 8.7km) where a house exhibits a home-made, white *borne* whose cap is blue and decorated with the gold stars of the EU. The column shows: Rome 548 Sofia 1278 Athènes 1928 Berlin 1991 Helsinki 2541 Stockholm 2691 and, on the side: LU SAN JOANS 0km (i.e. the name of the house 'Saint John's') which, if you ask me, is a touch heavy-handed on the humour front.

About 6 kilometres on, at 1099m, an unmarked Col de Végautier from which it is all downhill into the Défile du Chaudan and the high (actually low) road back to Nice.

COL DE PINPINIER 1130M

Eastern approach from D17 527m

LENGTH: 20.5KM
HEIGHT GAIN: 738M IN TOTAL, AS THE ROAD DESCENDS TO 392M
MAXIMUM GRADIENT: 8%

Puzzlingly there is another D10 to the south, roughly parallel to its northern twin, which leaves the road out of Roquesteron just beyond the chapel to Notre Dame d'Entrevignes.

The narrow road, marked 'difficult or dangerous' on the map, descends for the first 3 kilometres, below Sigale up on its hewn-rock observation platform, down the valley of the Estéron, twisting through olives, past old *borne* stones, oaks, cypresses to the left in a brief flourish of trim gardener's pride and out again into wilder country, bare rock and this long slope of a road, as into an open-cast mine.

At 3km, 392m, the Pont du Riolan, the Gorges du Riolan joining from the right and the road beginning to climb.

Aiglun (619m, 8km) is heralded by a profusion of azaleas and robinia (*pseudacacia*), and another large stone civic archway over the road with faded painting on the pediment 'AUBERGE DE CALENDAL' (the advertised inn nowhere in evidence).

1.5 kilometres on down, a steep drop of around 9%, into the impossibly tight Clue d'Aiglun (523m), the side-wall and stone parapet making a conduit barely the width of a car. A board advises on the '*pratique de canyonisme*' and gives a list of ordinances ('*Arrêtés Préfectorales*') governing the practice of abseiling down into the subterranean caves and plugs which perforate these canyons, together with safety measures, including what equipment to take (individual and team) and what precautions, as well as specific times when madness of this variety is officially permitted.

Inch down into the confines of the Clue to a tiny bridge over the Estéron and across it into a strictly one-way tunnel, 100 metres long and dark, so take care. Phew, this ride is very dramatic: it has the feel of an old contraband route through bandit country, trains of mules with muffled hooves swaying up the ascents, the big baskets on their back stuffed full with loot, driven by hirsute, scary-eyed smugglers toting antiquated, long-barrelled fowling pieces.

The climb starts on the other side of the tunnel, creeping tight round a blunt buttress and on up into Les Tardons (700m, 11km). Clumps of purple saxifrage sprout from the rock. At 13km, 718m, Le Collet (*collet* – *so* yearning to be a grown-up col) and flat for a way. A crossroads below Le Mas with the D110 – a side loop avoiding the col via Les Sausses – then a fine 1 kilometre causeway of new tarmac into the village (830m 16.5km) and a hotel/restaurant which caters for marriages and banquets.

On through sentinel pines and a good surface to the col, which has no marker, just a gap in the pinewoods and a sign for the Piste de Pinpinier forest trail. The descent is broader and smooth through a similar wildness for 4 kilometres to a cross roads at c.1135m with the D5 at a sort of clearing among trees. A view west towards a skyline of brooding mountains.

Col de Bleine 1439m

Mediterranean exploration

LENGTH: 5KM

HEIGHT GAIN: 310M

MAXIMUM GRADIENT: 7%

The 5 kilometres which lead to the col on a fairly mild gradient have a decided air of urbanity, after the yokel nature of the Pinpinier, for this is the way to Grasse, don't you know? The col is another in a clearing of trees and drops into an amiable, straightish descent round mild bends to the main D2 and on towards the coast, via Saint-Vallier-de-Thiey on the Route Napoleon and a good spot for lunch [see RIVIERA]. Napoleon passed through on 2 March 1815 with the kernel of his force, some thousand men, and rested on a bench under an elm in the town square. The romanticised story of that halt has his men exhausted but, please, they had been on the road for less than a day, had covered no more than 30 kilometres *and* they were professional soldiers. True, the road was no better than a rough track, despite Napoleon having ordered the construction of a road in 1802. (Provençals have never been quick to heed orders from the north. See page 276) A column bearing his bust erected in 1870 marks the spot.

This whole area repays wider exploration and there are a number of routes we have looked at but not included here for want of space. But you will find some great riding over climbs away from the coast, not necessarily to any great height but hard enough, in the hinterland of some of the better-known cols. The proof of their attraction for the curious is that a large number of cyclists ride them, nosing out hidden routes, letting the road take them where it will. Because of its position near the Mediterranean, this area will stay open to bikes most of the year round, too, and is an ideal playground for the autumn, after the sun has lost some of its intense heat.

Not far from Saint-Vallier is the Souterroscope de la Baume Obscure, a network of underground caves, galleries and grottoes opened by speleologists in 1958 in which may be seen strangely shaped stalactites and mineral encrustations on the chalk walls, cascades and an underground river, pools and curious rock formations.[29]

The underground river flows into La Siagne whose name bespeaks what was, originally, marshland. Provençal *sagno* is French *marais* (marsh) and the lower stretches of the Siagne's valley had a reputation for insalubrity: fetid stink, insects, poor ground.

29 For more information, see: www.baumeobscure.com/souterroscope.htm

La Madone d'Utelle 1174m

Southern approach from
Saint-Jean-la-Rivière 288m

LENGTH: 15.5KM

HEIGHT GAIN: 886M

MAXIMUM GRADIENT: 8%

Since I have been so acidulous about her on occasion, perhaps the girl should have some attention paid exclusively to her, in redress. That said, despite the vast broad outreach she has achieved since her first appearance on the world stage largely thanks to her championship by monks as their spiritual mother (etc.) she's hardly mentioned in the Bible – three times – so it ain't just me.

Two roads follow the Gorges de Vésubie to Saint-Jean, the lower D2565 which hugs the course of the river Vésubie and the upper D19, tracing the line of Paganino's new 1433 salt route [see page 254]. Just beyond the village of Duranus on this route is a jutting crag called the Belvédère du Saut des Français.

The Provençals have been inveterate opponents of Paris, the nominated capital of a notional France after the landmass of what had been Roman tripartite Gaul had split into a number of autonomous counties and dukedoms. Named for the insignificant Gallic tribe, Parisii, which occupied the island which became Ile de la Cité, Paris was chosen as their seat by the Merovingian kings in the 5th century AD. As for the Provençals, ever vilified as the slack southerners, they had no willing truck with the chilly northerners who claimed suzerainty over them, and when Paris proclaimed the Revolution it had sponsored and which, thanks to the courage and heart-warming responsibility of its citizens, it carried through on behalf of all Frenchmen and women even if they didn't speak the language, which most didn't, the Comté de Nice, looking as much eastwards to the Republic of Genoa as north to some fiction of authority, repudiated both Revolution and the Republic it declared. The Niçois answered to their own traditions and loyalties; not caring to lose their Catholic religion in return for some pale, secularised and state-ordered version of Christianity, they resented bitterly the imposition of laws and requisition of goods and foodstuffs by representatives of the so-called 'National Assembly' in Paris while their young men baulked at being dragooned into the revolutionary armies. Nor did they agree with the execution of monarchs. Toulon held out against the Republican 'blues' as the soldiers of the revolutionary armies were known, Lyon revolted against the revolution and when, in 1793, Nice was occupied by the Republicans, local resistants fought back. The revolutionary soldiers looted and burned but these redoubtable local men were no pushover. The Republicans suffered a defeat and the men of Nice brought a batch of their prisoners up to this crag and told these 'Français' to 'jump for the republic': a vertiginous 300 metre drop into the rocky defile of the river. That 'Français' carries all the weight of their contempt, loathing and disgust: they were men of Nice, *not*, emphatically not, *Frenchmen* not in manner nor custom nor language nor heredity nor allegiance nor affinity. *Non, non et non.*

From the belvedere, the road spins away 4.9 kilometres down to Saint-Jean.

On the low road, 6.5 kilometres from the junction with the main D6202 from Nice in the Défile de Chaudan, note the elegant broad-spanned stone bridge over the Vésubie by the Cros d'Utelle. The bridge was part of the Route du Sel and in Cros ('hollow' in Provençal), there remains a fine example of the original path, with bouldered steps, cobbled treads, a containing low parapet, now daubed with the familiar red and white *tache* of the designated footpath.

From Saint-Jean the D32 winds up round a

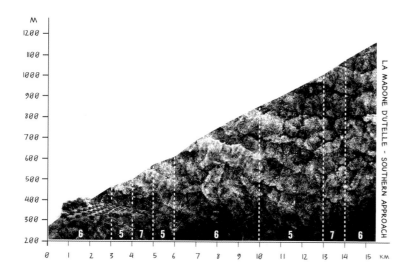

succession of hairpins through neatly- maintained olive groves, terrace by terrace on rapid lifts with views of the swishing snake's tail of the road below, the deepening gorge and the beetling cliffs of the Saut des Français. At 8.6km, 795m, Utelle itself sits on a projecting shelf with a wide panorama of the Vésubie gorge, the Forêt de Turini (east) and the Gordolasque mountains of the Mercantour below the border with Italy (north) no more than 25 kilometres away. When the traverse between the valley of the Tinée (west) and that of the Vésubie north of the gorge (east) was best effected by this route, Utelle occupied an important strategic and commercial position.

The ride up to the Sanctuary of the Madonne d'Utelle (on the D132 side road) is worth it for the view alone, but it is, too, a pleasurable detour on a road which trips nimbly up the bleached mountainside. At around 2km the wide and open road noses into trees and, as if atrophying in the shade of that bosky screen, it narrows sharply. Two kilometres on, it emerges from the shadows on a right-hand hairpin but, blinking in the sun, dodges straight back in as the slope eases again. The gradient is a steady 5–6%. At 4.6km once more away from the trees and onto the bare mountain without benefit of shade, a huge perspective from which the road drops timorously down as if dizzy with vertigo and scared to look out over the abyss. (Let it be said: quite a hairy ascent and an altogether jittery descent.) The road creeps gingerly round to another big hairpin and on to the broad plateau on which sits the Sanctuaire, a raspberry-fool-pink building with restaurant, hotel, boutique adjoining.

The sanctuary was founded in 850 AD by Spanish sailors in gratitude for the Madonna's intercession on their behalf during a terrible storm at sea – the Mediterranean is notorious for its sudden lethal

'blows' – and rebuilt in 1806. The high festivals of the sanctuary's year fall on 15 August, when the Virgin was assumed into heaven, and 8 September, the day of her nativity in Jerusalem.

The sanctuary is on an itinerary known as the Route du Baroque, a catchment of baroque edifices and monuments across Nisso-Liguria – Liguria and the old county of Nice – from San Remo to Nice and north as far as Saint-Etienne-sur-Tinée and Tende.

Beyond this great vantage point spreads the panorama of the Alpes-Maritimes and the Mediterranean littoral.

From the junction with the side road to the sanctuary, continue on the D32 through an unlit tunnel into a lost valley in hillbilly country. The surface is sorrily rough and, on the far side of another tunnel at a right-hand bend, a notice warns: '*Attention chaussée étroite sans glissières ni parapets*' (narrow road, no metal barriers, no parapets).

A stunted pine, a *pin à crochets*, stands all alone on a rock above the bend – like a sentinel on one leg with cape outspread or a cormorant drying its wings. Potholes here and there though generally visible, trees, a debris of loose stones at a quite wide verge which makes the road seem not so narrow, rain drains aslant with grills but not proud of the surface.

Some stretches have been poulticed with fresh tarmac but the gremlins up the mountain have chucked a lot of stones down onto the road.

There are a number of dumped, wrecked cars that have given up their wheezing combustive ghost, and now seem to function more as mechanistic installation art – the modern equivalent (perhaps) of the steers' skulls in the desert, lost in parched neglect to the scavengers, never to move again. Others appear to be still just in use, drawn up by a caravan, an encampment of what the French call *marginaux*, 'hippy outsiders'. For this is a lost canyon

of automobile wreckers, an extended roadside breaker's yard, where a decrepit campervan has its bonnet stuck into an alcove of the mountain side wall beside the carcase of a wrecked motor as if it had rolled home blind drunk one night, pitched into a pleat of rock, couldn't make it to bed and died of a fatal seizure.

Away from the pit of the rock walls, the road perks up and descends fast through trees on a smooth surface, twisting into the occasional hairpin, past still more broken jalopies and a fig tree, 'neath which to sit on baking hot days for its sumptuous shade, like Nathanael in the Bible. At 12.2 kilometres down the descent, La Tour (603m) is a tiny village with an old people's home. And from here a major disappointment, a cruel deception.

The COL D'ANDRION at 18.2km, 1681m, across the tiniest and narrowest of bridges – a real crossing of no return – from La Tour is a perfect gem: startlingly beautiful, long, very hard – the final 9 or so kilometres hardly falter below 9 and 10% – cutting up into untended woodland and the upper reaches of a hugger-mugger of mountains through some of the wildest areas in the region, for long used by the French military as an elite training ground. There is one thing, one thing only, against the Col d'Andrion: it's a dead-end. The dejection I felt when we got to the top was profound. On the way we passed an inscription on a rock, amongst other scrawled evidence of the erstwhile military presence, which reads: '*NON ACETO SUDORE VICTA RUPES*', a clear reference to Hannibal, 'You do not conquer a cliff with either acid or sweat.' A good enough motto and the allusion is to the Carthaginian's method of breaking through rock falls in the foothills (see Livy): he ordered his soldiers to light and stoke fires to raging heat under the rock and then douse the roasted boulder with cold vinegar. The effect of the chill liquid – which is also a mild acid – on the by now friable rock was to shatter it, perhaps not all at once but by degrees, both of heat and repetition.

From the col, the tarmac leads to the Granges de la Brasque (1687m), 2 kilometres further on, a rather spooky clutch of wooden hutments, most now deserted but one or two showing glimmers of marginal human activity and occupation. Once a military training depot, the huts were latterly occupied as a summer *colonie de vacances* – a holiday camp in the heart of nature for schoolchildren. Now abandoned, the Granges reinforce the air of gloom up here and added to the powerful sense that here was a climb we could not include. For what followed explains why.

The map shows a road, a passable road. The road does not exist. The asphalt fuses with a broad forest track which plunges, I mean *plunges*, off down the mountainside like a manic MTB descender, packed earth for a distance and smooth enough before the trouble starts: a litter of rocks and boulders, cauldron-sized potholes, ruts and furrows, ridges and blisters of extruded mud and… taut hairpins with neither barrier nor side wall.

You know, by now, how intrepid your photographer and I have been when called upon to prove our mettle. We do not seek trouble but neither, in the matter of work and commitment to life in all its manifold richness, do we do problems.

This road was, therefore, ours to negotiate. It was, by now, quickening dusk. Turning back was not an option, for the day's light was fading and, whatever faced us on this side, it was a shorter drop to a likely stopping place for the night. The abiding fear was that the shorter drop might turn out to be the shortest and speediest drop of all – straight over the edge.

It was horrible, no getting away from that, but nerves held and, when the wretched rusticity of that unmade parlous track melded, once more, with asphalt in the outlying suburb of Roquebillière, relief was complete. And in Roquebillière, the Bar des Sports, the only place that looked halfway open and alert to human life that dark evening, may not appear very prepossessing from the outside but its rooms have just been refurbished and are excellent. The welcome is friendly. They do not take credit cards. Le Jardin along the road is a splendid restaurant and there is a fine, well-stocked bookshop close by.

On 24 November 1926, a huge mudslide swept away a large part of Roquebillière-Vieux (the old, original town) at 585m and the village of Belvédère, its neighbour, as well as the tram line between Roquebillière and Saint-Martin-Vésubie up the valley. Landslides and disastrous slippages of rock have destroyed the village six times since the 6th century AD and six times it has been rebuilt, but after the 1926 calamity, which a number of the old houses did survive, the original site was abandoned and Roquebillière was reconstructed in the vicinity of the 15th century church further down the mountain.

The road west from Saint-Martin-Vésubie across to Saint-Sauveur-sur-Tinée at the foot of the long ascent to the Bonette crosses the Col Saint-Martin (1500m), a broad highway, 8 kilometres from Saint-Martin to the pass at gradients of some 5–7%. Off the road in Colmiane, near the col, and just opened is the only *luge d'été* (summer luge run) piste in Europe as well as downhill courses for MTB (VTT – *Vélo Tous Terrain,* 'all-surface bicycle').

Col de la Porte 1057m (Col Saint-Roch 991m)

Northern approach from Lantosque 447m

LENGTH: 14.4KM

HEIGHT GAIN: 610M

MAXIMUM GRADIENT: 8%

From Lantosque, an antique village built on terraces across a ridge, take the D73 towards Loda, overlooking the main valley road which runs parallel to it below on the other bank of the river. At 1km, 425m, a flight of stone steps on the left-hand side-wall begins a walk up the cut of a tributary stream, the Saint Colomban. Somewhere up there lies the Col de Turini.

2km, 470m, quite shaded, a smooth surface, downhill a distance and then climbing once more but at no more than 5% at 3km, 510m. The gorge begins to broaden here opening its arms to the south, to the sun and the balmy sea airs as do we, in surprise and gratitude.

(An early-season bike race near Draguignan, not far away, is called 'the English race' because rain invariably drenches it.)

Past a hairpin at 3.8km, 560m, the trees thin out and afford less shade on a stiffening gradient, around 6.5%. Loda (635m, 5.2km) is a tiny settlement but you would not know it by the solemn grandeur of its church. Out of Loda and down onto a broad sweeping left-hand bend with a low slide of rock accumulated to the left. Painted 'GO' and 'ALLEZ' encourage various names unknown to us but testify to an amateur race or *randonnée* (excursion) using this by-way. In ancient Provençal tradition, there are houses perched in stepped courses all round the hillside of this hanging valley as we scoot further down into a cut of this tributary – the Frace – of the Vésubie.

From 7.2km, 590m, over the Pont de l'Infernet (Provençal, 'a dry place') the confluence of two tributaries and up again at a heavier toll on your legs, 6–8% into a constricted throat of the stream which rides at the col. 9km, 670m, intermittent shade, at 9.4km, into the open. More names daubed and a defiant '*PASSERON*' stencilled here and there. An approximate 'They shall pass' or the Provençal sparrow? 11km, 820m, an auberge and camping *à la ferme*.

An altogether bosky ride now on an aptly rougher surface, sunlight dappled through the trees, languorous bend, 12km, 890m, out from the tree cover and a wooden sign for a walk to La Gabelle [see page 122].

The Col de Porte – '*ALLEZ AURELIE*' in white, '*AURELIEN*' in red, is here called des Portes and a wooden cross surmounts a stone plinth. A 2.5 kilometre drop down to the Col Saint-Roch at a broad meeting of roads: left towards the Col de Turini, right a quiet route back to Nice, and straight on for Lucéram, another alternative for the return to the coast.

From Lucéram (645m) to Saint-Roch

LENGTH: 5.8KM

HEIGHT GAIN: 346M

MAXIMUM GRADIENT: 8%

The short hop from Lucéram to Saint-Roch on the D2566 is twisty and consists of a regular 5–6.5%, easing off on the final stretch to a mild 4%. (The D2566 swings west out of Lucéram.)

Way above the rooftops of Lucéram, a sizeable mediaeval town in a hollow between two ravines, a stop on the Salt Route, the mosaic-tiled cupola of a slim clock-tower announces the 15th century church dedicated to Sainte Marguerite whose symbol is a dragon and whose story a fictitious romance. It might be a minaret, in red, yellow, green, blue, black enamel scales. And, on what were the upper limits of the town, can be seen the bulky remains of the original defensive curtain wall and blockhouse turrets with open galleries

The D21 begins in Lucéram and heads directly north for 10 kilometres to meet the D2656 at La Cabanette heading for the Col de Turini north of the Col Saint-Roch. It's a steep corniche road, nagging at 8% all the way, a dense crotchet-work of hairpins tying off the straights at either end, largely without shade, a series of stone revetments supporting the road in the determined effort to crank it up the side of the *rigole* – what the French call a drainage gutter – between the Cime de Rocaillon to the left and the Cime de Mouréou to the right.

At around 3km, 845m, into the open with a clear view of a col way up to the left, where the shallow sides of two *cimes* (summits) meet in a dip.[30] This is the Col du Savel, lying below the Saint-Roch to the south.

'*NIQUE LA POLICE*' scrawled on a wall (fuck the rozzers – *niquer:* to have coition with). A crucifix watches over the Col Saint-Roch.

There is a 12.6 kilometre steep drop left from Saint-Roch into Coaraze, over the Col du Savel (972m, 1.3km) on a chancy surface, the rock wall hugging the road close most of the way. A tablet set into it proclaims this to be part of La Route du Soleil linking the valleys of the Alpes-Maritimes. In Coaraze, Le Jouncas ('the rush') restaurant serves specially prepared salads and an excellent *myrtille* (bilberry) tart – the crème brûlée with *génépi* (a local liqueur) sounds toothsome, too. Rainbow-hued parakeets twitter in cages, a yappy dog broadcasts its twitchy neurosis on the balcony overhead.

From Coaraze through Bedejun ('good nosh')

and down to Nice: a good, long ride, full of interest – houses, twists and turns, trees, gardens, shrubs. This road, the D15, turns off the D2204 running north-east of Nice towards the Col du Nice (412m) near L'Escarène at La Pointe and makes a good exit into some real altitude and a huge variety of cols on offer in this hinterland of Nice, away from the urban sprawl. A sign reads '*La Forêt est Sacrée*' (the forest is sacred) and so we should and must regard it: no fire, no pollution, no rubbish. La Pointe-de-Contes is where the outreach of the city begins.

30 A *cime* is a cabbage head, then the crown of a tree, then the top of anything, therefore a summit.

COL DE CASTILLON 707M

From Menton, sea level

LENGTH: 15KM

HEIGHT GAIN: 707M

MAXIMUM GRADIENT: 5%

Mentioned en passant as a way into the country behind the coast. This southern approach is the only route for other traffic so its picturesque qualities are slightly marred when four-wheelers bedevil it. However, it's manageable and an arterial favoured by the local cyclists heading for the following clutch of cols above Menton which are, therefore, taken here in combination as a prelude to the Col de Turini.

We met a number of those locals one Sunday in June riding a *cyclosportive* (an amateur long-distance cycling event) the *Cimes du Mercantour,* organized by the Vélo Club de Breil-sur-Royau. (The Mercantour -- which formed part of the Italian royal hunting estates until 1861 – is the mountainous national park established in 1979 and includes the major valleys of the Ubaye and the Verdon.) The route crosses the Cols de Brouis, Castillon, Saint-Jean, Braus, Ablé, Orme, Turini and back over the Brouis. The clubmen and -women were a cheerful crowd. One of them, from Roquebrune (whose club has its own cyclosportive, *La Roquebrunaise*) said to me, through a broad smile, 'Down there, on the coast, you're braking the whole time because of the traffic but up here it's quiet, the roads are empty, the birds are singing.' Amen to that.

COL SAINT-JEAN 642M & COL DE BRAUS 1002M

Ascent via the D2204

LENGTH: 14KM

HEIGHT GAIN: 60M

MAXIMUM GRADIENT: 8%

The D54 turns off from the Col de Castillon, one of those meditational by-roads which so enthuses the man from Roquebrune, around 7 kilometres of easy riding in a tranquil between-wheres. At the nominated col, it turns left onto the D2204 which climbs at a steady 5% for just over 5 kilometres with a motiveless stretch of ill-tempered 8% 2 kilometres from the Col de Braus.

COL DE L'ABLE 1149M & COL DE L'ORME 1005M

Across the Plan Constant

LENGTH: 6.6KM

HEIGHT GAIN: 180M

MAXIMUM GRADIENT: 6%

Rustic away-from-it-all, these two. The road has the beckoning feel of a childhood holiday exploration, roaming off into unknown woods and fields at the carefree risk of getting lost. The gradient is unchallenging, no crankier than 6%, and an oddity: the highest point comes at the Plan Constant (1185m, 4.3km) an open flat area from which the road dips gently for 2.3 kilometres through scrub woodland to the unmarked col and continues its downhill slide to a sweeping right-hand bend on which sits the Orme, also unmarked, although there is a kilometre stone giving the height at 1190m – in contradiction of map and altimeter.

Col de Turini 1607m

From the south-west from l'Escarène 355m

LENGTH: 30.2KM
HEIGHT GAIN: 1252M
MAXIMUM GRADIENT: 8%

The road up the dusty gorge from L'Escarène has little shade, makes 5% for the first 5 kilometres, sees Lucéram coming just after 6km and raises its ante to 6.5 and 7%, gets a feel for the steepness and persists to just past the junction with the Col de l'Orme road, (980m, 11.5km). From here, look up to the *demilune* (crescent-shaped) revetments built to protect the road as it coils in tight hairpins round the arid mountainside. This is a hard-rock climb, exposed, parched, juice-free but sweaty along a balcony that winds up and up like one of those strait and narrow paths round a conical Mount Endurance to heaven in Non-Conformist engravings of the 19th century. Just as we are thinking that here, on this blistering stretch of road at an 8% which nags and nags at the legs seared with effort, there will be used gel packets scattered like torn betting slips at a bookie's counter, a white graffito on the metal barrier reminds us: '*C'EST PLUS FORT QU'EUX.*' So. The road decides, it's stronger than them – *cyclosportives*?

Ledge by ledge it goes, past La Cabanette (1350m, 16.5km) and the beginning of some tree cover, where the road broadens and takes pity, levelling out along a narrow ridge into the winter resort and *station climatique* (spa) of Peïra Cava, formerly a military post, below the eponymous peak. A café and restaurant.

The posting of soldiers hereabouts reminds us of just how fraught life in this region once was, vulnerable to incursion from the east, contrarily as

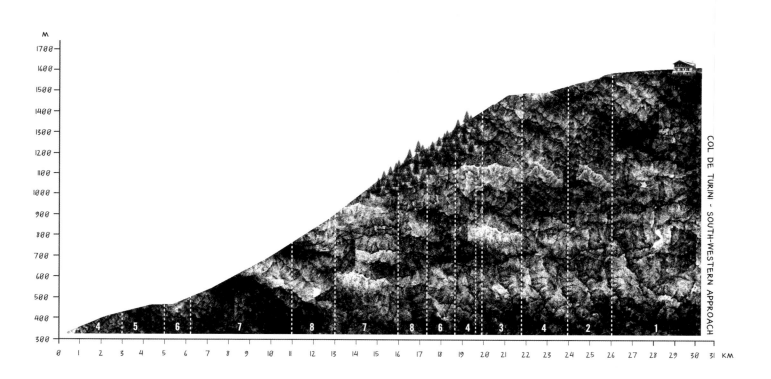

a launch-pad for aggression from within France which, as a united hegemony, had a long gestation. It was the Revolution which finally resolved a number of enduring dissensions by the homogenizing effect of law and an overarching statute book, a unity confirmed – set in stone – by Napoleon's imperial codification.

In 1792, the French revolutionary army overran Savoy and Nice, at that time held by the King of Sardinia. The following year, the Sardinian army backed by an auxiliary corps of Austrians waged a desultory war against the French army of the Alps around Briançon and the army of Italy in the valley of the Var. But in that year, a number of towns along the Midi mounted a determined counter-revolution against the government in Paris and a demoralized and ill-supplied force of 12,000 Republicans under General Brunet, was beaten off by a Sardinian army on the heights above the Turini.

From Peïra Cava (1420m, 18.8km), the road falls away on what ought to be a fast run towards the col, a 2–3% roll through shading trees, but with that undulation which can be murder on tired legs. The door of a small wooden cabin bellows: '*VIVE LES LOUPS MORTS*' (long live – in the singular – dead wolves, in the plural) – an ungrammatical, laboured attempt at bitter wit. The col is a wide blaze of open land, a Restaurant au Chamois to one side, offering a warm welcome to *motards* (motorcyclists).

Western approach from Lantosque 447m

LENGTH: 17.4KM
HEIGHT GAIN: 1160M
MAXIMUM GRADIENT: 9%

After 2 kilometres of no discernible gradient along the verdant valley of the Vésubie, turn off the D2565 onto the D70, noticing a deserted building, once a bar, with its defiant, painted legend above the door fading but still legible: '*MIEUX VAUT BOIRE ICI QU'EN FACE*'. There is no gaol, nor cemetery (the usual reference) nor even rival bar opposite but this now closed estaminet was telling customers it offered a better welcome than any sorry-set establishment over the road.

Now get some real climbing under the wheels. It's a pleasant road, full of movement, as kinked as a much twisted telephone cable, and, out of the small community of La Bollène-Vésubie (780m, 5km), the slopes start to bite and there is a vicious snap of 9% at 8km. It's leafy, a pleasing sense of making height, the encouragement of 'FIREFLIES' daubed on the road in yellow on one hairpin. Founded in 2000, the Fireflies ride the cols for a leukaemia charity and got their name that first year, when the riders were caught on a mountain after dark and made their way safely down the steep descent guided by a succession of fireflies twinkling in the verges of the road, a chain of sparkly glow-worm miniature emergency stud-lights.

Further up, a reminder of another epoch of violence here: a memorial to three young local men who fell heroically on 16 August 1944 in the fighting against the remnants of the German occupation. '*Morts pour la France*', with a cross of Lorraine on the stone.

Buttresses of rock project from the mountainside and, on the upper slopes, the road cuts through woodland, welcome shelter from any sun and some cool for punished leg muscles on the final 5 kilometres of up to 9% to the col.

The Turini has been included in the Tour de France on three occasions: 1948, when Louison Bobet won the 12th stage from San-Remo to Cannes; 1950, when Raphaël Géminiani took the 17th stage from Nice to Gap; and that climactic day on the 1975 Tour out of Nice, at whose conclusion Bernard Thévenet rode past an ailing Eddy Merckx on the final climb to Pra-Loup and into yellow.

Until a few years ago, the Monte Carlo rally crossed the tight switchbacks of the Turini in the dark and the stage was called 'The Night of the Long Knives', prompted by the swishing of the car headlight beams back and forth across the gorge like the thrust and parry of *Star Wars* light sabres.

7. Riviera

The Italian word *Riviera*, 'the sheltered coast of a lake or sea', has been applied to the Mediterranean littoral between La Spezia and Ventimiglia, on the border with France, since the middle ages. (Provençal, in a vowel shift which is quite common, says '*ribiera*'; thus Greek βίος – *bios* becomes Latin *vita*, and so on.) The Italian Riviera is distinct from the French which, to be pedantic, describes that section of the coast between the Italo-French border and the area round Monaco. The Côte d'Azur extends westwards as far as Hyères, close by Toulon, but it extends inland, too. The appellation was coined by Stéphen Liégeard, a minor poet (1830–1925) in a book with that title published in Paris in 1888. It is said that, after gazing out over the sea in Hyères, he was irritated by the way the English bandied 'French Riviera' about as if the entire coast belonged to them, and wrote: '. . . from this beach, bathed in the sun's rays, I baptize it, deservedly, Côte d'Azur' (from the deep blue, azure, of the marine waters). It is suggested that he coined the phrase on the analogy of Côte d'Or, the department in which he was born, in Dijon, which is nowhere near the sea but is famous for mustard the hue of old gold.

When the English milords and toffs arrived on the southern French coast, drawn by the sun and, more pertinently, the casinos – gambling was illegal in England – they began to refer to the 'French Riviera'. Little they knew of geographical division. Other chancers arrived, too, men without private income – imagine – almost certainly frowned on by the upper crust, not quite strawberry leaf, don't you know? Like the man who 'to Monte Carlo went just to raise my winter's rent'. Dame Fortune smiles. 'And now I've such lots of money I'm a gent.' He returns to Paris and:

As I walk along the Bois Boulong
With an independent air,
You can hear the girls declare
'He must be a millionaire.'
You can hear them sigh and wish to die

You can see them wink the other eye
At the man who broke the bank at Monte Carlo.

This part of the French south coast was colonised by Greek merchants from the 7th century BC. They set up entrepôts round the Bouches-du-Rhône, estuary of the great trading route into the heart of the Celtic princedoms, at Olbia (Saint-Pierre de l'Almanare near Hyères), Massalia (Marseille), Antipolis (Antibes) and Nicoea (Nice). This commercial stimulus was fundamental to the evolution of the Celtic La Tène culture, a wonderful flowering of craft, particularly in the working of bronze, iron and gold – jewellery, vessels, adornment, tools and weapons. Whether it was these early Greek settlers who introduced the olive or the later Romans is open to question, but the Romans certainly traded in olive oil as well as pottery and wine. (The Roman definition of a barbarian is often cited as being someone who eats butter, not oil, and wears trousers which, the knee-length short trews of the legionaries apart, the Romans considered very below the salt.)

Our nomenclature then is, in the precise sense, off-beam, but, stretching the point, *Riviera* has a seductive chime to it and may be jobbed in to embrace both Italian and French sides of the littoral. The climbs do probe a certain distance inland but we have confined them to the immediate hinterland of the starting points of our rides: San Remo to the east, destination of one of the great classic one-day races, Menton, Villafranca, Nice, Cagnes-sur-Mer and Mont Faron to the west, which scrapes in *just* to the definition of Côte d'Azur and what the English idle rich lumped in with their 'French Riviera'.

Be aware that even on this coast, the sun does not always shine and that snow may fall in late autumn, even a few kilometres inland from San Remo.

✧ RIVIERA ✧

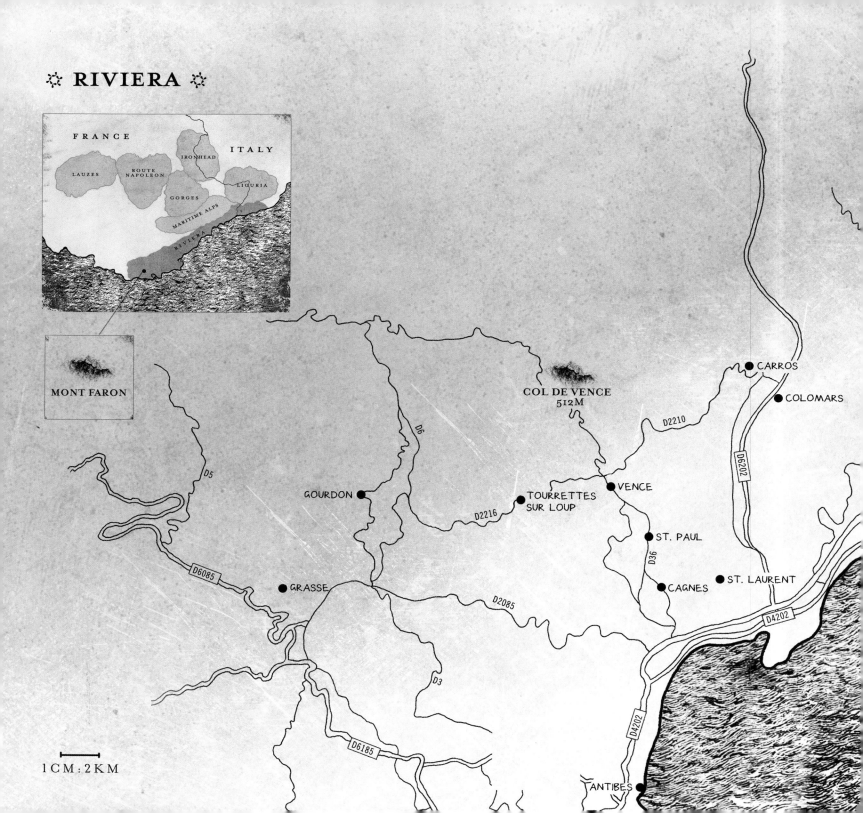

FRANCE

ITALY

LAUZES

ROUTE
NAPOLEON

IRONHEAD

LIGURIA

GORGES

MARITIME ALPS

RIVIERA

MONT FARON

CARROS

COLOMARS

COL DE VENCE
512M

D2210

D6

D6202

D5

GOURDON

VENCE

D2216

TOURRETTES
SUR LOUP

ST. PAUL

D36

ST. LAURENT

D6085

CAGNES

GRASSE

D2085

D4202

D3

D6185

D4202

ANTIBES

1 CM : 2 KM

POGGIO 150M

The ascent from the east

LENGTH: 2.5KM	
HEIGHT GAIN: 100M	
MAXIMUM GRADIENT: 6%	

In the north-westerly Italian province of Liguria alone there are four locales named Poggio, another called Poggio Favaro as well as a Poggialto and a Poggi but, to the racing cyclist and the clued-up amateur aficionado both, there is only one worth mention: *the* Poggio, outside San Remo. The name simply means 'hill', related to Provençal *puy* and Catalan *puig*. *The* Poggio owes its celebrity to its inclusion, since 1960, in the Milan–San Remo, 'La Primavera', the Spring classic, longest of them all – around 300 kilometres – inaugurated in 1907. Lucien Petit-Breton won that debut ahead of the first of his two consecutive victories in the Tour de France later that same year.

This Poggio, a suburb of San Remo, 5 kilometres to the east above the coast road, rounds off a leg-sapping roller-coaster of five minor hills along the coast: Capo Mele (65m) at 244km, 51.9 kilometres to the race finish, Capo Cervo-Mimosa (77m) at 46 kilometres, Capo Berta (130m) at 39 kilometres, Capo Cipressa (240m) at 21 kilometres, Capo Verde (45m) at 9 kilometres. The Poggio was added to this string of tormentors to make the race harder for sprinters looking to tuck in with the bunch ready to break clear for the final scrap on the Via Roma. However, the fact that sprinters have dominated the podium in recent years – Erik Zabel (four times), Mario Cipollini, Oscar Freire (twice), Paolo Bettini, Alessandro Petacchi – suggests that the Milan–San Remo preserves its core nature: a contest for galvanized-iron *rouleurs* (literally 'riders who roll' like the ball in the roulette wheel) with strength, endurance and finishing speed *and* Italian fast men,

(with willing teams), who thirst for this grand seafront showcase win on home turf.

Raymond Poulidor took his first big win as a professional – beating 'The Emperor of Herentals' Rik Van Looy, no less – in 1961, by (he said) changing up to a high gear just below the brow of the Poggio and kicking for home. The man who, with a ready grin, became the darling of the crowd, arrived on the Via Roma sunk in an unfamiliar privacy: no smile, eyes shut, spent, locked in relief and incredulity. Brian Robinson was robbed here in 1957, when, on a winning lead, he was told to sit up and hand victory to his team leader, Miguel Poblet. Sean Kelly won here twice but kept his big early-season effort for the Race to the Sun, the Paris–Nice, which he won seven times, and seven times is Eddy Merckx's all-time record for the Milan–San Remo, in the days when a big win at the start of the year ensured fat contracts through to its end. I saw Merckx winning his last Primavera in 1976, on a black and white television. He attacked again and again on the sinuous descent of the Poggio, got caught, attacked the very instant the bunch clawed back to his wheel, a sudden furious burst of speed until they were too weak or depressed to follow any more and he raced clear onto the Via Roma, alone once more, across the line right arm aloft, his face alight with joy.

The organizers of the 1968 Giro d'Italia used the Poggio for the 5th stage –149 kilometres, a kind of circuit of San Remo but climbed in the opposite direction from the Milan–San Remo, that is west to east. The stage was won by the Torinese Italo Zilioli, who beat second-placed Eddy Merckx by four seconds. Merckx wasn't unduly alarmed though. He'd put over two minutes into the likes of Gianni Motta (the 1966 winner), Felice Gimondi (winner in 1967), Franco Balmamion (laureate in 1962 and

'63). He'd already won two stages, and the response of Tuttosport (a sports news agency), somewhat hysterical, certainly premature, was that Zilioli had 'rescued the Giro' from the Belgian's stranglehold. In fact Merckx went on to dominate this, the first of his subsequent five wins of the Italian Grand Tour. However, no Italian had won Milan–San Remo since Loretto Petrucci in 1953, so it was heartening for the home crowd to see an Italian on the podium in the famous cycling mecca.

That descent is a real facer: a drop of some 150 metres in 3 kilometres, a narrow road crimped round wickedly sharp hairpins. There is no space for tactics. Laurent Fignon, who won the race twice, said he rode for 250 kilometres at the tail of the bunch, saving his final effort for the Poggio.

Consider this as a Riviera club hill climb, a brisk dash off the main coastal strip of the Riva Ligure. Cicero described the ancient Ligurians as 'mountain-men, tough and coarse', Cato said they were a breed of shysters. Take your pick: hard men at the head of the bunch or opportunists biding their time *in* the bunch.

The climb winds on an open road past curtain walls spilling flowers, cultivated terraces, fruit trees, long views of the sea and the marina, rows and rows of greenhouses, some in sorry disrepair, thistles sprouting through the broken, grubby panes. At 40m of height, around 0.5km, a curious tarmac graffito, the stencilled outline of a jousting knight on a bike with the legend PETA, who was the Roman goddess of prayer and entreaty, but may (of course) be short for Petacchi (which means 'bomb ketches'). Either way, you may pray that you don't explode as the gradient tightens at around 1.6km up to the intermediate suburb of Bussona and the cypress and cedar-shaded Santuario Madonna della Guardia set back off the road.

The last 500 metres into Poggio itself – the tiny town plonked atop the hill – has been marked on the road by a helpful dauber. From here you launch onto the sharp hairpins and, perhaps, think yourself into the hectic oblivion of the pros who are still in the hunt, caution tossed to the still air. It's a jinking dash down to the tiny spout of road which shoots them past the bar and *tabacchi e sale* (salt) at the bottom, through a funnel of houses, the municipal soccer pitch and the riotous rococo edifice of the Villa Nobel to the left and out onto the road on the outskirts which shortly fuses into the famous Via Roma. The race doesn't always finish there now, but its essential spirit must, surely, hover around it still.

Passo Ghimbegna 898m

North from sea level at San Remo

LENGTH: 19KM	
HEIGHT GAIN: 898M	
MAXIMUM GRADIENT: 8%	

Head north out of central San Remo from Piazza Colombo – on Saturdays a bustling market place – across a smaller piazza, Largo Volta, onto Via San Francesco Massa (a bike shop on the right a short way along). Continue on a winding, steep road towards the Santuario Nostra Signora della Costa and on past it towards San Romolo. This is Saint Romulus of Genoa whose name, in Ligurian, is Roemu. Thus the eponymous saint, who lived and died in a cave nearby, is celebrated both at sea level and altitude.

The road twists and turns through the upper suburbs at an impatient sharp incline as if wriggling feverishly to be free of houses, shops, cramped tenements, nodding dutifully at the iced-caked edifice which is the Santuario de Madonna della Costa and eventually breaking clear of urban and ecclesiastical excrescences around 3km, 200m. However, there is a hidden gem to be found here: the old walled village of La Pigna, the quiet mediaeval corner of San Remo old town. Built and fortified by the inhabitants of San Remo in the early Middle Ages as a refuge from piratical Saracen raids, it's still perfectly preserved: a warren of tiny squares, terraces, covered alleys and crinkum-crankum, narrow cobbled streets, some overhung by the lower storeys of the tight-packed houses. Outside one doorway, a bike chained up, surely the least practical of modes of transport in this quarter. *Pina* means 'pine cone' and *pigna*, 'a cone-shaped ornament'. The construction of La Pigna, curling round the hill above the city, recalls both.

In the Piazza dei Dolori (The Place of Sorrows) stands a balconied house, marked with a heraldic shield, once the palace of the Podestà (from Latin *potestas*, 'power'), the town mayor, appointed by the state government. From San Giacomom (240m, 3.6km), a grand view of the city below opens out although the onion dome of San Basilio, the extravagantly ornamented Russian Orthodox church – built by the Russian community in 1912 – near the seafront isn't, alas, visible. (Opposite it, there is a very helpful Tourist Office whose personnel will phone a hotel for you and book on the spot.)

On, past the Santuario and through the upper suburbs of north San Remo. At 7.4km this most delightful balcony of a road overlooking the waters of the Mediterranean noses into greenery, trees, shrubs, flora silvana, and then flattens out for a short breather into a string of small communities: San Borello (615m), Bevino (720m), San Romolo (800m), each, apparently, jealous of its discrete identity. No civic homogenisation up here.

This is fine riding: rural seclusion, bursts of wide open sky, a sudden slide down through woodland on a rougher road at 5.2km, 1040m, and at 7km, 1000m… *funghi* country. Tall and gangly sweet chestnuts with fertile mulch around their toes, spore-beds of the sought-after *porcini* mushrooms, known to us as penny bun or king bolete. A shady glade, the road snaking through, *castagne* (chestnuts), a musty fragrance and tasty *porcini*… essential filaments in the gastronomic core of Italy.

At the bottom of this descent a crossroads marks the unsigned Passo Ghimbegna, left to Baiardo, right for back to the coast, straight on towards Vignai (no vines in evidence now) along a road squeezing itself between the gauntlet of trees before emerging into the open with a broad view of the densely wooded valley back coastwards. It climbs gently and on into coppices of spindly limes and sweet chestnut and, at about 3 kilometres from the crossroads, a left turn goes off to Carmo Langan, climbing steadily to some 1470m at 11.2km when the descent begins at between 5 and 9% with San Giovanni del Prats ('Saint John of the Meadows') at 14.9km, 1250m… a house and a church.

Colle Termini di Baiardo 950m

Southern approach from Capo Nero 45m

LENGTH: 21.2KM	
HEIGHT GAIN: 905M	
MAXIMUM GRADIENT: 7.5%	

Just below San Romolo, where the road takes its right turn to Baiardo (at 716m) and the Ghimbegna, turn left towards Perinaldo and a bare 3.5 kilometres to the Colle Termini di Baiardo, which lies on the far side of a short tunnel. [This conical hill was sacred to the Celto-Ligurians. See LIGURIA.] Just before it, in a picnic area, an information board speaks of *ilex* (the evergreen oak), *populus tremula* (*le tremble* in French, our aspen), *ilex aquifolium* (holly), *roverella* (dwarf oak? *Rovere,* fr. *robur,* is common oak), *quercus pubescens*. This last, typical of the low mountains behind the Mediterranean littoral, has a similar wide distribution in the dry, chalky soil as that of the vine and favours warm, sunny slopes. It owes its name – which might be translated 'teenage oak' – to the downy flock ('bum-fluff') which covers its young branches and the underneath of its leaves. Pubescent oaks are similar to the marcescent oak whose leaves do not fall in autumn but wither to dry brown on the twig and drop only in spring, perhaps from embarrassment at the bonny show of sprouting green shoots all around. The wood of the pubescent is not much good for working but its roots encourage a mulch beloved of the precious truffle and you will see truffle hounds in this neck of the woods. There are, too, raptors – Peregrine falcon, Royal or Golden Eagle, buzzard, (*buteo buteo*) and it must surely be the dream of any cyclist panting to the end of a long, arduous climb to have the strength to rise up as on eagles' wings. Another illustration helpfully depicts the '*escrementi mammiferi*' for the discerning wild-lifer who wishes to marry spoor to droppings: *capriolo* (roe deer), *volpe* (fox), *tasso* (badger), *faina* (marten), *cinghiale* (wild boar), *riccio* (hedgehog).[31]

The descent from the Baiardo towards Capo Nero, a promontory at the west end of San Remo's limits, is notable for the wonderful views of the city, the bay and the marina which soon open out in the wide vista beyond your front wheel. To start the descent, retrace the way back to the junction near San Romolo and turn right towards Gozzo and Coldirodi. Starting through close woodland, the road takes a kilometre or two to settle into its rhythm on a flattish gradient and then, emerging into the open round 850m it begins a long, winding drop to the coast. It also, of course, makes an alternative to the easterly route out of San Remo. For a longer circuit from the Baiardo, continue straight on west from the col towards Perinaldo and the long Valle Nervia which slices through the ranges bordering France, wherein sits Dolceacqua below the Colle di Langan [see LIGURIA].

At the lower end of the more direct route due south to the sea and the intestinal twisty worm of hairpins leading to the Capo Nero, below Coldirodi, someone has painted in large letters on a wall '*BIANCHI BASTA*' (white enough). The *tifosi*, you must know, are nothing if not fervent in their rivalries… the Italian word is applied to someone suffering from typhus fever.

Along the coast road west from Capo Nero, there is a bike shop in Ospedaletti's main drag.

Southern approach from Capo Nero 45m

LENGTH: 21.2KM	
HEIGHT GAIN: 905M	
MAXIMUM GRADIENT: 7.5%	

Take the SP80 towards Coldirodi (5km) and when you get there turn round and drink in the glorious panorama of the pearl of the western Riviera. Two kilometres further on, at a hairpin, a junction with a road from Ospedaletti, continue right and another junction (222m, 8.3km) with a road back down to San Remo. Two more kilometres further on at 245m, the gradient begins to tighten and between 12.5km and 18km the slope bites hard with a remorseless grip of between 7 and 7.5%, finally evening out for the run-in.

Recommended tour: a counter-clockwise loop out of and back to San Remo.

LENGTH: 87.5KM	
OVERALL HEIGHT GAIN: 1955M	

From Capo Nero through Coldirodi and on to San Romolo (847m, 21.3km) left to Perinaldo (566m, 27km) and on to Apricale (273m, 38km) and Isolabona (108m, 40km). Northwards to Pigna (288m, 48.8km), Castelvittorio (389m, 51.5km) and the hilltop village of Baiardo brooding over the Passo Ghimbegna (898m, 63.5km). Take the SP55 to Ceriana (308m, 71.7km). The road levels out for some 4 kilometres and then climbs up into Poggio di San Remo (162m, 81km) from which the drop down to the Via Aurelia, the coast road, 84.5km, and the fast bowl into town.[32]

---

31 In San Romolo you may find one of the largest chestnut trees in Europe, dating from around 1200 AD, nearly six metres in diameter.

32 The hinterland of San Remo aches to be explored and this account can give but a taster of the cornucopia on offer. Supply yourself with a Carta dei Sentieri e dei Rifugi, issued by the Istituo Geografico Centrale, (IGC), scale 1cm = 500m, number 14.

COL DE LA MADONE 927M

North from Menton

LENGTH: 13.8KM

HEIGHT GAIN: 927M

MAXIMUM GRADIENT: 11%

This was Lance Armstrong's favourite training ride when he lived in Menton.

The coastal town, sheltered by a semicircular screen of mountains from the Mistral and reputed for its oranges, lemons and olives, seems to have paid protection money to the Counts of Ventimiglia in their walled *castello* on the Italian Riviera a few kilometres to the east before the end of the 10th century, until the Genoese families intervened in the 12th century. Genoa in the middle ages? Think New Jersey, think Sopranos. In 1364, at the climax of the continuing turf war in the prosperous mercantile port, Carlo Grimaldi, *capo di capi* of the Guelphs, (pro-Pope), one of two big Genoese families, moved in on the Ghibellines, (pro-Emperor), holed up on

the mattresses in Monaco, just along the coast, and made them an offer they couldn't refuse. Kissing the old town and the stinking portside streets goodbye, the Grimaldi family moved their end of the vendetta and Genoa business to the fastnesses of Monaco and Menton from where his soldiers could see the opposition coming a long, long way off. It may have been one of their 18th-century-made men who summed up the way of things: '*Son Monaco sopr'un scoglio, non semino, e non ricoglio, eppure mangiar voglio*' (I'm on a rock, I'm Monaco, I don't harvest and I don't sow but I... don't... starve).

According to the English writer Augustus Hare, by 1890 Menton's two bays had already 'filled with hideous and stuccoed villas in the worst taste... pretentious paved promenades have taken the place of the beautiful walks under tamarisk groves by the shore. Artistically, Menton is vulgarised and ruined...' William Webb Ellis, the Rugby schoolboy who, famously, during a football game 'picked up the

ball and ran with it', is buried in Menton. Gracious the town may not be to some eyes, but there are palm trees, sea breezes and a sort of melancholy grandeur, still.

Along the coast road towards the west end of town, near Cap Martin, find the Hôtel Impérial and turn off on the D23 towards Sainte-Agnès and Serres de la Madone.

The first kilometre of the climb from sea level, up through the town limits, is a scorcher, 11%, levelling out onto a ledge and right towards Sainte Agnès to a more manageable fluctuating gradient, 3–7%. Houses built on terraced ledges in what is a near perpendicular slope below the road and costly slices of real estate cut in terraces for the view and the postal address. Even 5.1 kilometres on, the road is still trying to shake off the scrub end of the above-town development, decidedly a stretch of tarmac that has grown used to riders, some of them famous, in anonymous training gear, pounding

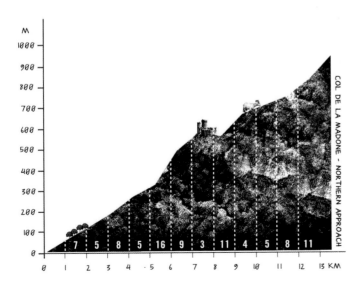

the kilometrage over and over and over again with scant regard for surroundings or anything much but heart-rate monitor read-out and time intervals. Tight hairpins signal the crank of gradient, too, around 8% to 6km where a low parapet wall marks the beginning of something more identifiable in the way of scenic interest – a view of the sea and the town – as the stone slabs of the cliff to the right burst out of their green leaf cloak like an expanding chest popping the buttons of a too-tight, pigeon-breast, Italian-cut shirt.

The road narrows at 6.6km and stays that way, maintaining its 8%. At 7.2km appears a crag with castle atop it, looming over the small town of Sainte-Agnès. Sharp right turn into town, very sharp left on to the col where the metalled strip gets the feel of untrimmed limestone, ploughing upwards, as it does, to the picturesque nowhere, an exposed ledge hewn out of the mountainside... a nice enough metaphor for will-power.

A short way on, look down over Sainte-Agnès: she died for her faith, which is too much to ask of any cyclist, even the most dedicated. Just up ahead, the ridge juts out like a chin in the direction of Cap Martin. Now, *menton* as you must know, means 'chin', and the French for a slap-up feed is 'getting stuck in up to your chin' so, if that doesn't have enough resonance for you as you ride up the Col de la Madone with thoughts of your reward, I don't know what will.

At 10km, 660m (the sign reads 695m though I feel obliged to say that my altimeter is not, by nature, quarrelsome but a most obedient item), a further stretch of this stony ledge leads into a short tunnel (10.5km) through which, occasionally, will skitter a large flock of goats. Gentians grow in the wayside rocks but if you have not yet observed plush blue-purple gentians in these hills you have not been

paying attention. Now, any goat will eat a gentian if it is not chivvied by the goatherd – I've seen the giddy critturs at it – but, then, any goat left to itself will eat pretty well anything.

Another tunnel at 10.7km where the road squeezes in awful tight like a leg into one half of drainpipe jeans and at 11km, 725m, a doorway in a wall to the right gives onto a room, whose dark and moist interior may once have had an express use but is now a fly tip: cables, car seat, junk.... From 12.4km, 820m, the shallow V of the col appears, off to the left at 11 o'clock (viz. military style of targeting) and at 13km, a wee bothy to the right probably does service of an electrical nature. Feel the pulse, feel the surge, there is but 800 metres to go.

It's a bleak enough col with hazy views way over north to the Pic de Baudon and its hinterland of neighbouring cols and south to the roulette coast, the Côte d'Azur... which puts me in mind of the vélodrôme and the flat zone of blue at the foot of the banking. It was the austere theologian Pascal who dwelt much on probabilities and may be said to have invented the ultimate game of chance, *roulette*. That was the word he coined for the making of a cycloid curve. Imagine a fixed spot on a wheel rolling along a flat surface: the arc described by that fixed point – think of a shallow dome – is the cycloid curve. Thus the bike circling the track may be seen as a ball spinning round the big, notional roulette wheel of the track. Does not the croupier spin the wheel clockwise and send in the ball anti-clockwise?

From the col, a snaky drop for 1.4 kilometres at around 6% into a sharp left-hand bend followed by a tunnel. The road ahead is nicely visible, skating along the slopes of this noted maritime alp. Is that a concrete works down there? A foul blot on landscape, whatever it is. There are more tunnels but they are short and pose no obstacle on this raw

stone road with its selvage of sunken boulders. A flying descent, for sure, and the occasional sharp hairpins come with plenty of warning. At 3km, around 700m, a couple of big hairpins, left and right, lead onto a smoother surface and at 3.7km, 660m, the junction with the D53 and a sign offering Saint Pancrace. The D22 drops on towards La Turbie.

Since this littoral was first colonised by Greeks, I hope that this Saint Pancras is he of Taormina in Sicily, venerated by the Orthodox Church, not his namesake of Rome, about whom nothing is known, save his curious attachment to a large railway station in London. The Sicilian – see introduction to Menton, above – Pancrazio, is the patron saint of jobs and is partial to parsley. Greeks decked tombs with parsley because it stays green a long time.

There is a shrine to San Pancrazio above Ventimiglia and the Counts of Ventimiglia held Menton until it passed – ha ha, euphemism – to the Genoese. Pancrace is one of three saints - namely Saints Mamert, Pancrace and Servais - known to the French as *saints de glace*, 'ice saints', from that period of their festal days 12–14 May, when there is often a sudden drop in temperature. A very ancient and clearly dotty tradition. So that rounds off the story of this Col de la Madone nicely. As for its dedication to the Madonna, you will know from the earlier volume on the Pyrenees that she gets absolutely everywhere.

Col d'Eze 512m

From Nice, sea level

LENGTH: 9.2KM	
HEIGHT GAIN: 512M	
MAXIMUM GRADIENT: 11%	

The Col d'Eze overlooks the French Riviera from La Grande Corniche (literally, 'the great high coast road') and, though of no great height, has its niche in professional cycle racing as an uphill sprint – there's no other way to ride so short a hill – in the Paris–Nice, for instance. There are other approaches to it other than from Nice, notably, east of Nice from Beaulieu-sur-Mer or from near the Cap d'Ail, through the village of Eze. Either of those rides up from the sea to the Corniche is what mountaineers would call severe, I mean, severe: short and horrendously steep, so these unnamed killers deserve consideration if not description.

Head north out of Nice from sea level in its eastern quarter along the Boulevard de l'Armée des Alpes and turn right onto the road to La Grande Corniche and Observatoire de Nice, MONACO and MENTON (there is a signpost) opposite the Avenue des Diables Bleus. [For *Les Diables Bleus*, see the description of the Bonette/Restefond in IRONHEAD, page 53.]

At the foot of the climb, set into a marly wall on the right of the road, are memorial plaques to '*ELLIOTT ZBOROWOSKI décédé à cet endroit le 1 Avril 1903*' (killed here on 1 April 1903) and '*Notre camarade WILHELM BAUER 30 mars 1900 CAN*' (which is Club Automobile de Nice). Both men were motor racers. The contemporary fad was for racing cars up hills and mountains often attended, as here, with disastrous, if not fatal, mishap. [Mont Ventoux was a celebrated uphill speed challenge, see that description in LAUZES.]

The first ramp, clawing its way out of Nice for some 2 kilometres, is hard, very steep indeed, the surface hacked a bit, the buildings to either side dusty, shabby and neglected. At 1.2km, the view opens to the left by an old pension, all on its own, a fine building lost to its past, its paintwork faded, its doors and windows asleep. Palms and shrubs overhang the long wall to the right, cypresses and olive trees line the route past the dwindling presence of houses and a few shops. At 2.9km, pines muscle in and we pass the hotel La Forêt and, when we were there, an over-geared cyclist. At 3.4km the road flattens and dives mildly along a cornice. Around 4.5km what might be a Hollywood Gothic mansion, angular, turreted, overblown, its walls striped with red and terracotta horizontal bands in a lurid display of poor taste. The gradient over the next 2 kilometres is pretty lenient. At 5.5km the D33 from Villefranche feeds in – a real horror to climb, that one – and the gradient stiffens as if in answer to what the immediate competition has to offer. The D3 at 6.3km shoots down (right) to Eze village, another stinker. (Friedrich Nietzsche, the German philosopher and regular good-time guy, enjoyed trotting down this road to the beach below Eze in the course of many summers he spent here. 'Is not,' he wrote 'life a hundred times too short for us to bore ourselves?')

For some way, *borne* stones mark the 0.5km intervals. A bit further on, the sky pulls out to reveal a wide, long view of the coast below: the bays, the marinas, the luxury boats and yachts, the cruise liners at anchor, Cap-Ferrat and the small peninsula enclave of Saint-Jean-Cap-Ferrat – Somerset Maugham's home till his death in 1965 – and Villefranche, known as Villafranca, 'free town'. (Charles d'Anjou, Count of Provence, founded it in the early 14th century and accorded it commercial privileges in keeping with its royal pedigree. Anjou being way up in the north-west of France, this gives some indication of how widely patronage was distributed and what clout the Counts of Provence enjoyed.) From here, see, too, the road curling slantwise round the cliffside way ahead and on down to the right towards Monaco. At 9.2km the road dips away to the col. There is no sign and one wonders why the slightly lower ground should claim the site of the col, unless it be that this stretch looks more like a neck between two haunches of rising ground. Here, set back from the road and a sweeping dirt lay-by, is a hotel, the Hermitage du Col d'Eze, with violet shutters and walls the yellow of mango fruit. A grove close by of *pin à crochets* (mountain pines), and, next to the hotel, a small tranquillity of palm trees, pampas grass and lissom cypress trees, usually heralds of a graveyard... 'Come away, come away, Death, and in sad cypress let me be laid...' (*Twelfth Night* Act II, sc. iv)

Mont Bastide, the low height to the south of the col, was first a Celto-Ligurian town and later a Roman legionary camp.

Col de l'Ecre 1106m

Southern approach from Pré-du-Lac 400m

I was sitting at lunch in Saint-Vallier-de-Thiey one sunny afternoon in August, a pleasant little town on the Route Napoléon – craft shop, town museum in an upstairs room behind the church, several bars and the alfresco restaurant by a broad sward of grass, when two cyclists pulled up, propped their machines against a tree and called for ice cream. I gave them time to cool their palette and then strolled over and engaged them in conversation. This does not always bear dividends. Your cyclist is an unpredictable creature, caught on the hop by someone who does not obviously look like one of their breed *and* my shorts were of the casual rather than close-fit variety. The response may be one of suspicion or monosyllabic caution. However, my accent is good, my unassuming demeanour seemed to strike a chord and the male of the couple did not interpret my accosting them as a brazen act of flirtation with his squeeze. It wasn't, but there's never any telling. Suffice it, then, to say that they told me about the Route Napoléon [see that sector] *and* pointed me towards the Col de l'Ecre, a favourite amongst cyclists whose regular rides criss-cross the hinterland of the Côte d'Azur. They looked quite well on it and there's no substitute for local knowledge.

Along D3

LENGTH: 14.5KM	
HEIGHT GAIN: 706M	
MAXIMUM GRADIENT: 13%	

A splendid ride up to a viewing point (c 500m, 1.6km) over some fairly stiff gradient and following the course of a stream, the Combe, till it and the road diverge at around 3.2km, 625m, then on through the Bois de Gourdon up to the tiny village of Gourdon itself (758m), perched on what must seem, to anyone unfamiliar with Provençal domestic architecture, to be not a very promising site for so much as a house let alone a clutch of them and, to boot, a castle, originally a Saracen fort, 9th–12th centuries, enlarged and modernized in the 13th century by its new Provençal owners and completely rebuilt again in 1610. Tourist shops, perfumes and hand-blown glass, painting on silk, polished stones, gingerbread, local fabrics etc. – a regular bazaar.

The climb from Gourdon on the D12 is exposed, running like a sloping gallery in a mine, cut into the living rock, a long pull of 6.5 kilometres, a steady 6%, best done in the autumn when the sun, often ferocious in these parts, is milder of joule.

The summit (no ceremony) comes at a sharp left-hand bend where the dead-end to the hamlet of l'Ecre joins the road. Better to turn left just before that on a narrow bucolic road, strictly a *chemin*, to Les Claps (signed hereabouts as Le Clap, which is Provençal for '*éclat de pierre, blocaille, têt*' – splinter of stone, stone-fall, a fired clay pot). This *chemin* cuts across the stony Plateau de Caussols and is a delight. The air is filled with the fragrance of resin exuded by the budding cones of *pins à crochets*, the plateau is open, stones and boulders dot the arid earth, the trees stand shyly apart and halfway across, away from the road, a curious round building with conical roof (familiar in mountainous areas across France, the summer hut of shepherds, in Provence a *bòri*: the neat corbelling requires no timbers and some *boris* are fine indeed, like large dovecotes, constructed with expertly interleaved thin stones, their rooftop sometimes capped with a stone cone and ball finial. This rather delicate example of the genre has had a lower collar added). Wild lavender grows. Hang-glider aficionados hurl themselves, willy-nilly, off the nearby cliffs.

The *chemin* rejoins the D12 which continues across a broad expanse of pastureland south over the Col de Ferrier into the excellent lunch-stop in Saint-Vallier.

By way of Pont-du-Loup and the Gorges du Loup

LENGTH: 26.5 KM	
HEIGHT GAIN: 706M	
MAXIMUM GRADIENT: 9%	

The Loup River rises on the north side of the Montagne de l'Audibergue along whose southern flanks runs the Route Napoléon. It flows eastwards in the loom of Le Gros Pounch round the lower fringes of the Plateau de Calern atop which sits the CERGA observatory. (The Centre d'Etudes et de Recherches Géodynamiques et Astronomiques carries out specialised research in measuring movements of the Earth and the development of astronomical instruments.) In the vicinity of Cipières it swings south and, some 5 kilometres on, begins the cut of the great cleft which makes the Gorges, a tightly enclosed ravine notable for a series of spectacular cascades. The upper Gorges stretch for some 5 kilometres to Pont-sur-Loup and continue through the less impressive lower Gorges to the sea at Bouches-du-Loup near Cagnes-sur-Mer.

From Pré-du-Lac (400m), 6.5 kilometres on the D2210 down to Pont-du-Loup (197m) and into the ravine, a magical enclosed way, a green and pale light dappled tree-lined tunnel with flittering leaf skylights and a hieroglyphic of solar scribble on the road beneath your wheels, climbing, climbing, not knowing quite where you are, pushing forever on and the closeness of the rock to one side, the river to the other and the chutes of water tumbling and sheeting in cool jets down the side of the ravine at the Cascade de Courmes, Cascade des Demoiselles and Saut-du-Loup in quick succession (around 371m at 3.7–4km from Pont-du-Loup). The lacework of fronds and leaf immediately close overhead on the road make this a very intimate gorge, a beautiful ride. The gradient hovers round 6% with blips of 3-4.5%.

At the bridge at Bramafan (470m, 5.5km) turn left onto the D3 and 5 kilometres up the ramp on the other side of the gorge to Gourdon.

Mont Faron 584m

From Toulon 14m

LENGTH: 5.5KM

HEIGHT GAIN: 570M

MAXIMUM GRADIENT: 11.4%

Head north from Toulon on the D46 into Les Moulins, D46, and at a traffic lights, turn right onto the Avenue des Moulins, then left onto Chemin du Fort Rouge, climbing all the way, on a twisty road through the upper suburbs. Note, as you go, a house called AMNESIA – its number is 768, that is the number of metres along the road from the start point [see earlier]. Here spreads out your first view of the great harbour and port of Toulon, France's principal naval base. The peninsula of Saint-Mandrier projects eastwards from the larger promontory of Cap Sicié – a good ride up there to a wonderful vista from the high point at Notre-Dame du Mai – to form the haven. Early in the French Revolution, Toulon, in revolt against the regime in Paris, remained loyal to the royalist cause and handed the harbour over to ships of the British navy commanded by Admiral Hood. There followed a three-month siege by the Republican army. It was ended after the 24-year-old Napoleon Bonaparte, a junior artillery officer, directed his fire so accurately and with such effect that the ring of forts, including that on Mont Faron, fell to the besiegers and Hood was compelled to withdraw his fleet. Two sanguinary men on mission from the Convention (parliament) in Paris then subjected Toulon and its citizens to savage reprisal for their treachery.

Toulon was bombed by the Italians in 1940 and in November 1942, 60 ships of the French Mediterranean fleet were scuttled to prevent them from being taken by the Germans. In August 1944, battalions of shock troops swarmed up the slopes of Mont Faron and, after fierce fighting, eventually drove the Germans off this prime defensive position on 22 August. They came back and the bloody tussle went on for another month. At last, French forces under General Lattre de Tassigny took the city and 18,000 Germans were captured.

From Amnesia, into overhanging spindly pines and along the Chemin du Fort Rouge. At 1.2km a T-junction: right to Centre Ville, left to Mont Faron on a wider road which suddenly narrows dramatically into a big right hand bend, 'MONT FARON 5km' painted in pale green on the tarmac. At around 2km, a walker's piste to the right and a big left-hand hairpin reveals a mighty panorama of the sea roads of Toulon, the dockside installations, the vast expanse of the harbour, the inner quays, the shipping in the lanes.

The map reads Route du Faron but this road is called Chemin de la Baume. Since this balm, we are told, 'eases suffering, calms pain and anxiety', be comforted because the way from here is very straitened, very steep and very scary: a thin ribbon of metalled shelving, the bare edge falling sheer away into the abyss, a white line marking its side. The mountainside has an unforgiving look to it, like the emotionless face of a *rouleur* on the rivet (in extremis): bare rock scored with weather, sparse pines, crags. This is the *garrigue*, the arid terrain of Provence – their word *garriga* comes from *garric* (an oak tree –dwarf variety, hereabouts) and a pre-Celtic word *carra*, 'stone' – with chalky subsoil, brush vegetation. The road is shored up, should you take a peek, with stone revetments. The view is stupefying,

but keep focus. Vertigo may strike the unwary.

At around 2.5km, a lonesome, cracked pine and a blue disc enclosing a white arrow, indicating that this is a one-way clockwise ascent of Mont Faron and really no place for a car. Bushy pines.

At 3km, a belvedere followed by another heavy stint of gradient. 300 metres to a big right hand hairpin and up, up, up… a long view to the north-west towards Mont Caume, which appears to be Provençal for 'bare rock summit'. A picnic area in the scant shade of gaunt conifers looking out over the valley between this great boss of geology and the next. A bit further on, a restaurant next to the station for the cable car and, round a left-hand bend to the top of this part of the climb and the memorials to the men who died in the fighting of August–September 1944. Stone plaques set into a wall, a Sherman tank on a plinth, Théâtre de Verdure (open-air theatre, literally 'theatre of greenery') on the mound above the wall, part of the drive to reinforce Mont Faron's reputation as a fresh-air, verdant lung for the city of Toulon, burdened as it is with maritime and other fume-belching industry.

A steak house – the Rotisserie du Drap d'Or – along the road a way and then the Mont Faron zoo.

There follows a descent onto the ridge. Off to the left stands La Chapelle de Notre-Dame du Faron, a low-roofed building fronted by a fencework of iron railings. Seven hundred metres of flat, a turning right to the Memorial and the *téléphérique* (cable car), straight on to Toulon. A road sign warns against smoking and cautions: '*Feux interdits*' - No fires.

The road meanders steadily downwards for around 2 kilometres, briefly climbs again but on a mild gradient, in the shade of pines – a blessing in

Col de Vence 963m

summer heat. A flat stretch of about 200 metres to a parking area and grand perspectives north and west over the encircling hills. A short hop up and here is the summit itself, and the Guinguette au Chat Perdu (a marmalade cat by the evidence of the sign). A *guinguette* is a popular café offering food, drink and dancing, generally in the open air amid trees and by grass. The banks of the Seine were once lined with them – most famous, perhaps, the pleasure garden of the Ile de la Grande Jatte, near Asnières, 7 kilometres west of the city, across the river from the banks on which sit the swimmers in Georges Seurat's pointilliste painting *La Baignade*. Guingettes also feature in Zola's novel about sexual passion, murder and the excoriations of guilt, *Thérèse Raquin*. The zoo specialises in breeding cats, it appears. Near the *guinguette* is the fort, as forbidding as all such grim foci of bellicosity are, on its dominating high ground, and here begins the descent, a one-way road, what one might call a rude descent: very tough, albeit largely in shade and on a wider road than the other side, less exposed, the minimal protection, but protection at least of a parapet wall. A huge panorama opens out as if you were taking to the open air off the heights of Toulon. At about 5km, new tarmac and a roundabout. This is where the suburbs of Upper Toulon begin and up this way, we believe, come the races, Paris–Nice, Tour de la Méditérranée and the time trials of the Mont Faron hill climb. Federico Bahamontes won it five times between 1955 and 1964. Pictures of hill climbs in 1930 show a savage stone and pebble-strewn grit road up here, horribly precarious, bare leprous white rock overhang all but scraping at the riders' shoulders.

Southern approach from Vence

LENGTH: 9.8KM

HEIGHT GAIN: 325M

MAXIMUM GRADIENT: 7%

The old walled town in the centre of Vence makes a nice stroll. In the tiny, flagged place through the Porte du Peyra (built in 1441, one of five ancient gateways) a fountain, dating from 1822, dispenses the mineral water of a stream 'La Foux' which issues from a source above the town in the *baous*, a range of limestone escarpments enclosing this immediate inland from the coast. (The word is derived from *balc*, related to Italian *balco*, 'scaffold', our 'baulk', meaning a beam, thence a projecting platform and a ridge.) A marble plaque listing the amount of different minerals present. Five of the *baous* are named. North-east from Vence: Baou des Blancs, Baou des Noirs, Baou de Saint-Jeannet, Baou de la Gaude and Baou Super Gattères, much frequented by rock climbers and by the superfit walkers who aim to scale all five in one day. Inside the walled town, a plethora of touristic and artistic emporia. Vence is known as the 'City of Art'; the painters Raoul Dufy, Chaim Soutine, Henri Matisse, Marc Chagall and Jean Dubuffet worked here, and the Fondation Maeght in nearby Saint-Paul de Vence houses a superb collection of modern art. D. H. Lawrence spent his last days in Vence and died there, 1930.

Many cyclists use the Vence as ingress to the varied riding in the hills above the coast. The roads up to the town are quiet enough early in the morning. I talked to several who had ridden up from Antibes and they were enthusiastic about the circuit. Early morning is cooler, too, although all the rides in this sector may best be enjoyed in late summer and early autumn. The continuation of the Gorges du Loup, for instance, leads on to the Gréolières les Neiges at 1430m and on through the Clue de Gréolières and north towards our ROUTE NAPOLEON.

From Vence town centre take the D2 out onto the steep exit past the Hôtel de Charme. A sign tells you: '963m 9km (to col) 477m (left to climb) 5%'. A bridge over La Lubiane and a balcony road. Note the numbering of the houses indicating the metrage distance from town – the regular system in rural France (and New England). 527m 8km 5%, where a memorial celebrates the liberation of Vence by Allied troops 27–29 August 1944. On this spot were found five bodies of men from the Forces Françaises de l'Intérieur (FFI – the French Resistance), who 'died so that France might live', the bodies of four American soldiers 'dead on active service', those of two sisters, named Zimmer, and a boy of 14, '*victimes du destin*' victims of fate. All blown up 'by Nazi mines'.

402m 7km 7%, and suddenly the road breaks out into the *garrigue* (scrubland). Views of the sea through the thin haze of heat and on a parapet '*A LA VIE A LA MORT*' in red paint, presumably a declaration of undying love, but there is neither name nor attribution of desire. The Baou des Blancs stands high (673m) off to the right amid the surrounding hills of Lower Provence. The rest of the way does not shift from an ingrained 6–7% and there is no shade. However, this is classic Provençal landscape, limestone plateau with pubescent oaks and scrub vegetation. 2.8 kilometres from the col the Ball Trap Tir Club de Vence has a wooden cabin and their clay-pigeon range. Look back over the *baous*, the scored crevices cut by the precious sources of water, the sea, the great sweep of the Baie des Anges, Antibes.

Just short of the col, a stables – one of many in the vicinity – La Cavetière Ferme Promenade Cheval Poney, an emergency phone and the col sign by which grows purple-flowered wild mint and a splendid *tilleul* (lime) tree.

The Rules of the Road

The internal shifts of professional bike racing are easy enough to explain but to anyone not versed in the codes of loyalty, sacrifice and team commitment, they seem bizarre, impenetrable. The boss of the peloton, *le patron*, a senior champion to whom the rest must, by the old code, at least in some measure, defer, is somewhat outmoded now, not because the bunch is more democratic but because it is harder for a single rider to achieve, let alone merit, such domination. Bernard Hinault was the last to exercise that sort of feudal authority, not that it was always honoured. His order to call off the attacks was ignored by rivals fed up with his arrogant manner and physical bludgeoning in the 1985 Tour, for example. The American, Greg Lemond, chafed at his boss's seeming perfidy during the 1986 Tour, his first win, and the explanation – that Hinault had attacked so ruthlessly in order to kill off the opposition, *not* to discomfort his young team mate – had a queer ring to it, for sure. Lance Armstrong had all the attributes of a genuine patron in the Tour, save that many in the peloton did not respect him nor did they warm to his gaucheries… handing his rival Marco Pantani victory on the Ventoux – unthinkably crass – and then referring to him patronisingly as Elefantino. However, to the Paris–Nice. Eddy Merckx had signed for the Peugeot team when he turned pro in 1965, the year that the team's boss, Tommy Simpson, won the Worlds' Road Race.

In the 1967 Paris–Nice, Merckx won the stage into Chateau-Chinon and took over the lead. However, on the Col de la République, a few kilometres to the south-east of Saint-Etienne, Simpson went on the offensive and took the leader's white jersey from Merckx, who had believed that being leader on the road meant that he had automatically become leader in the team. Two days later, he was out in front, on his own on the climb of Mont Faron, Lucien Aimar, Bernard Guyot and Simpson all chasing. The team car driven by Gaston Plaud, the Peugeot *directeur sportif*, drove up alongside Merckx and told him to wait for Simpson. He had no option. He waited and, for the next 25 kilometres, towed his boss – who, naturally, did no work – and thus helped him to win the race.

ACKNOWLEDGEMENTS

My first thanks, as ever, to Simon Mottram, director of *Rapha*, whose vision and commitment to the broader cause of cycling has not only given stimulus to an entirely different, and welcome, attitude to what has for so long been considered a poor man's pastime in the UK, but has backed a number of offshoots from *Rapha's* central business, of making clothing, one of which is this series of books about the mountains.

I write this on the morning of *Rapha's* fifth birthday party. The Romans called a five-year period a *lustrum* and, at the end of the cycle, the censors, their most senior magistrates, conducted a purificatory ceremony. The rites involved a solemn procession round the object to be purified by officiating priests bearing materials invested with magical properties. Some people feel like that about bike componentry.

To Pete Drinkell, photographer, driver, font of common sense, a man of nerveless cool and unfailing good humour, generous companion of the trips to garner ground research and this remarkable portfolio of photography, I owe an enormous debt. The work is made so much easier with perfect complicity in the sharing of different aspects of it and Pete is not only the complete professional, he is a sterling friend, too.

In the *Rapha* office, Joe Hall has managed the project of this second volume in the *Massif* series from start to finish and has been of huge help in every way: calm, easygoing, responsive and efficient, he has fielded much of the basic organisational work which has lightened my load significantly. Andrew Maxwell Hyslop edited with his customary thoroughness, courtesy and unfailing good humour. His aim is of course to root out and highlight discrepancies in information, contradictions in data and infelicities of style (*mea culpa*) and, above all, to make the text as good as he can make it. This he has done with the deft, light touch of a French polisher's pad. Mike Curtis proof-read the text with eagle eye, diligence and expedition as well as providing the list of Italian equivalents for bike parts.

Herbie Sykes, now resident in Italy and a considerable student of Italian bike racing and social history, as his book about Franco Balmanion (*The Eagle of the*

Canovese) amply demonstrates, provided me with valuable references, friendly response to importunate enquiry, astute comment as well as timely loan of a video of the Giro crossing two remote climbs in Liguria. This latter supplied detail for the story of that day which would otherwise have been denied me.

Lucy Hudson of the Italian Department in the University of Reading proved to be a veritable tiger in helping me elucidate a problem in linguistics. I emailed out of the blue, on the flimsy pretext that I had once taught at the university and my daughter is completing a doctorate there. However, taking on the task, unfazed, she prodded, cajoled, urged and besieged various Linguistics experts who proved either dilatory or flummoxed or both. There was, sadly, no conclusive decoding of the conundra so I have had to resort to an educated guess.

Jonathan Bacon is a cheerful individual whose work on the design of the book deserves a fulsome plaudit; Ben Aquilina's line drawings are utterly delightful and Neil Wass, at Manson/TMG Horizon Printers, has brought the whole thing to a sumptuous conclusion. To all three, hats off.

On my first trip to the Alps, my baptism of riding mountains was l'Alpe d'Huez, which will be described in the next volume, and I concluded that excursus with the ride up Ventoux, which does find place in these pages. Of my particular experience on that monster, in the teeth of a ferocious mistral, I wrote in more general terms: 'Mountains are rarely, if ever, finished with you' and it is true. This book is testimony to an abiding passion, a deepening understanding, and the absolute privilege of ever closer acquaintance with mountains, rooted in that truth.

Graeme Fife 2009

Author's Note

For all you nerds out there who are ferret-quick to pounce on an inconsistency and trumpet it as a howler, your crowing is unhelpful, misplaced and unseemly. Amid the clamorous contradictions of those mechanical slaves upon which we rely – altimeters, odometers, books, maps, road signs, guides and sundry web-based reports – the discrepancy of a horizontal or vertical metre here and there matters not one iota. If there *are* those of you to whom the actuarial exactitude of statistics matters more than the uplift of simply being in the mountains and riding them for the joy, the suffering, the overwhelming satisfaction with which they load us mortals, a taste of eternity, then this book probably ain't for you. Your nit-picking letters and e-mails are certainly not for me.

All translations in the text are by the author.

ESSENTIAL REPAIR VOCABULARY

Note: Don't forget that, although it is better to be able to ask for exactly what you need, you can always point and rely on the international language of bike shops. Mechanics in most small garages are happy to help out with running repairs on bikes.

English	French	Italian
Adjustable spanner	clef (clé) anglaise	chiave registrabile
Allen key	clef hexagonale or à six pans	chiave a brugola
Bag	sacoche or musette	borsello
Battery	pile	pila
Bike	vélo	bici
Brake	frein	freno
Brake block	patin de frein	pastiglia del freno
Brake cable	câble de frein	guaina del freno
Brake lever	poignée de frein	leva del freno a mano
Brake hood	cocotte	coprisupporto
Broken	cassé (-ée)	rotto
Cap	casquette	cappellino
Cassette	roue-libre à cassette	casseta/pacco pignoni
Chain	chaîne	catenary
Chain rivet extractor	dérive-chaîne	smagliacatena
Chainwheel	plateau de pédalier	guarnitura
Cleat	cale-chaussure	tachetto
Crossbar	tube horizontal	tubo orrizzontale
Down tube	tube diagonal	tubo obliquo
Forks	fourche	forcella
Frame	cadre	telaio
Front	avant	anteriore
Gear cable	câble de dérailleur	guaina del cambio
Handlebar	guidon	manubrio
Handlebar tape	tresse pour guidon	nastro manubrio
Headlamp	phare	luce anteriore
Headset	jeu de direction	serie sterzo
Head tube	tube de direction	tubo di sterzo
Helmet	casque	casco

English	French	Italian
Hub	moyeu	mozzo
Inner tube	cambre à air	camera d'aria
Jersey	maillot	maglia
Nut	écrou	dado
Oil	huile	olio
Pedal	pédale	pedale
Pump	pompe	pompa
Pump up	gonfler	gonfiare
Puncture	crevaison (verb: crever)	foratura (verb: forare)
Quick-release hub	moyeu à blocage rapide	mozzo sganci rapidi
Rear	arrière	posteriore
Rear lamp	feu arrière	luce posteriore
Rim	jante	cerchio
Rim tape	fond de jante	nastro paranipples per camere d'aria
Saddle	selle	sella
Saddle post	tige de selle	reggisella
Screwdriver	tournevis	cacciavite
Shoe	chaussure	scarpa
Shorts	cuissard	pantaloncini
Socks	chaussettes	calzini
Spoke	rayon	raggio
Sprocket	couronne	pignone
Stem (of handlebar)	potence	attacco manubrio
Tights (bib tights)	collant (collant à bretelles amovibles)	salopette (also bib-tights)
Tyre	boyau / pneu	copertura
Valve	valve	valvola
Washer	rondelle	rondella
Water bottle	bidon	borraccia
Wheel	roue	ruota

INDEX OF CLIMBS